Live in the Love of Mary

MARY
AND
OUR LOVE

By

Reverend Zygmunt V. Szarnicki

Zygmunt V. Szarnicki

j.pohl associates

Published by
J. POHL ASSOCIATES
1706 Berkwood Drive
Pittsburgh, Pa. 15243
(412) 279-5000

ISBN 0-939332-22-1

THE AUTHOR

Reverend Zygmont V. Szarnicki was ordained for the Diocese of Pittsburgh on March 4, 1945. He attended St. Mary's College and SS. Cyril and Methodius Seminary in Orchard Lake, Michigan and studied Theology at St. Vincent Seminary in Latrobe, Pennsylvania.

He served in a number of churches in the Diocese of Pittsburgh during his fifty years as a priest. His association with parishes dedicated to the Blessed Mother were as follows: Our Lady of Perpetual Help in Natrona Heights, Our Lady of Czestochowa in McKeesport, SS. Mary and Ann in Marianna, the Assumption in Bellevue, Holy Family and Immaculate Heart of Mary in Pittsburgh, Pennsylvania.

During his priesthood, Father Zygmunt V. Szarnicki read and studied from many books and other writings concerning Our Blessed Lady. He visited many of Her shrines. He talked to many people devoted to Our Heavenly Queen. His own reflections are recorded in this book. To mention or list all his references would take pages. For convenience and brevity none will be mentioned, nor will the lectures and personal experiences be listed.

May the reading of this book bring to our minds more clearly that the Mother of Jesus loves us and we are to love Her.

ACKNOWLEDGEMENTS

Many persons have contributed to the gathering of the material in this book and to its preparation and printing.

I owe gratitude to my parents who inspired me to love the Blessed Mother, to my professor and pastors who led me in the knowledge of the Blessed Lady, to the groups with whom I traveled to Our Lady's Shrines in the United States, in Canada, in Mexico, in France, in Portugal, in Spain, in Italy, in Poland, in Germany and in the Holy Land and to The Legion of Mary.

Further gratitude is given to James and Jean Shanley who were the guiding light to have this book printed and to Mr. Randy Duva of Pittsburgh, Pennsylvania.

May Our Blessed Mother bring blessings to all who contributed in any way to the printing of this book.

In gratitude and Thanksgiving,

Rev. Zygmunt V. Szarnicki

DEDICATION

*I dedicate this book to the memory of my parents,
Adam and Magdalena (nee Poniatowska)
Szarnicki who gave me life and direction.*

INTRODUCTION

Many books and treaties have been written concerning the Blessed Mother by saints, scholars and devotees. Although I am no saint nor a scholar, nonetheless I love the Virgin Mary and I am devoted to Her.

This writing is not a dogmatic document but rather an expagression of a son who has visited many a Marian shrine and saw the love and devotion of the pilgrims. If by chance my love of the Virgin Mary was lukewarm before these visits, it surely grew with each pilgrimage to Her shrines.

What struck me first was the devotion and fervor of the multitudes. No matter where the shrine is located, there crowds gather to honor and love our Blessed Mary. Yes, the shrine itself had and has its beauty and attractiveness, but the people's love and their expressions of love in prayer, song, attendance at Mass, the reception of the sacraments, the processions, the walking on their knees and the feeling of being in a most holy place brought awe into my being. I am positive such a feeling was aroused in you as you visited the many shrines of Our Lady and especially so in those shrines where She Herself appeared.

Each adventure to a Marian Shrine brought a desire to know Our Mother better. As I learned more, I now wish to pass on to others some information concerning the Mother of Jesus and the Mother of us all.

This is not a complete account and dissertation on Mary nor an account of all of Her appearances nor all of Her shrines. What is written should be enough to motivate all to be more inquisitive about Our Blessed Mother, and it is my hope that all of us will have a greater love and devotion to Our Blessed Mother. May our love of Mary increase as years go by until we have the greatest love when we see Her face to face.

TABLE OF CONTENTS

— PART I —

REFLECTIONS ON THE LITANY OF LORETO OF THE BLESSED MOTHER OF JESUS

WRITING ON THE LITANY
OF OUR BLESSED MOTHER

The purpose of these articles on the Litany of Loreto is to foster an ardent devotion, reverence and filial love toward our Blessed Mother that, through this love, She as a good Mother may protect us here upon this earth and lead us by our hand to Her Son when He calls us home.

To have this greater love for Mary, Our Mother, we must know more about Her. We shall attempt to foster this love in the explanation of each title of the Litany we recite in Her honor. The following articles will promote the understanding of Her titles and foster love of Our Blessed Mother.

After the invocations of the Blessed Trinity to have mercy on us, we say, Holy Mary.

Holy means to be like unto God, to be without sin, to be in sanctifying grace. Mary, a young girl of about fifteen years of age, was to be married to Joseph when the Archangel Gabriel came to Her and told Her She was holy, She was in sanctifying grace. He said, "Hail full of grace, the Lord is with Thee." Not only was She in sanctifying grace, but She was full of grace.

It was fitting to sanctify Her first because it is most proper that the creature with whom the Blessed Trinity was to have such an intimate connection as to have Her be the Mother of Christ to be holy.

From the Gospel we adhere to the words of the Archangel that Mary is holy since She is full of grace and from the practice of the Church in reciting the prayer "Hail Mary", where we say "Holy Mary" we acknowledge Mary as holy.

In Mary, grace was increased during Her life by meritorious acts, by being the Mother of Christ, and by receiving the plenitude of the Holy Spirit, our sanctifier.

O Mary, Keep us under Your protection and bring us to be united with the "Holy of Holies" and live with Him forever.

THE MEANING OF THE NAME OF "MARY"

There are various meanings of the name of Mary: namely, illuminatrix, the one illuminated, Myrrh, Star of the Sea, a drop of the sea, mistress, the beloved, the best, the powerful. There is one meaning which is favored and used most often by modern writers and this meaning, coming from the old Egyptian language, means the beloved of God.

The first time the name of "Mary" is recorded in the Sacred Scripture is that of the sister of Moses and Aaron whose name is written today as Mariam.

It seems most likely that God ordered Anna and Joachim to name their Daughter "Mary." God has ordered the names of others who were chosen by Him for special tasks and it follows that He intervened here, too. God changed the name of Abraham, Sara, Jacob, and He ordered the name of John the Baptist and Jesus.

The name of Mary has its special meaning and the first is "Madonna." This is a title of glory resulting from Her being Queen. As Queen, She rules over the Heavens and earth. She sits on a throne along with the King of Kings.

A special honor is given Her by an individualistic veneration which is known as "Hyperdulia" which is that special veneration given and due Mary alone because She is the Mother of God, the most exalted in dignity of all the angels and saints.

The name of Mary signifies Light, for She is the one who enlightens and the one who brought the "Light" of the world into the world. She knew more about Christ and about God than any other person on earth. It was She who directed the Apostles and the early Church. She guided the Church in choosing the Gospels to be placed in the Bible. She continues to enlighten the Church and many writers, artists, and working people.

Mary has helped the faithful throughout the centuries. She will help us and all people until the end of the world. May we address Her often under any title or all titles as we ask for help. May She help us as we travel along our way to eternity.

O Mary, You are most powerful before God. Pray for us that we may know Christ and love Him as You knew Him and loved Him.

THE POWER OF THE NAME "MARY"
AND THE BATTLE OF VIENNA

On September 12th of each year, the Church celebrates the feast of the Holy Name of Mary to commemorate the great victory won over the Turks at Vienna in the year 1683. It was only through the invoking of the holy and powerful name of Mary that Europe was saved from the inroads of the Turkish hordes.

All of Christian Europe was threatened with destruction in 1683 from the great armies of the Mohammedan infidel Turks. Country after country fell under their powerful armies. Thousands upon thousands of Christians were murdered. The Turks marched through Hungary into Austria and laid siege against the city of Vienna. Fifteen thousand troops tried to defend the city against 200,000 Turks. What made matters worse was a fire which broke out in one of the city's churches and this fire was sweeping down upon the munitions arsenal. Everything looked black for the Christians. They were certain of their own and the city's destruction.

On August 15th, the feast of the Assumption, all the soldiers and the inhabitants of Vienna prayed to Mary and invoked Her most holy and powerful name. They placed their whole life and city into the hands of Mary. Immediately after, the fire was checked and put out. New hope and courage came upon all in the city. More prayers and more invoking of the name of

Mary was heard throughout the city. Mary, save us. "Mary, help us" was heard everywhere.

There was a time when everything looked as if lost. The army could defend the city no longer. The Turks entered the city and were destroying everything they laid their hands on and killed everyone they came across. Suddenly, a huge battle cry is heard. A great army of Poles led by their King, John III Sobieski entered the city in its defense. The people cried with glee, "Mary has come to our aid." King John, now joined by Prince Charles of Lorraine and his German army, went to offer Mass in honor of Mary. Sobieski served the Mass and received Holy Communion.

Great world leaders had a deep, warm devotion to the Mother of God. We are Her children as much as they were.

> *O Mary, we Your children turn to You for help. We are in danger daily for the devil is never asleep. We are in physical danger, too, for many sicknesses attack us. Spare us from the current plagues of cancer, heart attacks, strokes and AIDS.*

The priest gave his blessing in the name of Mary to the united forces. Inspired with all confidence, King Sobieski exclaimed, "Let us go now, for the Virgin will be with us." Whereupon, with unusual courage, the armies rushed upon the Turks who, panic-stricken, fled for safety. A complete victory was won and Christendom was spared from the impious hands of the Turks.

King Sobieski and Prince Charles returned to the altar of Mary and returned solemn thanks. The captured green standard of the Turks was given to the Holy Father, Pope Innocent XI, who laid it at the feet of Mary. This Pope ordered the feast of the Holy Name of Mary be celebrated every year in memory of this great victory.

King John III Sobieski returned to Poland bringing some booty to be placed in the Shrine of Our Lady of Czestochowa which Shrine he visited before he led his army to Vienna. He returns to thank Our Lady.

Some booty is in the museum in the Wawel Castle in Krakow. The headquarter tent of the Turkish general may be seen in that former residence of Polish Kings.

The power of Mary is very great. Calling upon Her and using Her name with devotion, brings Her to the aid of everyone. In time of danger from our enemies or in time of trouble, we should call upon Mary for help. When the devil and the fire of the flesh tempt us to commit sin, we should flee to Mary and call upon Her for aid.

> *May the sweet and powerful name of Mary be upon our lips most often, but especially at the time of our death. Mary, my Mother, help me now and at the hour of my death. Protect me when I am most weak. Spare me from the inroads of Satan. Be at my side to win the greatest victory possible - my eternal salvation.*

HOLY MOTHER OF GOD

Is it not strange that we should call a human being the Mother of God? How is this possible that a woman could give birth to a person who is God? But yet that was possible and that happened nearly two thousand years ago when a Virgin by the name of Mary gave birth to Jesus Christ who is God.

This is a truth of our faith that the Blessed Virgin is truly the Mother of God. We have the inspired words of St. Elizabeth who was filled with the Holy Spirit to prove the truth from The Sacred Scriptures, for she said (Luke 1, 43), "and whence is this that the Mother of my Lord should come to me."

Your mother gave birth to You as a person although she, by being fertilized by your father, generated only the flesh while God created the soul; yet by that merit we all call her mother of our total person. In like manner, Mary conceived and gave birth to the person Jesus Christ. Christ had two natures - the Divine and the human. Therefore, truly Mary is the Mother of God since Jesus is true God and true man.

In a way, Mary participated in the fecundity of the Father who generated His Son from all eternity while Mary generated Him in time. She has a special affinity to Her Son because from Mary Jesus took His humanity, She was with Him during all the days of His earthly life, and She shared in His passion. Also, Mary is called the Spouse of the Holy Spirit since She conceived by His overshadowing.

From this dignity of being the Mother of God, Mary obtained all Her privileges, Her sanctity and Her high position in Heaven.

Mary, from Your place in Heaven, we who honor You as the Mother of God beseech You to gain graces and favor for us so that we may be loyal children of God and You.

Of the many scenes presented to us by our faith, literature and art at Christmas time, there is one in particular which moves my heart to tenderness. My heart is affected every time I see a mother hold an infant and especially so of a newborn child; but somehow my heart beats differently when I behold Mary and Joseph in complete ecstatic adoration of the newborn Jesus. I rejoice in the Nativity scenes.

In my mind's eye, I see the picture of Mary and Joseph in adoration of the Infant. Yes, it is easy to look at a painting, no matter by what great artist, of the Nativity or at a manger arrangement with Jesus in the crib. I see the improvised crib. I look at the long promised God-man. I observe Mary and Joseph as they behold Jesus.

My eyes turn to Joseph for a moment. His face is radiant and I can see it is spellbound. I let him remain in his ecstasy and silent adoration as I turn to Mary.

Mother Mary, how fortunate You are to give birth to Your Lord. As You behold Your Child, You cannot believe... but it is true...

You, yes You, gave birth to Your Creator, Your Redeemer, Your God now come into flesh. Look at Your Son, the true God and true man for whom all creation groaned and awaited.

What can one read in or from Your face and eyes as You behold Your Son? I read joy, love, and submission to God's will. I read gratitude for the honor the Father has bestowed upon You by selecting You to be the Mother of His Son. I see peaceful astonishment, a deep reverence, a spellbinding awe, and admiration beyond description. I see You in sweet love and devotion. Your face is so mild and lovely while Your eyes radiate happiness and softness.

In Your whole demeanor I see a willingness to be of assistance to others. You who were submissive and cooperative to the will of God are now ready to bear anything and everything to accomplish Your sublime mission as the Mother of God, the protector of Christ, and the Mother of all mankind.

Your mind is in deep thought as to what will be the course of Your Son, what will be His future, how will You fulfill Your dutiful task as His Mother, how will You raise Him, and will all the people recognize Him and accept Him as the Son of God? Definitely You are concerned about His future and that of Your own.

As You gaze upon Your Infant, Your loving heart beams love for all who accept Your Son. O, how You wish all mankind will accept Him, recognize Him, love Him and obey Him and His request of "Come follow Me."

Another question comes across Your face: Will mankind accept Me as its Mother? O Mary, I do see in Your face an all-embracing love for the whole Mystical Body of Christ of which each one of us is a member.

As You adore Jesus, I join in that adoration and express my love of Him and of You and I venerate You as the Mother of God and my Mother.

May all people's hearts glow with some of the love You possess. I ask You to open all hearts with love for Jesus, with love for You, with love for their immortal souls, and with love for everyone of our human family for we all make up the Mystical Body of Christ, Your beloved Son.

MARY, THE MOTHER OF GOD I

Not all people believe as we Catholics believe today. Not even all Christians believe the same. Take a look at how many Christian Churches are in any community. What makes them different? Definitely their doctrines are at variance with that of the Catholic Church.

The Blessed Mother's position in our faith has been attacked and denied in the early Church and it is still being denied. Is Mary the Mother of God or not? Some argue against that title and truth of the Catholic Church. They claim that, if Mary were the Mother of God, then She must be a goddess. This conclusion everyone denies; nor does that reasoning follow true logic; for example, the mother of our president is his mother but she is not a president; the mother of a

7

football player is his mother but she is not a football player. To say Mary is a goddess is most erroneous.

The question of Mary being the Mother of God plagued the Church after the Council of Nicea because the doctrine of Jesus Christ was not understood correctly by some. Some held that Christ was two persons. Others claimed His Divinity united with His humanity later and remained distinct forming two persons in Him. Nestorius seemed to have that misunderstanding as some have even today.

To solve the problem in the early Church, a council was called at Ephesus by the Emperor Theodosius II in 431. Bishops from the Eastern and African Churches plus delegates from Rome played their part. Nestorius and John, the patriarch of Antioch, were placed against St. Cyril of Alexandria and his followers. The true doctrine was hammered out and the hero was St. Cyril. Nestorius held Mary was the Mother of Christ, but not the Mother of God, that She gave birth to the human body and not to the divine person. Mary gave birth to the temple of God, but not to the God-man. Nestorius' argument was that Mary was the "CHRISTOTOKOS" (the Mother of Christ) and not the "THEOTOKOS" (the Mother of God). His idea was that Mary was only the Mother of Christ, in whom God (the Logos or the WORD) later came to dwell.

The true doctrine was established at Ephesus and made clear for all Catholics that Mary gave birth to a LIVING PERSON who is TRUE GOD AND TRUE MAN, that this Person is Jesus Christ, the Son of God, the Second Person of the Blessed Trinity, Who always existed with the Father and the Holy Spirit, but Who in the love of God for man was born in time for our salvation, but never stopped being God although He came on this earth and became man.

O Mary, we firmly believe that You are the Mother of God. We firmly believe that, when You accepted the will of God to be the Mother of His Son and at the moment of the conception, the Divinity and humanity were united in ONE PERSON TO WHOM You gave birth. This Person is Our Lord and God. In truth You are the Mother of God, of Our Lord Jesus Christ.

As we believe You are the Mother of God, we also believe You are our Mother because Jesus gave You to us in the person of St. John the Apostle, when He said, "Mother, behold Thy son; Son, behold thy Mother."

As You nurtured Jesus, taught Him, protected Him, followed Him, believed in Him and adored Him, help us to be like You. Also help us to love Jesus as You did and help us to love You. Increase our love and devotion. May we show our love of You by honoring You with our prayers, veneration of You and Your icons, and above all, by following Your requests of "Obey My Son and follow My Son." Be at our side now and at the hour of our death. Present us to Your Divine Son. May we see You and be with You in Heaven where we shall be with God forever.

MARY, THE MOTHER OF GOD II

The Apostles went through the world teaching Jesus. Their teaching came to us in the creed we call the Apostles' Creed. This Creed seems to be easy and simple. We can have a fairly good understanding of it.

Then came the Greeks, whose mind was a philosophical one. It wanted to analyze everything and every truth of the Apostles' Creed. As the Greek schools attempted to rationalize the faith, questions and controversies arose. There were many which caused councils to be called.

The first council was that at Nicea which resulted in the Creed we recite every Sunday. The council's big question was: Did or does Jesus have the same nature as God the Father? That is why we say in the Creed today "God of God, Light of Light, true God from true God". The council settled that question with the answer "YES". JESUS HAS AND HAD THE SAME IDENTICAL NATURE AS THE FATHER.

Another question came up and sometime we hear of it again: Is Mary the Mother of God? Some even say or said that Jesus did not know He was the Son of God until later in life or perhaps at His baptism. O, I wish these theologians would leave our faith simple and easy as the Apostles gave it to us.

Because of these questions another council was called and in 431 at Ephesus these questions were brought onto the discussion floor. Two factions were especially noted: One led by Nestorius, the Bishop of Constantinople; the other by St. Cyril, the Bishop of Alexandria, Egypt. Nestorius claimed Mary to be the carrier of Christ and not the Mother of God because that would make Her a goddess. Even women opposed him saying that they gave birth to a living person and not a clump of flesh. Nestorius was defeated and exiled. St. Cyril's position became the doctrine of our Faith. Mary is the Mother of God, because She gave birth to the living Person Who is both God and man.

On New Year's Day we commemorate this doctrine of our faith. It is good to know the truth of our faith and all its doctrines but more important, is to live the faith.In our living the faith and truth about the Blessed Mother, we have a great respect and love of Mary, we honor Her, we venerate Her, we hold Her in high esteem and we pray to Her for help.

We should not only know and honor Her as the Mother of God, but also we honor Her and hold Her as OUR MOTHER.

> *May the Mother of God, the Mother of Jesus, the Mother of us all be with us during our life helping us on our way to eternal life and may She be with us at the moment of our death to lead us to Jesus.*

HOLY VIRGIN OF VIRGINS

A virgin is a person whose body remains intact, that is, no sexual act was committed. Of the countless virgins, Our Blessed Mother is considered and venerated as the Virgin of all virgins.

Our Mother Mary, because of Her vocation and selection, was conceived without sin. She was full of grace. She conceived Christ through the power of the Holy Spirit and not by human contact. Although She was married, She remained a virgin. The Lateran Council in 649 declared Her to be the Perpetual Virgin; that is, a virgin before, during and after the birth of Jesus Christ.

Because of Her privilege, grace and position in our salvation economy, She ranks first among all virgins, saints and angels.

> *O Mary, most Holy Virgin of virgins, obtain the graces necessary for all of us to remain holy and in the love of God. May we have the grace and strength to respect our bodies and the bodies of all males and females be it in single or in married life. O Virgin of virgins, pray for us.*

MOTHER OF DIVINE GRACE

The first time we hear of Mary and Grace is when the Archangel Gabriel appeared to Her and said, "Hail full of grace the Lord is with Thee." Grace is that special help from God for us to get to Heaven.

Grace is divided into actual and sanctifying grace. Sacramental graces are those which come through the sacraments. They are actual and sanctifying graces.

Sanctifying grace is that grace which makes us holy and pleasing to God. From the angel's words we know Mary was full of grace and, therefore, most pleasing in the eyes of God.

In the Litany of Loreto, one title for Mary is the Mother of Divine Grace. But, Jesus is the Author of all grace. It is Jesus who gained and merited all grace for our salvation by His coming upon this earth, suffering and dying for us. It is He Who established the sacraments by which we can get all the graces necessary to make us holy and pleasing to God and get to Heaven.

Since Mary is the Mother of Jesus Who is the Author of all Grace, consequently She is the Mother of all Jesus did. Therefore, She is also Mother of Divine Grace.

It is a theological conclusion that all graces come to us through Mary just as Jesus came to us through the maternity of Mary. Mary is called the Almoner of God because She dispenses God's graces to us.

In our religious life we pray to Mary to help us in our daily life so that our faith may be strong, that our hope will guide us through life to attain Heaven, and to strengthen the love of God and fellow man. In particular, we pray that Mary is at hand at the hour of our death. We know that even when we are dying, we being more helpless than ever in our adult life, we are in need of God's grace and we ask Mary to be at our side with all graces so that we may die in the love of God.

> *O Mary of Divine Grace, God filled You with grace from the very first moment of Your conception and He strengthened You*

with grace all the days of Your life. May we through Your intercession have the graces to live according to the Will of God and to attain a life of everlasting happiness.

Since God is the Author of Grace and Jesus merited all grace because of His life, death and resurrection, how can we say Mary is the Mother of Grace?

We justify the title by this reasoning: Since Mary is the Mother of Christ, She is also the Mother of all Jesus was and did. Therefore, She is the Mother of Grace which Jesus won for us.

Since Jesus and grace come through Mary, we claim Mary as the almoner of all grace, that is, She is the dispenser of grace by a special privilege since She is so favored by God.

Grace is that special help merited by Christ aiding all to gain Heaven. Grace is understood as Actual, that is, it comes and goes when needed to do good and avoid evil. It illuminates the mind and strengthens the will to do good and avoid evil.

Sanctifying grace is that spiritual gift of God which makes us holy and pleasing to God. This grace comes primarily to us through the sacraments.

O Mother of Divine Grace, obtain all the help I need to avoid sin, to do good, and to remain in love of God. O Mary, help me with God's grace.

MARY, THE MOTHER OF CHRIST

Our faith testifies that Jesus Christ is the true Son of God, the Father, and the true Son of Mary. The Gospels give us all the proofs necessary to assert that Jesus was born of Mary and that Jesus is the Son of the Father.

The first General Council of Nicea wrangled with the question of how Jesus was true God and true man. The conclusion was that Jesus had the same nature as the Father; as Son, He always was, always is, and always will be. It was only in time that the Son of God was conceived by the power of the Holy Spirit, gestated in the womb of the Virgin Mary and was born of Our Lady as the God-man, Jesus Christ.

The word Jesus means Savior for Jesus came to redeem mankind. The word Christ means the Anointed One, that is, the natures of God and man were united into one Person to Whom Mary gave birth. It is our faith that Jesus Christ has two natures: divine and human; that He is only ONE PERSON; that He has both a human and divine intellect and will.

It is not the purpose of this article to prove the identity of Jesus Christ as God and man. The purpose of this article is to stimulate our love of Jesus and Mary and, since we are explaining the Invocations of the Litany of Loreto, we are concentrating on Our Blessed Lady and Her privileges in the process of our salvation.

Mary, who gave birth to Jesus and raised Him, knew Jesus better than any other person who lived upon this earth. Being in Heaven now with Her Son, She

11

knows Him even better. She loved Him most tenderly when He was upon this earth and now She loves Him all that much more since both are in Heaven and He has granted Her all the honors due Her as the Mother of God and the Mother of Christ.

Because of Her tremendous love for Jesus Christ, Mary also has a tremendous love for you and me and for all mankind. God created all mankind; Jesus redeemed all mankind; God wants all mankind to live with Him in Heaven; Jesus opened the gates of Heaven for all who love God. Since Mary is the Co-Redemptrix and Our Advocate, She desires all mankind to come to the knowledge of Her Son, to love and serve Him by keeping the covenant with God, and to come to eternal bliss.

"Loving Mother of the Redeemer, Gate of Heaven, Star of the Sea, assist Your people who have fallen yet strive to rise again. To the wonderment of nature You bore Your Creator, yet remained a virgin after as before. You who received Gabriel's joyful greeting, have pity on us poor sinners." Lead us to Your Son and eternal happiness, O Mary, Mother of Christ and our Mother.

MARY, MOTHER OF THE CHURCH

How could Pope Paul VI in promulgating the "Lumen Gentium," Light of the Nations, give Blessed Mary the title of Mother of the Church? This title has been inserted in the Litany of Loreto.

We Catholics have no problem with that title. Perhaps other Christians may object, but they have already objected to Mary's position in our salvation. How much of Marian theology is accepted by our Christian brethren? Do they accept Mary as the Mother of God?

We Catholics adhere to the Gospel truth that Mary is the Mother of Jesus. Since Jesus is true God and true man, then Mary is the one who gave birth to Jesus, the God-man. Consequently, She is the Mother of Christ Who is God and, therefore, She is the Mother of God.

Jesus Christ is our Redeemer. Mary is the Mother of the Redeemer. She is also the Mother of the redeemed because Jesus gave Her to us to be our Mother when He said, "son behold thy Mother, Woman behold Thy son."

Our Lord identified Himself with people. He tells us, "I am the vine, You are the branches." Again He speaks of one sheepfold of which unity He is the Good Shepherd and we are His loyal following sheep.

The faithful constitute the Mystical Body of Christ. When we are baptized we put on Christ says St. Paul. Now baptized persons have Christ living in them. "Now live I, not I, but Christ living in me," says St. Paul.

The logical conclusion from the Mystical Body of Christ is that Mary is the Mother of the Mystical Body of Christ, but the Mystical Body of Christ is the Church. Therefore, we say and believe that Mary is the Mother of the Church.

O Mary, how wonderful was and is Your role in the salvation of mankind. You gave birth to Jesus, You reared Him, You were present at His teachings and miracles, You suffered along with Him at the crucifixion, and You were present with the Apostles on Pentecost Sunday. Your role is not over until all mankind is with God. Guide us, Your Church, through the stormy waters of our life and history. Lead us as Your devoted children to Your Son, keep us close to Him, and bring us to eternal glory.

MARY, OUR MOTHER

"Woman, behold Thy Son." "Son behold thy Mother."
(John 19, 26-27)

During the crucifixion of Her Divine Son, Mary received an unusual privilege from Jesus. This distinct honor is called the Universal Motherhood of mankind.

Our Lord knew His end was coming. As Our Lord looked down upon the small group of the faithful who were near the cross, He saw the pain His Blessed Mother was enduring. Truly this is the time when the sword pierced Her heart as was prophesied by Simeon.

Since death was near, Christ had to complete His last will and testament. Already He committed His blood to the Church, His garments to the enemy, a thief to Heaven, and soon He would commend His body to the grave and His soul to His Father. There were only two beloved treasures remaining - His Mother and His beloved disciple, John. "Woman, behold Thy son." "Son, behold thy Mother." "And from that hour," writes St. John about himself, "The disciple took Her to his own."

These words of Christ have a much greater meaning than what they seem at the moment. The Church, guided by the same Holy Spirit Who inspired St John to write these words, holds that St. John represented all the redeemed of Christ. By giving Mary to John, Christ gave Her to all of us.

The Blessed Virgin Mary is truly our spiritual Mother, for She is the Mother of Jesus Who, by His passion and death, makes it possible for you and me to be the adopted children of God. It is Mary who cooperates with God in giving us Jesus Who also is our supernatural life and food.

As a true Mother, She takes care of us. She shows Her love for us by obtaining graces for us. She constantly intercedes for us. She appears at times upon this earth bringing consolation, direction, graces and cures to Her children.

Mother of God and our Mother, help us to love You and Your Son above all. This we do when we avoid sin, receive the sacraments, recite the Rosary, Litany, and the "Hail Mary." As Your true lover may we never worry about our salvation, for You are praying for us sinners now and at the hour of our death.

"O Mary, my Mother, be gracious to me."

MOTHER MOST PURE - MOST CHASTE

Purity and chastity pertains to absence of sinful sexual activity. It can mean also a complete absence of sexual acts. Persons who vow chastity are to keep their bodies intact. Only in married life proper sex acts are sinless.

Because Christ was most holy and pure, it behooved that He be born of a most holy and pure mother. We hold Mother Mary to be most holy and most pure.

Mary's purity is proposed to our belief by the following arguments:

1. From non-divinely inspired literature (the Gospel of St. James) we learn of Mary as a baby was given to the sterile Joachim and Anna through a special privilege and providence It is related that Mary spent childhood years in the Temple and there remained a pure virgin. A virgin is one whose body is intact.
2. Mary consented to Archangel Gabriel's words only after She learned Her virginity would remain intact.
3. Mary remained a perpetual virgin even though She was married to Joseph, a most holy man who received all the graces for his position in our salvation process.

Although purity and chastity in our modern day of pornography and sex license are scoffed at by some, nevertheless, these virtues are fostered by the Church and religious families. Purity and chastity are the safeguards of happiness, health of body and mind, and means of attaining eternal glory.

MOST CHASTE: Because of Mary's position and virtues, She is the model and example for us Christians. She inspired and inspires all good people to refrain from sinful sexual activity. She obtains graces to defend these virtues of excellency. By Her example and help, She encourages all to live a pure and chaste life according to their vocation. With the grace of God, all can refrain from sinful sexual acts.

Because of the beauty and excellency of these virtues, each and every one of us should strive to possess holiness of body and soul. This should be done by:

1. Prayer - The Blessed Virgin's love for God was the greatest and it was demonstrated by Her constant prayer.
2. Reception of the sacraments is absolutely necessary for holiness and purity.
3. Mortification of the senses: eyes, ears, taste, touch, and hearing is most beneficial to avoid occasions and temptations of sin.

O Mary, Most Pure and Chaste, help me to live a holy life pleasing to God, to Jesus, and to You. May I realize that God lives in me and I in Him. Keep me in God's and Your love. Keep me pure and chaste.

MOTHER INVIOLATE - MOTHER UNDEFILED

Mary is the Mother Inviolate. The word inviolate means unspoiled, unbroken, unstained, unprofaned. But in the life of Mary, it means no sin and no concupiscence for evil. There was no passion, no inclination, no desire for evil in Mary.

This special privilege was given to Mary because She was to be and is the Mother of God. From the very first moment of Her conception, She was filled with grace, making Her the Immaculate Conception. This grace kept all passion in obeyance. It was checked. But, when Christ was in Her womb, all vestige of concupiscence was removed. Thus Blessed Virgin Mary became in reality the "Mother Inviolate." This grace kept Her pure and holy. No one violated Her body; no sin entered Her soul.

> *O Mary, Mother Inviolate, pray for us and obtain the grace needed for us to shun sin, run away from sin, and grant us the strength to reject sin.*

UNDEFILED: When we say "Mother Undefiled, pray for us," we profess two truths, i.e., that the Blessed Mother was uncorrupt in body and soul.

The soul of Mary was and is uncorrupt because She was full of grace. By the special privilege of Immaculate Conception, She was preserved from the original sin and its effects. She crushed the head of the serpent, the devil. In Christian art, She is pictured standing on the head of the serpent. Christ crushes the devil.

Defile means to make corrupt, dirty, pollute, to violate the chastity of. Undefiled means the opposite: incorrupt, clean, unpolluted and chaste. It was and is fitting and proper that God chose such a maiden who was virtuous. It was and is proper that Christ should be conceived in a most holy and pure body. It was and is proper that Jesus gestated in a holy tabernacle, the immaculate body of Mary.

It is our Christian faith that Mary is most pure and most holy in body and in soul. Nothing could defile Her because of the amount of grace received.

As to the uncorruptness of Her body, we all profess the truth of Her assumption into Heaven. On the third day after death, She was taken into Heaven where She lives in Her glorious resurrected body. No, Her body did not become dust.

> *O Mary, keep us in the love of God. May our souls be ever holy. May sin and temptations be ever so far from us. May our bodies and souls appear full of grace before God. O Mary, Mother Undefiled, keep us pure.*

MOTHER MOST AMIABLE

From Her Heavenly home, Mary shows the same love toward all as She did upon earth. Only more so because She knows more of the secrets of God than when She lived in Nazareth.

Because of Her love for us, Her care of us, Her good deeds toward us, we call Her most Lovable and the Mother most Amiable.

15

Why is the Blessed Mother Lovable? Why is any mother lovable? It is only natural for children to love their mother. We all know the qualities of a mother. Mary had and has all of the characteristics of a mother to the highest degree. If religious and national heroes are lovable because of their goodness of character and dedication to idealism, then Mary, whose character is one of the greatest, is most amiable. She was the great heroine at the time of Christ's conception, birth, life and death. After the Ascension, She remained an example, an encouragement for the Apostles and faithful.

We breathe with pride when we speak of the great battle of Bunker Hill, Gettysburg, Meuse Argonne, Corrigedor, Okinawa, because heroism was shown there. Our bosoms swell with pride when we mention Loreto, Lourdes, Fatima, LaSalette, Guadelupe, because Mary's graciousness was and is shown there.

We all should learn more about Mary. We all should study Her life as it is recorded in the Scriptures and in Tradition. We should read about Her apparitions, Her requests, Her messages, and Her concerns for us. The more we know of Her excellence, the more we shall admire and love Her.

Mary is indeed most amiable and the most lovable. We are to love Her as She loves God by imitating Her.

> *Mary most lovable, teach us to be like You in our accepting God's will in everything May we follow Your example. May we not only say or repeat "Thy will be done," but actually execute God's will as You did. You said, "Behold the Handmaid (servant) of the Lord, be it done to me as You say (will)."*

MOTHER MOST ADMIRABLE

Natural and Divine Positive Law demands that children love, honor and respect their parents. The natural tender love and attachment of an infant toward its mother is most evident. Even our Lord, although being God, loved, obeyed, honored and respected a Creature, His Mother.

What made Holy Mary so admirable that the Son of God loved, obeyed and honored Her? What makes all Catholics and Orthodox revere Mary?

God loved Mary for everything that She was. He considered Her humility and Her complete identification of Her will with His will by a total submissive love.

Our Lord knew very well the privileges Mary received, Her extraordinary sanctity, Her dignity as Mother of God, Her love of God. For this reason, Our Lord obeyed, respected and honored His Mother. He gave us an example how to venerate Her. For about thirty years, He was subject to His earthly Parents.

Our Lord set His Mother on a throne in Heaven as Queen of Angels and Saints for all of God's creatures to admire.

King Solomon, who is an Old Testament figure of Our Lord, represents a symbol of the admiration of Christ for Mary by his respect for his mother. One day, Bethsheba came to see her favorite son to ask for a favor. King Solomon came down off his throne, took his mother and placed her upon his own throne.

Then another throne was set up for the king's mother and she sat at his right hand. The king said to her, "My mother, ask, for I must not turn away my face."

There is a sacred statue of the Mother Most Admirable in the Church of Monte Berico, Italy. Most Catholic churches have a statue or picture of Our Blessed Lady. It matters not who the artist is who carves or paints an image of Our Lady. We admire not so much his artistry, but the beauty and holiness of Mary. Our minds transcend from the image to the person. We are in awe as the image of Mary enters our mind. We cannot help it but be in admiration of the most holy and most powerful Mother of Jesus.

O Mary, as we admire You for Your perfection of holiness, power and position in our economy of salvation and Your glory in Heaven, may we not only bask in Your goodness and authority, but obtain the effects of Your perfections so that we may become more and more like You and Your Son.

MOTHER OF GOOD COUNSEL

Pope Leo XIII added the title, Mother of Good Counsel, to the Litany. We may wonder why.

This title has its foundation in the Prophet Isaiah, who called the Messiah, the "Counselor." Our Lord gave all the advice needed for a happy life upon this earth and in Heaven. The Gospels are full of this advice.

Besides being the Mother of the Counselor, Mary is a counselor in Her own right. Since She is sinless, everything in Her is good. The counsel or advice She gives is good also.

Did you ever see a child who did not turn to his mother for advice? The love and understanding a mother has of her own child can't be found in another human being. The advice mothers give is always weighed and determined after deliberate thought, taking all circumstances into consideration, especially the intimate knowledge she possesses. Added to this, Our Blessed Mother loves us and every soul.

Who of us will say we need no advice? Original sin darkened our intellects and weakened our wills. We study and study and still there are vast subjects about which we know little or nothing. Besides, we do forget so easily.

It is no wonder the Catholics turn to Mary for help and counsel for She knows the secrets of God and is the dispenser of Divine Grace. Besides, She has a great insight and knowledge of all of us because She is with God through Whom She knows all that pertains to Her.

In the Gospel at the Wedding at Cana, Mary tells the waiters, "Do what He tells you to do." We know Mary advised the Apostles and first Christians. She continues to advise all Her children. St. Dominic sought advice from Mary to combat the heresy of the Albigensians. Her advices also were given at LaSalette, Lourdes, Fatima for happiness, peace and salvation.

We, too, are to seek advice from Mary in all our serious undertakings, especially in the choice of a vocation be it in religion, marriage, or single life.

Mary, Our Mother, wants us to live with Her Son in Heaven. Repeatedly She visits us telling us, directing us, leading us, advising us, obtaining graces and favors for us.

On the feast of Mother of Good Counsel, the Church prays that we cling to Her counsels and attain Heaven.

O Mary, Mother of Good Counsel, pray for us. Obtain the wisdom for us to make proper decisions so we may please God today and every day of our lives.

MOTHER OF OUR CREATOR

We attribute a title to the Blessed Mary which seems strange to many. Because we call the Blessed Mother the Mother of Our Creator, we are accused of making Mary a goddess and even putting Her above God. Since Mary is only a creature of God, how then can She be called His Mother?

There was a time before creation - if it may be called time - when God only existed. We express that faith when we say, "I believe in God." This God then created Heaven and earth.

Our Faith further tells us that there are three persons in this one God: God the Father, God the Son, God the Holy Spirit. Our Faith tells us that God the Father is the Creator, God the Son is the Creator, God the Holy Spirit is the Creator. But, there are not three Gods nor three Creators. There is only one God, one Creator. The persons of God are equal in all respects. Since creation - to make something out of nothing - requires omnipotence, God the Father is omnipotent, God the Son is omnipotent, and God the Holy Spirit is omnipotent. Hence, when Mary gave birth to Christ, the Son of God, She became the Mother of the omnipotent Creator Son. Therefore, Mary is the Mother of Our Creator.

Because Mary is so close to God, She has partaken in many of the effects of God. Just as nearer to the fire, the more intense is the heat; so, too, with Mary who, being more close to God than any other of His creatures, acquired the greatest of all benefits and privileges from God. Among these benefits there are two special ones: most potent and beauty.

Mary's association with God has made Her most powerful. From the time of the Feast of Cana, She is practically commanding God to do what She desires. This we can see by the effects of Her power with God. During the history of Christianity, we see many miracles effected through the intercession of Mary.

All creation shows forth the beauty of God. Who will say there is no beauty in the world: the sky, the stars, the moon, the forests, the fields, the flowers, the human being - everywhere we turn we see the beauty of God's creation. Yet these are as nothing in the comparison to the beauty of the body and soul of Mary. Since the most beautiful souls among people are the saints, Mary's beauty arises far above all for She is Queen of all and is holiest of all Saints.

Mary's beauty and power are so great because She is the nearest to the source of power and beauty. She who was created by God became the Mother of the Creator when She gave birth to Christ.

Oh how wonderful and beautiful is the work of God! How thrilling it is to have Mary, our Mother, as the Mother of Beauty, of God Omnipotence, of God and of Our Creator.

O Mary, Mother of Our Creator, pray for us. Obtain for us the wisdom to appreciate all creation, to enjoy all creatures, and to come to a greater knowledge and love of You and our Creator.

MOTHER OF OUR SAVIOR

Is there any question of Mary's Motherhood of Jesus? There should not be for the whole New Testament testifies to the fact that Mary gave birth to Our Savior. St. Luke writes in Chapter 2, 11, "In the town of David a Savior has been born to You, Who is Christ the Lord."

The teaching of the Apostles was (Acts 5, 31) "God exalted Him with His right hand to be Prince and Savior." St. Paul testifies (Acts 13, 23) "From His offspring God according to promise brought to Israel a Savior, Jesus." And again St. Paul writes (Titus 3, 6) "Whom He has abundantly poured out upon us through Jesus Christ, Our Savior."

St. John in his First Letter writes (1 John 4, 14) "That the Father has sent His Son to be Savior of the world."

We need to profess Jesus as Our Savior and Lord. We need to profess Mary as the Mother of Our Savior and Lord. Christ is our acknowledged Redeemer and Mary is our Co-Redeemer because of Her cooperation with Jesus in the process of salvation.

How is Jesus a Savior and does that title really belong to Him? Jesus is the only One Who could and did satisfy the penalty of sin. Sin and especially mortal sin is infinite because it offends an infinite God. This offense requires an infinite apology. The only One Who could satisfy sufficiently to an infinite God for an infinite offense is Jesus, the God-man, Who did it by His suffering and death which is of infinite merit.

Our Lord gave the power of forgiving sins to the Apostles who, in turn, gave it to priests who receive it at their ordination. Every time we receive absolution in the Sacrament of Reconciliation, we meet the all-merciful and loving Christ, the forgiving Father, and the sanctifying Holy Spirit. Yes, in the Sacrament of Penance we meet Our Savior and Redeemer and experience the effect of His infinite mercy.

As the Blessed Virgin Mary brought Our Savior into the world, She continues working for the salvation of all peoples. Her mind of interest in the salvation of mankind is the same as that of Her Son.

O Mary, Mother of Our Savior, may You ever be at my side and especially when death comes. Pray to Your Son for us and obtain the grace of sorrow. May we receive mercy and forgiveness and may we see Our Savior face to face.

VIRGIN MOST PRUDENT

What is prudence? Here we speak of it as an infused intellectual virtue of correct reason by which we judge things according to the will of God. Its job is to advise, to help us judge correctly, and requires us to obey its urging for everyone's good.

Prudence requires:

1. Memory - a true retentiveness of faith, truths and conclusions.
2. Understanding - a view from all angles and a deep perception of consequences.
3. Docility - seek advice from others for two or more minds are better than one.
4. Knowledge of things - a vast knowledge of various subjects helps one to make better judgments.
5. Foresight - looking to the future - what will be the result or effect of our decision.
6. Circumspection - seeing under all circumstances.

Prudence as a virtue resided in a most perfect degree in Mary since prudence abides with grace and wisdom. Mary is full of grace and the seat of wisdom. Although Her intellect was not darkened by original sin, She passed judgment upon all Her acts. Before She consented becoming the Mother of Our Lord, She deliberated and consulted the Angel. Once She made the decision, it was irrevocable.

All through Her life She prudently considered Her actions as how to please God. She knew that fulfilling the will of God pleased Him most. From the Gospels we see how She acted taking the journey to Bethlehem, to Egypt, obeying Joseph, and in dealing with Her neighbors. She did not boast of Her position nor brag about Her Divine Son. She kept all these things locked up in Her heart.

In our life there are many practical, weighty decisions we will make. We need help. The devotee of the Blessed Virgin Mary knows where to turn for help. He knows who is Most Prudent and most willing to help.

O Mary, Virgin Most Prudent, help us to make correct decisions and please God in all our actions.

VIRGIN MOST VENERABLE

We are a race of hero-worshipers. Every age admired its military leaders, its idols of the stage, sports arena and arts. New York City gives a ticker-tape parade to generals, swimmers of the English Channel, football champions, etc. Babe Ruth was the idol of nearly every American boy and so was Davey Crockett.

Our religion gives vent to our nature of hero-worshiping. We do honor the great heroes and heroines of our faith. We place them upon our altars and venerate them by praising them, asking them to pray for us and by imitating some of their virtues.

Of all the Saints in Heaven, there is one who is the Most Venerable. She was selected by God Himself for this exalted high honor. He picked Her out to be the Mother of His Son. Because of this privilege, She was laden with every gift and honor. The angels saluted Her. St. Joseph and St. Elizabeth admired Her. The Apostles revered Her, the faithful all down through the ages have shown and still show their great love and respect to Her. The works of artists, musicians, architects, and builders have perpetuated the expression of their love for Her. The lives of men have been drawn to sanctity because of Mary.

Mary's excellence has given Her an unusual place in the hearts and minds of the faithful. She is the Most Venerable.

Because Catholics place Mary in Her exulted position of worship, we have been branded as idolaters or we worship Her as a goddess. How foolish and rash is that statement!

True the first Commandment does prohibit the worship of a creature as God. If we Catholics worshiped Mary as a goddess, then indeed we would be idolaters. Mary's worship is not adoration, for adoration is that worship which pertains to God alone. Mary's worship is veneration. It is the highest kind of honor, love, and respect given to a creature. This we call Hyperdulia. Dulia is the ordinary honor and respect given to God's friends who are already in Heaven. They are honored because they achieved something which is derived from the goodness of God. God is honored for the Goodness which He is Himself. Mary receives Hyperdulia and saints Dulia, while God receives adoration.

The best answer to those who accuse us of idolatry in our worship of saints is the answer we give to the invocations in our Litanies. We say, "God, have mercy on us." "Christ, have mercy on us." But we say, "Mary, pray for us."

It is not difficult to see why the Blessed Virgin Mary is the Most Venerable. Her great love of God with Her immaculate heart, Her complete identification of Her will with God's, Her honor as Mother of God and Queen of Heaven place Her in that August position.

The faithful, realizing the exulted station of Mary, have venerated Her in every possible way. And, in their love of Mary, two things are most noticeable: first, the imitation of Mary's virtues and, second, the taking of Mary as one's advocate.

O Mary, inspire us to live in great love of God as You did and do and intercede for us now and at the hour of our death.

VIRGIN MOST RENOWNED

"Virgo Praedicanda"... The Virgin is to be made known and to be known by all.

Of all the names of persons who lived upon the earth, there is one name, excepting that of Our Lord Jesus, which is most remembered and worldwide known. This Heroine's name is spoken of most tenderly now over two thousand years. God Himself magnified the name of Mary.

Why is Mary so renowned, so famous, so exalted by all?

1. She is famous for Her humility which was most pleasing to God.
2. Her greatest fame comes from the fact that She is the Mother of God.
3. Because of vocation as our Lord's Mother, She was worthy of a visit from an Archangel; filled with Sanctifying grace, preserved from original sin.
4. God loved Her in a special way for He bestowed upon Her all kinds of privileges and favors.
5. The Apostles loved Mary. They were encouraged by Her. They wept at Her tomb. They carried Her name and greatness everywhere they went. As they spread the Gospel of Christ, they spread the knowledge of Mary. As they fostered the love of Christ, they also included the love of His Blessed Mother.

Where the Apostles left off in praising Mary, the early Fathers of the Church took Her up. With this knowledge and love of Mary, the faithful throughout all ages and times have learned to know Her, love Her, and praise Her.

The praise of Mary is seen in hymns and songs, in paintings, statues and other works of art, in churches and shrines. Her name is given to churches, schools, cities, lakes and rivers.

She becomes the Queen of Poland and Ireland, the Patroness of America, the Protector of Mexico and all Americas.

Everywhere in the world, the name of Mary is known and loved. God wants Her glory, Her virtue, Her power, Her life proclaimed and praised. That is why He permits Her to visit upon this earth from time to time to remind people of Her love.

We, too, are to join in the praise of Mary and to help in making Her known and loved by more people. In Your contacts with other people, let them know Mary and let them love Her. She will take all who love Her and lead them to Her Son.

O Mary, help us to spread Your love for us so that all may know You and experience Your solicitude. May we rejoice in Your fame forever in Heaven.

VIRGIN MOST POWERFUL

Man craves power. This thirst for power begins early and lasts long: a child at play wants to be the leader; a youth strives for captaincy of a team or president of a club. Workmen want to be the boss; a soldier a general; every man a king in his own home, a woman a queen in her domain. Some think they are gods and goddesses. The whole world was theirs as for Alexander, Napoleon, and Hitler.

Earthly power is a blessing if used properly for a common good, but when abused it is tyranny. An absolute monarchy can be the best and worst form of government. The power of God was not nor is tyranny because He is most just. God has given power to Mary which power She also uses justly. Since She is next to God and greatest of all creatures, Her power is next to that of God's and, therefore, She is most powerful but not all powerful. Only God is all powerful; Mary is most powerful.

Whence comes Her power? The privilege and honor Mary received are all due to Her because of Her destiny of being the Mother of Jesus. Did She have God do favors for Her and fulfill Her requests? Absolutely.

What happened at Cana when the wine ran out? It was through Mary's request that She moved Jesus to perform His first public miracle.

The Gospels are written about Jesus. Very little is recorded in Scripture about Mary. But, ever since the Assumption until our present day, much is written about Mary, about Her apparitions, Her miracles, Her influence of changing the lives of people. To verify Her power before God, all we need to do is to visit Lourdes, Fatima or Guadalupe where we can see many documents of miracles and cures received through the intercession of Mary. If fortunate, we may witness a cure.

We repeat often the adage, "The hand that rocks the cradle rules the world." Mary's power before Jesus is great. When we run into snags, we should turn to Mary.

O Mary, Most Powerful, obtain for me all the graces and wisdom needed to lead a good life. By Your power, beseech Jesus for the strength to overcome sin, to acquire virtue, and attain everlasting life in Heaven.

VIRGIN MOST MERCIFUL

How is it possible for the Blessed Virgin to be most merciful when, in the first apparition at Fatima, She requested the three children to accept all the sacrifices and sufferings God would send them in reparation for sin and conversion of sinners? We know how much the children suffered because of the opposition of the people and government. Also, we know some of the sufferings St. Bernadette endured after she saw the Blessed Mother in Lourdes. How can we square up with the apparent contradictions?

The word mercy comes from the Latin "Misericordia," which means heart of misery, a torn heart. Did Mary ever have a torn heart? Yes, indeed, very much so. Do you recall Her Seven Sorrows? In most of Her paintings, why have the artists painted Her with a sad countenance? Is it because She suffered because of the cruel treatment Christ received and because of the burden of sin which Christ bore on His shoulders? Do you think the paintings of Our Lady of Perpetual Help or Our Lady of Czestochowa are happy pictures?

We know Our Blessed Lady has a sympathetic heart. She had concern for the young couple at Cana. She had concern for Jesus as He carried His cross and when crucified. The Pietà is a magnificent portrayal of Her sorrows.

Because She endured distress caused by the suffering of Jesus, She has concern for us who are the Mystical Body of Christ and we are Her children. We are confident Mary knows our problems and sufferings, sadness and troubles -

physical and spiritual. Therefore, She has empathy for all Her children because She is a loving Mother who is troubled by our misery.

We look to Mary because She is especially merciful to the sinner because sin is the greatest evil and makes one most miserable. She is merciful to the afflicted. She is most merciful to all in the fear of death for She brings consolation to them and inspires them to look to Heaven and for the mercy of God.

The Church realized the power of Mary and the extent of Her mercy for, in the early days of Christianity, the prayer "Hail Mary" was formulated. We ask Her to be with us at the moment of our death and we ask for Her prayers. It is a salutary practice to recite the "Hail Holy Queen... In all our afflictions we turn toward Thee, O Virgin Mary. Despise not our petitions, but in Your mercy hear and answer them"

> *O Mary, be at our side and obtain God's mercy and forgiveness for us. May we experience Your mercy now and may we see You and Jesus forever.*

VIRGIN MOST FAITHFUL

We have seen fidelity in this world. Couples are married twenty-five, forth, fifty and sixty years. Their attachment, their loyalty, their mutual self-sacrifice astonishes us. Yet love demands this loyalty and faithfulness.

The faithfulness of a mother to her sick child is seen by her continual attendance at his bedside. A mother's love demonstrates stick-to-it-tiveness as she will stay at the side of the wayward son and defend him.

The faithfulness of the Blessed Mother is far greater than any shown upon this earth.

1. She was faithful to Her love of God all Her life. No matter what difficulty of problem She faced, She did all to please God.
2. After She gave birth to Our Lord, She remained trustworthy and loyal to Him, remaining with Him until the end.
3. While She lived with St. Joseph, She as his wife was at his side sharing all the dangers, trials, hardships and work. She is a model for all wives in this virtue. If more of our women had Her as a patroness and practiced Her virtues, divorce would be extinct.

Mary loved St. Joseph. She had reverence for him, for She knew his position. Therefore, She trusted him completely. His reverence and trust was great, too, for he knew the sacredness of Her body, the sanctity of our soul, and Her uniqueness of vocation. He honored Her body and soul. And he did not dare violate the integrity of Her body, or lessen the sanctity of Her soul. But, rather, his love furthered Her sanctity. Such was the mutual trust and love of Blessed Mother and St. Joseph.

We are all required to love one another by the precept of Our Lord. Our love is to be a faithful and trustworthy one. The love of husband and wife is to be of a great faith, of a great trust, of a great reverence for each other, of a great respect of the soul and body. We are not animals, but children of God. We have immortal souls which are most sacred and they demand respect.

O Mary, Most Faithful, teach all of us to be faithful in our love of God and each other. Keep us adamant in our stand of serving You and even stronger to profess our faith and love and to avoid separating from You and God. Let us remember that it is he who will be saved who perseveres to the end.

MIRROR OF JUSTICE

Does a mirror distort a figure? There are those mirrors that do just that, but the ordinary mirrors we have in our homes reflect the image as it is. It is not strange that we like the image of ourselves. We can easily repeat the words "Mirror, mirror on the wall, who is the fairest of them all?" We are gratified with seeing ourselves, especially when we are happy and all dressed up.

How often are we told that our eyes, our face, and our disposition reflect what is inside of us. The eyes are the mirror of the soul, we are told. The face reflects joy, sadness, anger, trouble, concern, placidness and/or just plain nothing. "Your face is just a blank," we have heard expressed. "Your face reveals your inner happiness and peace."

Every person reflects the greatness of God to a greater or lesser degree, for we are created in the image and likeness of God. Our bodies reflect what God had in mind for us. Our intellect and will reflect the powers of knowing and choosing which God has in the highest degree. Our soul has the immortality of God. There is beauty, order in our bodies, and all body parts form unity and there is symmetry. The qualities come directly from God's wisdom and knowledge.

According to the image of God, mankind does act like God if he is in love with God and his fellow man. The attributes of God are exhibited in us human beings when we live in the love of God. A soul filled with the Spirit of God cannot help but manifest the fruits and gifts of the Holy Spirit.

The face of Moses after his meetings with God glowed with a certain light that people feared to approach him. The glory of God reflected from him so much that the people begged him to cover his face.

Our Blessed Mother was filled with the Holy Spirit and all His gifts. She was full of grace. Because God gave Her all the grace and privileges which came along with Her accepting the mission of being the Mother of God, Mary possessed the graces and privileges of being the Daughter of God the Father, the Mother of God the Son, and the Spouse of the Holy Spirit. Her will was to do the will of God. "Be it done to me according to Thy word."

Because of Her holiness, She reflects God's attributes. She reflects His justice.

O Mary, most just, we beg from You to be the recipients of all graces so that we, too, can reflect God's goodness, kindness and mercy. Instill in our hearts the Christian virtue of justice for all. May we render to all what belongs to them. May we give God the honor and glory which is due Him. May we have the highest honor for You and also reflect God's justice.

MARY, THE SEAT OF WISDOM

There is a story told about two brothers who were in the Dominican seminary in Italy. Hyacinth had no problem with the studies while the grades of Chester were very low. One day, as the two Polish youths were recreating in the monastery garden, they came upon a statue of the Blessed Mother. "Do you pray to the Virgin for wisdom?" asked Hyacinth. "No," responded Chester, "but I do pray to the Blessed Mother for graces to be holy." "If you want to become a priest and pass all your examinations, you better pray to the Seat of Wisdom for wisdom. We do want to return home as priests and bring our people to the knowledge and love of God." Chester did pray to the Seat of Wisdom. He passed his tests, was ordained a priest, returned home and was a missionary pastor in his own country. Some claim they were only relatives. He is known today as Blessed Chester while his brother is Saint Hyacinth.

Our Blessed Virgin is truly the Seat of Wisdom for She is the headquarters of God's wisdom. Her body was Christ's house and temple. Christ ruled from Her arms. We learned that Mary is the Daughter of God the Father, Who is all wise; She is the Mother of God the Son, Who is all wise; She is the Spouse of the Holy Spirit, Who is wisdom itself. Being so intimate with God and His wisdom, Mary was/is filled with wisdom and She was/is filled with grace. It is from this treasury and reservoir that Mary dispenses super abundances of wisdom and graces to all who call upon Her.

Wisdom is that spiritual gift by which one judges according to God's standard, according to His will. Human wisdom is attained by reason and experience, while Divine wisdom is a gift from God. This practical wisdom directs all our actions for the honor and glory of God and for our salvation and for the salvation of others. Wisdom gives reason for labor, for long suffering, for living upon this earth. We have been taught our faith from our parents that the beginning of wisdom according to Scripture is the fear of the Lord. It is wise to be sorry for sin and to despise sin. It is wise to long for Heaven. It is wise to offer one's self and everything one thinks, says, does, enjoys and suffers for the honor and glory of God and for one's salvation.

Wisdom fills the soul with certain divine attractiveness, making one's words and all actions acceptable to God. Deeds, possessions or lack of them, sickness or health accepted according to God's will brings us to glory.

As Christ learned many things from Mary by His human experiences, so, too, can we learn much from Her. It is no wonder that saints turned to Her for guidance, for wisdom, for grace. All saints attribute much of their wisdom to Mary.

O Mary, Seat of Wisdom, teach us how to live according to God's standard and direct our lives according to God's will that we

*may bring greater honor and glory to God and salvation to
ourselves.*

*Inspire us to judge others as God would judge them. May we
have the wisdom to be tolerant, to be kind and to be forgiving.
Guide us to use Your and God's standards when we see people
acting differently than we do. You along with God know all
circumstances while we humble beings do not. Wisdom, come to
me. Mary, Seat of Wisdom, help me to be wise.*

CAUSE OF OUR JOY

How easy it is to consider the Blessed Mother as the Sorrowful Virgin. Her
association with Christ during His Sacred Passion and the uniting of Herself
with His sufferings plus Her hatred of sin brings to our mind Her Seven
Sorrows. Even now, when She appears upon this world, She is grieved by the
sins committed by man. Yet, Mary is considered as being full of joy and is the
cause of it.

Joy is a pleasure or satisfaction we experience and which is brought about
in many ways:

1. God so created us that we find many pleasures in the creatures of the
   world. The blessings of God are everywhere. The trees, flowers, hills,
   plains, water, rain, snow, cold, warmth, the beauty of the sky, the order
   of plant life, and everything God has created can give us joy, pleasure,
   satisfaction.

   There are some creatures which require some consciousness of their
   good before they give pleasure, music, painting, sciences, books and
   the like. For a connoisseur of art, a painting will hold him spellbound
   for hours while to the unversed, it's just a blot of paint.

2. People are a greater source of joy. How great is the joy of the parents of
   a new baby? Association, friendship and love keeps life interesting and
   the world populated.

3. Our own good acts afford us pleasure. A kind word, a charitable deed,
   the extending of our goodness to our fellow man brings an
   unfathomable joy to our hearts. This is true because our goodness
   comes from God Who is goodness Himself and the consequences the
   participating in the joy of God. God is joy because He is love and He is
   the first cause of our joy.

Mary is the second cause of our joy because She is the Mother of God,
Mother of Our Redeemer. What greater joy is there in the world than that
brought by the knowledge of our redemption?

Joy is a characteristic of holiness. Mary is full of joy because She is full of
the love of God, sanctifying grace.

If we are to be truly joyful, we, too, must be in love with God and Mary. We
must be holy.

*O Mary, cause of our joy, fill our hearts with a great love of
God.*

SPIRITUAL VESSEL

What do we mean when we say that man is very spiritual or that man has no spirituality? Usually spirituality means:
1. a love of God
2. a life of sanctifying grace
3. an attainment of a greater degree of Christian perfection

Since the Blessed Mother is attributed with the beautiful descriptive title of "Spiritual Vessel," let us briefly consider wherein Her spirituality lies.

1. Love of God - love - deep devotedness - self-sacrifice - putting one's will in complete conformity with the Beloved's. Mary's love of God was beyond measure. As a Maiden, She vowed Her purity to Him. Her attitude throughout Her life was, "Behold Thy Handmaid, be it done to me according to Thy word." She asked others to do likewise as, at the marriage feast at Cana, "Whatsoever He shall say, do ye." She sacrificed Herself completely for His love.

    Then what mother does not love her child? Here Mary's Son is the Son of God. Her love for Him is more intense than the love of any other mother, for She knew who Christ was. She appreciated God that much more because She knew who and what He is.

2. Mary indeed can be called "The Spiritual Vessel," for She truly is a container of God. She was conceived full of grace. Christ was conceived in Her by the Holy Spirit and Christ lived in Her body. She was the most dear Daughter of God the Father. The great degree of sanctifying grace which She had made Her the Mansion of the Blessed Trinity all the days of Her life.

3. Spirituality is produced by a Christian perfection and Christian perfection is only possible by living a life of imitation of Christ. "Take up thy cross and follow Me." Who could possibly follow Christ in every detail more closely than Christ's own Mother? Mary identified Herself with Her Son. She shared in all His joys and sufferings. She offered Her whole life for the benefit of mankind just as Christ did.

And, even today, She still is concerned about the welfare of Her children. Not only does She speak to Her Son and to God the Father for them, but also Her concern for us has brought Her upon earth numerous times. She pleads with us to love God, to serve God, to pray, to keep away from sin, to do good and to observe Sundays.

O Mary, Spiritual Vessel, make us lovers of God and spiritual vessels, too.

VESSEL OF HONOR

A goldsmith molded a beautiful and artistic monstrance. Whenever anyone saw it, they were thrilled by its excellence and they praised its maker.

In a way, God is such a goldsmith Who formed a most beautiful and excellent vessel, the masterpiece of His handiwork, the Blessed Mother.

All the world for all ages admires the greatness and beauty of the Blessed Mother. This recognition of Her excellence and nobleness by all people is a way of honoring Her. The many shrines, churches and chapels named after Her; the numerous books, poems and hymns written in Her praise; the statues and paintings of Her - all these are external manifestations of the honor heaped upon Mary by the faithful.

All this honor rightly given to Mary, whom God created as His most perfect and beloved creature. He made Her full of grace, most pure, most humble, most loving, and kind. Everything about Her was marvelous and holy.

"Holy the womb that bore Him, holy the breasts that fed. But holier still the royal heart that in His Passion bled." (Newman).

This wonderful creature of God neither was nor is devoid of honor. Her complete life was a continuous praise and honor of God. For this reason, She is named "Vessel of Honor." God honored Mary and Mary, in turn, honored and honors God.

She honored God by Her life in the temple as a young girl and She honored Him by vowing chastity. She honored Him by giving Her will over completely to Him. She honored God by becoming the Mother of His Son and fulfilling His will in raising Christ and by giving an example to all how to love God and be obedient to His holy will. She honored Him during the Sacred Passion. She honored Him during the Death, Resurrection and Ascension of Christ. She honored Him by encouraging and teaching the Apostles and early Christians. She honored God in Her own death and Assumption. She sings His honor now in Heaven. She furthers His honor now in Heaven. She furthers His honor by teaching the faithful to love God better. Even to honor God, She leaves Heaven and comes upon this earth reminding us to love God.

O Mary, Vessel of Honor, make us into vessels which will honor God by our daily lives and deeds now and by singing His glory forever in Heaven.

SINGULAR VESSEL OF DEVOTION

The great love of the Blessed Virgin Mary had and has for God and the love the faithful have for Mary has given Her a special title, that of "Singular Vessel of Devotion."

Mary's love of God was complete; Her devotion to Him was total. She pledged Herself and vowed to be in God's service forever. She expressed Her consuming love by word and deed. She lived in the Temple, She gave Her will completely to God, She lived with God upon earth, She worked for Him. Her love of God was totalitarian as expressed by St. Paul, "Whether you eat or drink or whatsoever you do, do all for the glory of God." No human heart ever loved God as this heart of Mary. It is easy to see why Mary is titled as the Singular Vessel of Devotion.

1. The faithful, realizing the unique privilege and honored position of Blessed Virgin Mary, have made Her a Vessel of Devotion as no other of God's creatures. The honor and respect given Her is by far the greatest rendered to the Saints. This veneration merits a special name of Hyperdulia, the highest possible veneration of a saint. We know that Mary's sanctity is by far the greatest of all God's creatures, even greater than that of all the saints put together. God gave Her all this grace because She is the Mother of His Son, the Spouse of the Holy Spirit, the singularly privileged Daughter of the Father. She commands the love, honor, and respect which the Church gives Her.

2. The devotion to Mary is shown by the confidence the faithful have in Her. We title Her Mother, showing what trust and love we put in Her. We fly to Her for help in any distress or difficulty. We lean upon Her as we did upon our mothers when we were children. We know how good She is and how faithful She has always been to us. We know that Christ bequeathed Her to us. Christ, Who died for sinners, should give us a mother who cares very much for sinners, too. As He wanted them to convert and live, She also does the same.

3. Lastly, the devotion is shown to Mary by the love and affection we have for Mary. Who cannot love Mary, since She is so good, so beautiful, so great? Who cannot love Her who did and does so much for us? No matter where we go throughout the world, we shall find churches and shrines dedicated to Mary, and thousands and even millions of faithful come to those places dedicated to Her to honor Her and to pour out their love to Her.

Mary's devotedness to God is an example for all of us to follow. She respected God and gave Him the honor due Him, She placed all confidence in Him, She loved Him above all. May we honor and love God so much as to see Him forever.

O Mary, teach us to be devoted to God and to Your Son. Help us to respect God and to give Him the honor which is due Him. May we follow Your example and place all our confidence in God Whom You loved above all. Mary, stimulate our hearts to honor You, be devoted to You, and to love You. May our acts of Hyperdulia prove our devotion to You.

MYSTICAL ROSE

The "loveliest flower" that ever bloomed is a rose. There are more expensive flowers than the rose as the orchid, and more fragrant as the gardenia - but only the rose has that great public appeal. All peoples throughout all ages regard the rose as the queen of all flowers.

God has a beautiful flower garden of Saints and the rose therein is the Virgin Mary. Her sanctity, loveliness, and fragrance spread forth throughout all

Heaven and earth. And, because our human mind is incapable of completely describing Mary's beauty and greatness, faith has called Her the "Mystical Rose."

All the fine arts: music, poetry, painting and sculpture are employed to extol the beauty of the Mystical Rose. The human mind and heart work hand in hand in praising the Virgin Mary.

As the rose has two stages of beauty - that as a bud and fully bloomed, so, too, is Mary's beauty. The bud stage of Mary's loveliness is the period from the creation to Her Immaculate Conception. This is the era when God had Her in His mind. He knew from the very beginning that Adam and Eve would sin and His Son would have to come upon the earth to redeem mankind The thought of Son and Mother went hand in hand. The plan of redemption required a mother for the Son of God. In God's mind, He saw a beautiful Maiden, holy, lovely, and devoted. She was the loveliest of all His creatures and the one whom He loved most.

> *O Mary, may we through Your intercession be pleasing to God as You are to Him and as a rose is to mankind.*

The full bloom stage of the Mystical Rose covers the time from the Immaculate Conception on for all eternity. Now the flower is seen by all. Its fragrance diffuses itself over the whole of Heaven and earth. Mary, in Her full bloom, was in Bethlehem, Egypt, Nazareth, Jerusalem and on Mount Calvary. Her sanctity and submission to God's will filled Her completely and permeated Her whole being and Her works. As the perfume of a rose is highly volatile, so Mary's sanctity and loveliness volatizes most readily without becoming rancid or depleted.

It is not strange that, in many of Mary's appearances, there are roses - at Lourdes and Guadalupe especially.

Mary is the Mystical Rose, who makes fragrant our road through life to Heaven. Our fight with the devil, our difficulties in spiritual life, our difficulties in our physical life are made easier by Her and more pleasant and easier to bear. May we follow the aroma of this Rose to the Garden of Heaven.

> *O Mary, make our souls beautiful as a rose. May the odor of sanctity accompany our lives. We pray that, through Your power, we all may be most pleasing in the eyes of God as roses are pleasing to all peoples. May our good deeds rise in the eyes of God and man as an aroma of rose perfume. O Mary, pray for us and help us to be pleasing to God and helpful to man.*

TOWER OF DAVID

The enemies of man are many. All through the ages we read of wars, battles, and raids. To protect themselves, man built fortifications, be they in form of walls, towers, castles, trenches, or the atom bomb.

In the time of the Old Testament, the shepherds built towers for a defense. From these high towers they saw their enemies approach. Within these towers they hid their valuables, women and children. From the heights of these defenses they shot arrows and threw stones upon the invaders. These towers protected the whole of Judea.

From all times there was and is an enemy of man's soul. The devil tempted and won the battle with Adam and Eve. He also tempted Our Lord. No one is spared of his machinations.

Everyone is to build a fortification against the enemy of his eternal bliss. "Watch and pray, lest you fall into temptation," says Our Lord. We have much more assurance of victory when we watch and pray from within the protection of the Tower of David, which is Our Blessed Mother.

She is called the Tower of David because David was the greatest, most noble, most respected, most feared King of Israel. He united the country of Judea. He established Jerusalem as a Holy City, the home of the Ark of the Covenant of God. David was a symbol of strength, of prayer, of penance. David was a man according to God's own heart. He was a great lover of God, a great prophet, a prototype of Christ. And, from his house, Mary is born.

When the great King, Christ, came to Judea to establish His Kingdom upon earth, He established a most formidable force, a most sturdy tower, a great defense. When the devil fights for our souls, he has to fight the Blessed Mother, too. All who enter under Her mantle need not fear of error in faith, nor loss of virtue, nor loss of Heaven. She is that Tower which crushes the head of the serpent. Only they are lost who do not place themselves under the protection of the Tower of David.

> O Mary, the Tower of David, take us into Thy ramparts and save us. Remember, O most gracious Virgin Mary, that never was it known that anyone who fled to Thy protection, implored Thy help and sought Thy intercession was left unaided. Inspired with this confidence, I fly unto Thee, O Virgin of virgins, my Mother, to Thee I come; before Thee I stand, sinful and sorrowful. O Mother of the Word Incarnate, despise not my petitions; but in Thy clemency hear and answer me.

TOWER OF IVORY

We saw how the Blessed Mother under the title Tower of David is a formidable bastion of power protecting the faithful from sin and error in faith.

Under the title "Tower of Ivory," we see the beautiful structure of strength called purity.

Ivory among the Jews was a very scarce commodity, rare, expensive and, once possessed, it was fashioned into beautiful pieces of art. Its pliable nature gave way to the artist's knife. Its surfaces became brilliant with luster of high polish. The quality was of long endurance.

The Tower of Ivory as applied to the Blessed Mother has this meaning - a symbol of endurance, chastity, and beauty.

Ivory, besides having a quality of not rusting nor rotting, has a whiteness as compared to the Blessed Mother's purity. In Her purity is Her strength, for purity gives mastery over all spiritual evil. We speak of knowledge as a power and that it is. But purity of body is that power which gives perfect peace of mind, tranquility of passion, and security of gaining Heaven.

This beautiful Tower of Ivory was carved by God Himself. True, all God's creatures are beautiful: the raindrop, snowflake, the leaf, flower, tree, lakes, mountains, the sky. Yet far more beautiful is the creature called man for the human being was formed in the image and likeness of God. The most beautiful of all human beings is the Blessed Virgin Mary, for God took from Her body, blood and flesh for His Own Son. She had to be most perfect also. Her body was most beautiful, but Her soul surpassed all comeliness. Her soul, with its grace, love, humility and chastity, is so outstanding that it shines forth like a beacon light in the darkness, like a high, white tower to be seen by all.

O Beautiful Tower of Ivory, be not only our inspiration and example of purity and love, but also obtain for us that grace to conquer the devil and repel all temptation against purity. Mary, be our tower of protection.

HOUSE OF GOLD

Nothing is too good for God. Nothing too expensive, nothing too beautiful. The greatest talents and the most costly metals have been employed for the houses of God. The finest of gold and silver, stone and marble, the best in architectural and engineering designs have built the magnificent cathedrals and basilicas.

One of the most beautiful and costly houses of God was the temple built by King Solomon in Jerusalem. Eighty thousand men alone carved stones for the edifice. Three thousand overseers or bosses were placed on the many jobs. The oracle, the Holy of Holies, where the Ark of God was to rest, was made of the purest gold. Even the floors were overlaid with gold plates which were nailed with gold. Everything was covered with gold. The temple in Jerusalem was the House of God, and the spirit of God lives there.

God built a special temple Himself in Mary, His Mother. The plans for this house were made from all eternity. They were perfected in the Immaculate Conception. The flesh was of the finest gold of purity. The spirit was of the greatest amount of sanctifying grace. The mind was adorned by the gold of humility and prayer. Into this most beautiful and precious temple came our Lord to live, to take a body, from which to come to save the world by His love and grace, from which He came to become one of us.

No, nothing is too expensive for the Lord; neither heart nor life. Mary gave Her heart and life to God. This heart was pierced causing Her life to be spent in a palace of pain. The very depth of Her soul was wounded as She held Her lifeless Son's body in Her arms. Yet Her heart and life became more noble - a purer gold by these trials and tribulations.

O House of Gold, intercede for us that we, too, may be purified by our daily crosses and by God's grace be fitting temples for His residence in us.

ARK OF THE COVENANT

The devotion to the Blessed Mother as the Ark of the Covenant has its beginnings in the doctrine of St. Thomas Aquinas who lived in the thirteenth century. St. Thomas wrote that Christ, to whom the word Ark was first applied, took His flesh and blood from the immaculate and untainted body and blood of the Blessed Virgin. Thus, She was like the Ark of the Covenant of the Old Testament, for Both were made of the most precious and durable substances.

The first time we read of the word "ark" is in connection with Noah. God ordered Noah to build an ark to save all life. And, when the rains stopped, God made an agreement or covenant with Noah that no more deluges would visit the earth.

An agreement was made by God in Paradise to send a Messiah. This agreement God renewed from time to time with the patriarchs of Abraham, Isaac, and Joseph. He makes a further covenant with the Hebrews through Moses on Mt. Sinai in a form of promises and commands on two tablets of stone.

These tablets God ordered to be kept in a special chest, an ark made of cedar wood inlaid and overlaid with the purest gold and crowned with gold. This ark was carried by the Levites wherever the Hebrews went. They kept the ark in sight because it was most sacred and most precious. If anyone looked upon it or touched it unworthily, he was struck dead. For the spirit of God lived in the ark. This ark gave the Hebrew army strength. Victory was theirs at all times when the ark was in the front lines. The Hebrews made God the general of their army. God was the Lord of Hosts.

By carrying the ark seven times around the city of Jericho, the walls of the city crumbled. The Jews carried the ark into Jerusalem and there it found a worthy place of rest in the beautiful temple of King Solomon.

The ark passes out of the pages of history in the year 530 B.C. when Nebuchadnezzar sacked the city and burned the temple. No longer did the Jews have the ark.

Now, Christian faith applies the name "Ark to the Blessed Virgin Mary for She is like the Ark of the Covenant of the Old Testament.

1. The ark was made of acacia wood which is rare and estimated as incorruptible -so Blessed Virgin Mary is one of this kind. She has a body which is incorruptible, for after death She does not return to dust, but is assumed into Heaven.
2. The ark was covered with the purest gold - Mary's gold was Her super abundance of grace and purity.

3. The ark contained the two tablets of the ten commandments and the spirit of God was in it - Mary had the singular distinction to have the author of the Ten Commandments, God Himself, live in Her body.
4. The ark was blessed and sanctified unto God alone - Mary was blessed among all women and sanctified by the Holy Spirit Himself.
5. The ark was taken and placed into the city of Jerusalem - Mary, too, was taken into the new city of Jerusalem and placed on the throne near Her Son.
6. So as in the ark were two tablets of stone, in Mary at one time were two hearts - the most sacred heart of Jesus and Her sweetest immaculate heart.

O Mary, Ark of the Covenant, bring Thy Son to us and fortify us with His spirit. As the Hebrews of old marched into battle behind the ark, may we, too, march behind You through this battle of life on earth to conquer eternal victory.

MARY, GATE OF HEAVEN

The Church has adapted many passages of Sacred Scripture to the Blessed Virgin Mary. Among some of these is the section of the Prophet Ezechiel, Chapter 44, verses 1 to 3, in which the inspired word is, "Then he brought me back to the outer gate of the sanctuary, facing the east, but it was closed. He said to me: 'This gate is to remain closed; it is not be opened for anyone to enter by it; since the Lord, the God of Israel, has entered by it, it shall remain closed.'"

The adapted meaning is: Mary was a virgin before the birth of Christ and only He entered the Womb of Mary to take His humanity. After the birth, the gate was closed, meaning Mary remained a virgin. It is our faith that Mary was a virgin before the birth of Christ, during the birth of Christ, and after the birth of Christ.

The Jesuits have a motto, "Through Mary to Jesus." As Jesus came into this world through Mary, we are to go to Jesus through Mary.

Wherever we may go to any of the shrines of the Blessed Mother, She has one purpose in mind, "TO LEAD ALL PEOPLE TO JESUS AND TO ETERNAL HAPPINESS." Since Jesus is eternal happiness, Mary wants us to know Jesus, love Jesus, serve Jesus, and be with Jesus, Who said, "I am the Sheep Gate."

Our Mother knows better than all of us that the "WILL OF GOD IS TO BE DONE." She not only knew of the will of God, but She said, "Behold the Handmaid of the Lord, be it done to be according to Thy word." From the moment She knew She was to be the Mother of Jesus, She disposed Herself to the will of God and fulfilled every wish of God. We, too, are to say, "Thy will be done," and mean it.

Our Lord gave Mary to us as our Mother whom we are to respect, love and obey. He gave Her to us that She may take care of us, intercede for us, help us, and pray for us. Through Mary, the Gate of Heaven, we shall see and live with Jesus.

O Mary, You brought Jesus to us. Take us by our hand and lead us to Jesus now and especially at the hour of our death. May we enter Heaven because of Your goodness and love for us. May we rejoice with You and with God forever. Be our Gate of Heaven and let us enter into life of everlasting joy.

MORNING STAR

We are all fascinated by the sight of stars. But our appreciation of the stars is comparatively nothing to that of the sailors.

True, today the sailors do not depend too much upon the stars, nevertheless, a star is a sign of a clear night, a fair night. Before the time of the compass, the stars were all important to sailors. The stars gave them direction. The stars gave them assurance, consolation, certainty, and joy. As long as they could keep their eyes upon the stars, they knew all things were going right. On cloudy and stormy nights, the sailors prayed for a glimpse of the stars. Direction was lost, fear fell upon the men, many times hope was lost as well as the ship and lives just because the star was not there to direct them. The morning star was a cause for rejoicing.

To us upon this earth, the Blessed Virgin Mary is that Star of the Sea who shines at all times. There is no cloud big and thick enough to dim or blot out Her light. She is there shining at all times, directing and leading us through the rough sea of life to our eternal Port.

We all must admit that there are times in our lives when the sea of life gets plenty rough. The numerous temptations during our lives keep driving us upon the rocks of disaster. And there were times when we may have suffered some calamity. If we could only keep our heads and look to the Star of the Sea, all would be well.

St. Bernard gives us very sound advice when he said, "O thou who feelest thyself tossed by the tempests in the midst of the shoals of this world, turn not thine eyes away from the Star of the Sea if thou wouldst avoid shipwreck. If the winds of temptation rise against thee, if thou are confronted by the rocks of tribulation, look at the Star and call on Mary. If thou art agitated by the waves of pride, ambition, calumny, jealousy, look at the Star and call on Mary. If anger, avarice, the allurements of the flesh seem to engulf the frail vessel of thy soul, cast a look toward Mary. If thou art disturbed by the enormity of the sins, confounded by the foulness of thy conscience, terrified by the horror of the judgment of God, overcome by sadness, from the abyss of despair send up a thought to Mary. Let the name of Mary be always on thy lips and in thy heart, and while invoking Her intercession, do not fail to practice Her virtues. Following Her, thou canst not go astray; praying to Her, thou canst not be without hope; thinking of Her, thou wilt be on the right path; as long as She sustains thee, thou canst not fail."

From all the care Blessed Mary has for us, we can readily see why She is called the Star of the Sea, our Salvation.

O Mary, give us the enlightenment to look upon Thee when we are in temptation, in doubt, in distress, or/and in trouble. O Star of the Sea, pray for us and all will be well. May Your Star lead us safely to Port.

HEALTH OF THE SICK

From the beginning of Christianity, the Blessed Mother has been invoked by the faithful who were in some difficulty and especially when sick. Because their prayers were answered, Mary has been given a special title of "Health of the Sick."

It is only fitting that the Blessed Virgin Mary should be the Health of the Sick, for, as a true follower of Her Son, She imitated and still imitates His actions and labors for the same purpose Her Son had.

Our Lord came to save mankind. True, this is especially a spiritual goal, but, where can you read in the Gospels where Our Lord neglected to body afflicted. He went about everywhere healing the sick. No sickness was too vile or too far gone - no, not even leprosy. Our Lord's compassion for the afflicted knew no limit.

The Blessed Mother accompanied Our Lord and learned from Him how to love Her neighbor, how to pity them and how to help them. She learned more of the sufferings of the human body when St. Joseph died in Her arms. But, most of all, Her heart was wrung by the sufferings of Her own Divine Son. The three hour long lesson She received at the foot of the cross impressed Her heart indelibly.

The lesson of mercy and pity for the sick was learned well by the Blessed Virgin Mary for She has been taking care of the sick ever since.

Mary knows that, once a person is baptized, he becomes a member of the Mystical Body of Christ. She cares for the whole body, and, if a member is ailing, Her watchful eye is centered upon that individual.

Mary's power of intercession is indeed great. She constantly presents the petitions of Her children - and that we are since Christ bequeathed Her as Our Mother - before the throne of God. Her supplications are answered for Christ cannot refuse His Mother Her wishes.

We do not speak here of the spiritual health, the greater favor Mary obtains for us. True She is most interested in the spiritual welfare of every soul. She desires every soul to live in the love of God. She hates sins as God hates sin. She begs for grace for all and dispenses grace to all.

It is the physical health we are primarily concerned with in this article. And there are millions of proofs of return to body health by the "Health of the Sick."

Every shrine in the world has countless records of miraculous cures. Every type of sickness and in every stage of its intensity has been cured.

The faithful know the power of the Blessed Virgin before the throne of God. That is why, when we are sick, our petitions to God are placed into the hands of the Blessed Mother. Our simple faith in Mary is best exemplified by the story of a young boy at Lourdes. One whole week he awaited for a cure. Each day he was taken from his sick bed and placed into the cold waters of the Grotto's spring. Each day he was blessed with the Blessed Sacrament. On the last day of his stay at Lourdes, he begged Our Lord thusly, for a cure, "Cure me O Lord Jesus, because, if You don't, I'll tell Your Mother on You."

It is important for us to turn our mind, prayers, and eyes to Mary in time of sickness be it our own or someone else's. She brings help. She grants favors and grace. She changes the mental outlook on suffering. And, if it is God's will, body health and strength will be given.

> *O Mary, Health of the Sick, take care of all the sick now and at the time of death. Above all, obtain for us the grace to accept God's will in all things. May our sufferings be acceptable to God as a means of salvation. May we understand that through the Cross is our Salvation.*

MARY, REFUGE OF SINNERS

Among the attributes of God are mercy and justice. His mercy forgives but His justice requires punishment for evil and reward of happiness for the good. Heaven and hell are the final ends for all mankind.

During our Blessed Mother's appearances at LaSalette, She revealed Her difficulty of holding back the hand of justice of Her Son. Why? Sins demand punishment because of unfaithfulness and disregard of God's love. But, Mary is our Mother and Advocate who pleads for Her children. Every mother is most anxious about her children. If they are sick, She is a most solicitous nurse. If a child gets into trouble, a mother is at his side to help. If a child goes wayward, She worries and prays more than ever for his correction.

Our Lady's love for us is greater than the love of any good mother because Mary is our Spiritual Mother. It is Her prerogative to inspire and to grant graces and favors. As Mary appeared sad and even in tears, She must appear before the throne of God in sadness because She loves all people, even sinners. Even if tears will help, Mary will plead in tears before God for Her children. No one can resist the tears of a mother nor can God. Christ must give grace and even perform a miracle for the salvation of a soul at the request of His Mother.

Why did Mary appear on the earth? Why did She give us the scapular? Why does She request a daily Rosary? Why did She give a vision of hell to the children at Fatima? Why did She request the young nun, Catherine Laboure, to have a medal stamped? All this and more because of Her concern for us.

As God wants the conversion of sinners, so does Mary. If angels rejoice more over the conversion of one sinner than over ninety-nine just, then Mary's heart experiences joy, too, for She and Jesus want the love of all people, want all sinners to return to grace, and They suffered for the salvation of all.

The Hebrews of old had cities as sanctuaries to which they could flee for safety. The pagan Hawaiians had a haven to which to flee. Among Christians, the sanctuary in the church was a refuge and protection for criminals and sinners. Such a Refuge for protection is Our Blessed Mother. It is a Catholic solace to place ourselves under the protection of Mary. We should run to be under the mantle of Mary. Once there, we are safe and sanctification is ours.

O Mary, be our Refuge, be our harbor, be our solace, be our comfort and be our merciful, loving and caring Mother. Obtain all the graces necessary for us to remain secure in Your love. Protect us from the wrath of God and the fires of hell.

MARY, COMFORTER OF THE AFFLICTED

The difficulties in our life are many. We have difficulties with body and soul. The body has its infirmities and needs; the soul has its proneness to sin and its need of grace. But, there is no need to despair or to complain to God about our weakness, for in our weaknesses we can become great saints of God.

This is especially true since God has given us His Grace to help us and He has given His Mother for our protection and comfort.

During her life, St. Mary Magdalene de Pazzi had a vision of seeing a great number of ships in a storm. All seemed to be lost except one which came in safely with Mary at the helm.

Our life is like a stormy sea. The body and soul are so afflicted that no one is without a cross which we are to carry patiently unto glory.

At death there is a great danger to our soul because the devil tempts us in our weakest hour and faults. St. John of God, while dying, complained, "No Blessed Virgin Mary." Shortly She appeared to him saying, "John, why dost thou fear?" "My custom is not to abandon My children at hour of death." What consolation is this doctrine for us to have Mary as our Comfort.

After death, Mary continues to help. There is no pain in life as great as that of "Purgatory. Souls in Purgatory need Mary's help. To St. Bridget of Sweden, Our Lady said, "I am compassionate to My clients." Church teaches that Mary quickly frees souls from Purgatory.

She inspires families to pray, to have Masses said, to gain indulgences and merit and all to be offered for souls in Purgatory. She begs for liberation from Her Son for all souls.

St. Peter Damian tells of a story of how early Christians formed candlelight processions on eves of great feasts to the catacombs and large churches. One day in Rome, Marozia, who was dead for one year, appeared to her cousin in the Church of St Mary's. Her cousin was astonished and frightened. She spoke to her to identify her. She revealed that she was released from Purgatory by our Blessed Mother and came here with many others to thank Her. On Her feast of the Assumption, more would be liberated. To prove she was a true spirit, she told her cousin she would die in one year. That happened.

Mary, Our Comfort, pray for us. Protect us now and at the hour of our death. Plead our cause. Liberate all souls from the pains of Purgatory.

MARY, COMFORTER OF THE AFFLICTED: II

"Man, born of a woman, living for a short time is filled with many miseries."

(Job 14, 1).

How true is this statement! Personal and human experience verify Job's observation. We do not have to look far or long to realize our life has many physical and spiritual afflictions.

In our problems as children, we turned to our parents for help. In sickness, we, as all adults, turn to doctors, dentists, and nurses. In other problems, we turn to particular professionals. But, in physical or/and in spiritual difficulties, we turn to God, to Mary and/or to saints. Priests and religious may be of some help. But, above all, we turn to God. "O Lord, have mercy. O Lord, help me. O God, save me."

After God, we turn to Mary, for She is the consolation and comfort of the afflicted. We address Her as the Consolation of the Sorrowful. Mary knows desolation for She is the Sorrowful Mother. Do you know Her Seven Sorrows? She shows pity on all who suffer and turn to Her.

Our Blessed Mother is willing to console all afflicted. We have countless examples of Mary's consolation. The saints experienced all kinds of consolation in their trials and sicknesses. Countless number of people report many favors received today from the goodness of our Mother.

Mary, as a good Mother, takes Her children to Her bosom, caresses them, encourages them and shares Her sweetness and joy with them. Blessed are they who experience the embraces of Mary. Blessed are they who experience physical and/or spiritual cures. Cures are many at the Marian Shrines.

For Her children, Mary obtains grace of patience and resignation. Consolation was given many a Saint. "Your sufferings are gaining you a high place in Heaven." This consolation is wisdom for you and me. May we offer all we experience for the glory of God and our salvation.

Hearing such words from the lips of Mary have inspired many of the saints not only to bear patiently their ills but also to ask for more. In all our afflictions, let us turn to Mary for inspiration and consolation.

> *O Mary, Comforter of the Afflicted, pray for patience and the gift of long suffering for us. May we through Your intercession have that grace of long suffering now so that we may not suffer in Purgatory but be taken immediately into Heaven.*

MARY, HELP OF CHRISTIANS

St. John Bosco was in trouble. He had a school for boys who ran away from home and lived in hovels in Turin. He brought them together into a home where he fed them and educated them. On one particular day, he had no food but had a bag of chestnuts. As the boys came in for lunch, he had them put their hands into the bag and take as much as they wanted. All the time he was praying, "O

Mary, Help of Christians, help me." Every boy got chestnuts but the bag was not depleted.

The Christian navy was embattled with that of the Turks. The fleets met at Lepanto in 1571. For a time, the fierce battle seemed to be in favor of the Turks. By a special privilege, Pope Pius V in vision watched the battle. He could see from his place in Rome how the battle was progressing. He pulled out the Rosary and asked all of Rome and all Christians to pray the Rosary begging help. The battle ended in favor of the Christians. Pope Pius V attributed victory to Mary and the Rosary. It was that same Pope, St. Pius V, who established the Feast of the Holy Rosary to be celebrated on October 7th each year.

Again Europe was in danger from the Turks. The Moslem army marched past Greece, through the Balkans and came as far as Vienna. All of Europe was in danger. The Holy Father begged for help to save Vienna, all of Europe, and Christendom. Among the leaders of the army of Christians was King John III Sobieski. In 1683, this Polish King was selected by the other generals to be the commander in chief. King John III devised a plan to beat the Turks, but, before he assaulted the infidel forces, he and his troops met in a church dedicated to the Blessed Virgin. While at Mass, he begged for help from the Blessed Mother. Fortified with the help of God and Mary, he directed the assaults upon the Turks. The Turks were defeated, Europe was saved from the infidels, and Christianity remained the strong force of life in Europe. This victory was attributed to the help Mary gave to the Christians.

Mary, You gave help to many Christians in their problems and troubles. All of us Christians are in battle with the devil. We need Your help. Help us to fight impurity and evil of every kind. Help us against the atheists. Save us and our country. Because of You, may we all one day share victory in Heaven.

BLESSED VIRGIN MARY IS A QUEEN

"And a great sign appeared in Heaven; a Woman clothed with the sun, and the moon under Her feet, and on Her head a crown of twelve stars."

(Apos. 12, 1).

"Our Lord awaited the Assumption of His Blessed Mother, for He had a place of Honor and Glory prepared for Her. After forty hours in the grave, Our Lord takes His Blessed Mother into Heaven where She is greeted amidst the applause and joys of the Heavenly Court of Angels and Saints. What a joyful reunion of Mother and Son this must to have been! What pride does Joseph, St. Ann, and St. Joachim, King David take in Mary! What joy fills the heart of Mary as She sees the glory of God, the triumph of Her Son and the splendor of Heaven."

Mary sees Her Son sitting upon a throne, for He is the King of Kings, and this throne is with the throne of God the Father and the throne of God the Holy

Spirit. Near the throne of Her Son, Mary sees another throne and this is empty. But not for long, for the King of Kings, Who rules the whole universe, has His Mother escorted to that beautiful throne at His side. Mary is seated and immediately Our God places a crown upon Her head. One can easily imagine hearing the angels, the choirs of angels, sing out in beautiful harmony, "Hail, Holy Queen."

How is it that Mary is crowned Queen of Heaven and of earth by Her Divine Son? Our Lord, being the King of men and all creatures, so willed it that His Mother sits on a throne near His own throne.

The crown used by Christ in Mary's Coronation is a crown of justice. This is the reward for Mary's love of God and Her submission to His will. "Behold Thy Handmaid, be it done to me according to Thy will." (Luke, 1, 38), was Mary's motto. She lived for the honor and glory of God. She offered each thought, word and deed to Him.

This crown is also a crown of glory for all She underwent as the Mother of Christ. Here She shines forth as the Queen of Angels, patriarchs, prophets, Apostles, martyrs, confessors, virgins and all saints. She has received more grace than all put together. It is She who brings the Christ into the world for whom the patriarchs and prophets awaited, the Apostles served and the saints confessed. She suffered more than the martyrs.

This crown, one of glory, is also a crown of power, because, as Queen, She has been given the power to distribute the grace of God. She does give us the graces needed, She begs mercy for us and She brings blessings unto us. She, as a good Queen and our Mother, takes care of us.

Knowing the Blessed Virgin Mary's position in Heaven, we easily can praise Her and beg, with confidence, Her help as we do when we say:

"Hail, Holy Queen, Mother of mercy, our life, our sweetness and our hope. To You do we cry, poor banished children of Eve. To You do we send up our sighs, mourning and weeping in this vale of tears. Turn then, most gracious Advocate, Your eyes of mercy toward us and after this exile, show us the blessed fruit of Your womb, Jesus. O clement, O loving, O sweet Virgin Mary"

MARY, QUEEN OF HEAVEN AND EARTH

In Rome, before many dignitaries of the Church and fifty thousand faithful, Pope Pius XII formally proclaimed Mary the Queen of Heaven and Earth, and established this feast to be celebrated each year on October 31.

The miraculous picture, called the Salvation of the Roman People and which is claimed to have been painted by St. Luke, was brought from the Basilica of St. Mary's Major to St. Peter's. Here, before a tremendous gathering of venerators of the Blessed Mother, Our Holy Father placed a rich bejeweled crown on Our Lady's head.

Great must to have been the joy of all those present to witness such a ceremony honoring Our Blessed Mother. Seeing so many people in one place alone is exciting. But, to see our Holy Father, the Cardinals and Bishops, the miraculous painting of nearly two thousand years of age and then the crowning and the proclaiming of Our Lady's Queenship must have filled the hearts of all with triumphant joy and impressed their minds indelibly with the grandeur of the sight and occasion.

Our Lady had been addressed as Queen ever since the fourth century when St. Ephren, the Syrian, called Her by that title Our prayers to Mary often use the title of Queen. And rightly so, for truly She is a Queen.

Mary became Queen of all creatures when She became the Mother of God, the Creator of all. As Mother of Christ, She shares in all that He possessed and possesses. Then too, by being His Mother, She shared in His work of redemption. For this reason, She is called the Co-Redemptrix, that is, the Sorrowful Mother was the second cause of our salvation - Christ being the first. By cooperating with Christ in all His work, Mary shared in meriting us out of the power of the devil.

Truly, Mary is Queen of queens. As Queen, the highest honor and love given to anyone except God is directed to Her for this is Her proper due. The veneration of our Queen of queens is called Hyperdulia.

As we honor Our Lady, may our prayers have a most receptive and gracious ear.

> *As we cry from this vale of tears, may the Queen of queens dry our eyes by bringing peace to our minds and to the world, harmony and love to our families, and grace and joy into our hearts. We pray for these blessings.*

MARY, QUEEN OF ANGELS

From the writings of St. John the Evangelist, as recorded in the Book of Revelations, we read and conclude that the Woman crowned in Heaven is the Blessed Mother. She is crowned as Queen of all God's creatures and placed on a throne at the side of Her Son. Therefore, Mary is the Queen of all angels and all mankind.

Angels have a high dignity for they are pure spirits endowed with intellect and will. They are persons higher in dignity than we human beings. Here we speak of the good angels who now see God face to face.

The title of angel means a messenger, a function which he performs. This word comes from the Greek language and it means to announce. We know of angels because God revealed them to us. The Holy Scriptures have many references to angels. Definitely we cannot know anything about angels from our human reason. Nonetheless, tradition and human experiences have added some notions to our knowledge of angels; for example, angels came to the children of Fatima and one of them gave Holy Communion to them. We have been taught that there are nine choirs of angels, namely: Seraphim, Cherubim, and Thrones whose function is to attend to the throne of God; Powers, Virtues and Dominations whose function is to administer the universe; Principalities,

Archangels and Angels who attend to the needs of mankind. Among the lowest choir of angels are the Guardian Angels who are appointed to protect us.

We know more about angels from Christ Who tells us that, "Their angels see God face to face. He has given His angels charge over you."

From what we know about angels, we conclude they are most beneficial for all mankind. They have the power to strengthen us, to guide us in our ways, and to inspire us to do greater works for the honor of God and for mankind's benefit. It is said that St. Francis of Assisi had angels play music to comfort him in his sufferings. Perhaps that is why we paint angels as musicians. At least the angels sang at the birth of Christ and at the wake of Mary.

As God appointed angels to be interested in mankind and to aid mankind, Mary has a greater interest because of Her association with Christ Who came for our salvation. We are not left alone to work out our salvation. We have on our side angels and, in particular, our Guardian Angel and, above all angels, there is the love and solicitude of Our Blessed Mother.

O Mary, Queen of Angels, we beg You to see to it that each of us is always under Your protection and guided by the angels so that we may live in great love with You now and one day with perfect love in Heaven.

QUEEN OF PATRIARCHS

A patriarch is a founder of a family or tribe or is a ruler of a group of people or a section of the Church.

The patriarchal periods are divided into:
1. prediluvial, that is, from Adam unto the flood
2. semite line from Sem to Thare
3. Abraham, Isaac, Jacob, and his twelve sons.

King David is called a Patriarch, too. These persons are listed as men of great faith.

In the New Testament period, certain bishops of Sees are titled patriarchs: as of Rome, Constantinople, Antioch, Jerusalem and Alexandria. Among the Orthodox, Moscow and Bucharest are added.

In the Old Testament, God spoke to many of the Patriarchs in person or through an angel. To them God promised land, great power, great number of descendants, and a Redeemer. These leaders kept the faith whereas others around them fell into idolatry.

Abraham is considered the father of faith and, because of his faith, he was justified.

Isaac was a peaceful man who submitted himself to the will of God. He is a prototype of Christ because he was offered in sacrifice to God by his father.

Jacob was the blessed of God and the father of the twelve tribes of Hebrews.

Joseph was blessed by God after being sold by his brothers. He prospered in Egypt and saved his brothers from famine.

As the Patriarchs preserved and taught faith in God, so did Mary while on this earth and She continues to do so even unto today.

In all Her appearances, Mary rejuvenates our hope, tells us to keep our faith in Her Son, and stimulates our hearts to love God.

As the Patriarchs hoped for a Redeemer, they expected a Jewish virgin to give the Savior birth. They longed for the Messiah and the honor Mary was to receive.

Mary was crowned Queen of all peoples and She is the Queen of all leaders and founders of faith.

O Mary, we long for Your grace as Patriarchs longed for You and Your acceptance to be the Mother of Jesus. Pray for us now that we may be filled with joy knowing You are our personal Queen. Help us to believe, to hope, and to love. May we be Your subjects also in Your Heavenly home.

QUEEN OF THE PROPHETS

The hope in a coming Redeemer was kept alive by the prophets who called the Hebrews - Jews - back to the faith of the One True God and urged them to live according to a covenant made by God with them. The prophets were enlightened and inspired by God and they bravely related God's messages to the people.

God spoke to the prophets who, in turn, would say, "This is the Word of God." They were teachers who developed the knowledge and practice of the Law. They insisted the Law be kept. They also blamed the people for any misfortune because of their sins.

These seers prepared the way for the coming of Christ. They foretold the circumstances and events of Christ's life. These prophets were especially chosen and commissioned to work for God as the prophet Amos said, "I was a herdsman plucking wild figs and the Lord took me - and said - 'Go prophesy to My people, Israel.'"

Moses is considered the great prophet, lawgiver, and leader of the people. God spoke with Moses frequently and on friendly terms. Our Lord explained the writings of Moses to the Apostles. On Mount Thabor, Moses and Elijah appeared with Christ for both the Law and Prophecies reveal the mind of God concerning His Son's coming upon the earth.

The Old Testament prophets are listed as four great prophets because they wrote amply: Isaiah, Jeremiah, Ezechiel, and Daniel; and those who wrote less as the twelve minor prophets (short writings): Osee, Joel, Amos, Abdia, Jonah, Michea, Nahum, Habacuc, Sophonia, Aggai, Zacharia, Malachia.

St. John the Evangelist and Apostle wrote about things to come in the Book of Revelations. In this apocalypse, our Blessed Mother is a subject in the war against Satan and is victorious as Queen who has a crown of twelve stars.

Christ is spoken of as a descendant of King David and is to sit on David's throne forever.

A virgin forever, the Mother of the Messiah was subject of the prophets and the hope of Israel. Jesus is the King and Mary is the Mother of the glorious King and also the Queen of all peoples and especially of the prophets.

> *O Queen of Prophets, speak for us, keep warning us of God's wrath. Keep the promise of eternal happiness ever before us and also keep the fire of the love of God in our hearts. Be our Queen now and forever.*

MARY, QUEEN OF APOSTLES

Not too much is written in the Gospels about Blessed Mary because the Gospels are the Good News of Jesus and our salvation. Because the concentration is on Jesus, very little is known of Mary.

Did Mary know the Apostles? Definitely She did, for She saw Jesus a number of times during His public life. She was with Jesus at Cana of Galilee and during His Passion and Crucifixion. She was with the Apostles on Pentecost. She lived with St. John the Evangelist for a longer time until She returned to Jerusalem where Her time on this earth was fulfilled. The Apostles visited Her grave and they are the ones who gave us the first information of Mary being taken up into Heaven.

Jesus is the King of Kings and the King of the Apostles. Mary was crowned Queen of all. Consequently, She is the Queen of the Apostles.

Mary stayed with the Apostles after Jesus ascended into Heaven. She prayed with them and encouraged them. They must have experienced much consolation just being in Her company and having Her pray along with them.

As the Apostles were concerned and commissioned to "Go and teach all nations, baptizing them in the name of the Father and the Son and the Holy Spirit," Mary had and has the same interest. She wants all to come to know Her Son, to love Her Son, and to be with Her Son in Heaven.

Blessed Mary appeared and appears even now teaching us to be faithful to God, to fulfill His will, and to avoid sin. She has given us means of protection: the Rosary, the Scapular, the Miraculous Medal, and shrines which were built at Her request.

> *O Mary, Queen of the Apostles, be our Queen. Make us Apostles of You Son. May we teach our children the faith. May we keep our faith ourselves and practice it by receiving the sacraments most frequently. Help us to spread the faith and love of Jesus. May we as You and the Apostles strive to bring others into the Mystical Body of Christ, the One Holy, Catholic, Apostolic Church. Keep us loyal until the end.*

QUEEN OF MARTYRS

No human heart is so calloused that it is not moved to compassion and pity at the sight of a broken-hearted mother holding in her arms the lifeless body of her child. Charity urges us to help, if possible, the afflicted mother. The human heart springs forth great gushes of sentiments of love to such a sorrowful woman.

Many a heart was converted to God by the thought or sight of the Sorrowful Blessed Mother. Swords pierced Her heart during Her life, but, at the hour of the death of Christ, Her heart was crushed. The enormous spiritual sufferings, greater than any physical suffering, at the time of the Crucifixion brought about a spiritual martyrdom for Our Lady, the Queen of all martyrs.

This Queen of Martyrs has stimulated others to follow in the footsteps of Her Son. She fired their love to the greatest degree love could attain, for "Greater love than this no one hath that a man lay down his life for his friend."

The annals of Christianity are full of this consuming love. From the earliest days of the Apostles to our own day, we read of the great witnesses of faith in God. For Christ, each Apostle died a horrible death, the early Christian martyrs met death in the teeth of the lion, a fiery pillar, at the sword, on the rack, and by every conceivable way. Throughout the ages, the lovers of God laid down their lives in every country of the world. Even today the same continues. They show their faith by deeds - a death of witness of their faith.

Love must be tested and tried. Sacrifice is that test. If we shall sacrifice the comforts of our lives, the delights of the body and of our own possessions, we can say we do love. But only when love supersedes all things, even to the extent of giving one's life, then love is perfect and complete.

Our love of God is to be perfect. Mary will stimulate that love, give us consolation in our trials and sufferings, and obtain for us the grace necessary to withhold to the end.

O Mary, when our end comes, present us to God because of our supreme acts of love. O Mary, help us to love God totally.

MARY, QUEEN OF CONFESSORS

From the time of the First Pentecost, great and courageous men went throughout the world professing and teaching Christ and His doctrine. These men boldly wrote with conviction about Our Lord and of the life of a Christian. The Church attributes the title of Confessor to these men.

In face of opposition and unbelief, these champions of faith not only admitted their own belief in Christ, but they boldly taught by word of mouth, by writings and by acts of belief that Jesus is the Son of God and the Redeemer of humanity. Although they did not spill their blood for Christ as the martyrs did, many of them suffered a spiritual martyrdom by opposition, criticism and ridicule.

These are the men who were the preachers and teachers who carried the message of Christ to the whole world. They are the teachers of the faith and the witnesses of Christ. In their work as disciples of Christ, they practiced heroic virtues of Faith, Hope and Love. These men are remembered today because of their writings and of the living tradition of their personal history. Among them are the great confessors of the East, the Greek Fathers, and of the West, the

Western Fathers. Today these noble souls are listed among the doctors, pastors, and holy men.

To these men of faith, our Blessed Lady was their guide and model. As She professed Her faith in accepting the words of the Archangel at the Annunciation, as She accepted Her Son as Christ at Christmas, as She acknowledged Him as all powerful at the Wedding Feast at Cana, and as She loved Christ when He hung upon the cross, so too, the confessors profess their belief in Christ in everything He did and said. Mary was of deep faith and She helps others to have a great faith in God, in Her Son, and in the eternal life we are to have with all who love God.

> *Mary, Queen of Confessors, help us to profess our faith openly and bravely. May we confirm our faith by our actions. May we have the grace through Your hands to be known as men/women who not only believe but also live the faith in Christ and in the faith of His Church established by Him upon Peter. O Mary, we acknowledge You as Queen of all who openly profess their faith in Jesus. May You lead all believers to the glory of living now in faith, hope and love, and bring us into union with Christ in the world to come.*

QUEEN OF VIRGINS

A host of women have taken Our Lady as a model, guide and Queen. These women have dedicated themselves and their complete lives in the service of Her Son, Our Lord. As She gave Herself completely to God and to His service, so these countless virgins of all ages have done and still do today.

To follow Our Lord most closely, these women of great love have followed their Queen by saying: "Behold the Handmaid of the Lord, be it done to me according to Thy Word." They have taken the vow of obedience and thus deny their own will so that God's will may be fulfilled.

To be more like Our Lord and Our Lady, they have taken the vow of poverty.In perfect imitation of Our Lady, these noble women "know no man"; that is, they live a life of complete purity, chastity, and of self-denial and control.

These women who have dedicated their lives in imitation of Our Lady in the virtue of purity are similar to the Old Testament Ruth who loved Naomi so much that She accepted her home, people, God, and burial ground. Virgins have accepted Christ as their Lord and their Love. They dedicate much of their time to Christ, His Church, and to the people of faith. They love to spend time before the tabernacle of the Lord. They speak of a spiritual marriage because of their dedicated love. They aspire to be with Jesus forever just as His Mother is with Him forever.

> *O Mary, take care of all those who have dedicated their lives in virginity so as to be like You. May their love of Jesus keep them safe from the inroads of sin through Your help. O Mary, pray for all virgins and all people.*

48

QUEEN OF ALL SAINTS

As an artist paints a picture on his canvas, he has a model before his eyes and he paints accordingly. In a way, each of us is an artist painting, or better still, sculpturing ourselves after a model. We are striving for perfection in spiritual life. Our perfect model is Christ Himself. Then other models are the saints who imitated Him and especially so is the Blessed Mother, for She was and is nearest to Our Lord and imitated Him most perfectly.

The virtues acquired by saints differ according to the individual: poor, rich; well, sick; nobleman, servant; free, slave; learned or unlettered. All imitated Christ and His Mother according to their personality, abilities, and the graces given them.

In each of us, as was in the saints, is this something which cries out, "Reach higher, love God deeper, sacrifice for the love of God. Become more perfect and attain Heaven and happiness." This desire for spiritual perfection and happiness made people do anything and everything for God - even be a martyr. They left home in pursuit of an ideal; they gave up family in order to be more free in attaining their resolve. Many desired martyrdom so as to be in Heaven quickly. Willingly they gave up their lives to be with Christ. There are many saints in Heaven who have no special date on the Church calendar, nor are they on the altar, nor were they canonized.

Our heart takes courage to know God comes to our aid with this grace to overcome all weakness and to do all good and avoid evil, but it is most heartening to know others attained a perfect love of God. The saints attained that perfection. They also wish our sanctification and intercede for us that we can attain a great love of God.

Needless to say, the Queen of all Saints is most interested in our sanctification. She sets many examples for us of how to love God. She intercedes for us. She obtains the needed graces for us. She inspires us to overcome the world, the flesh, and the devil. Her appearances upon this earth have brought about the conversions of nations, the holiness of many, and their elevation to the altars. Wherever there was enkindled a spark of love of God in man's heart, Mary fed oxygen to it producing a bursting flame of love. Through Her love of souls, She brought many to the perfection of love.

> *O Mary, thou knowest how to love God best, teach us how to love Our Lord. Lead us along the road of love. Encourage us. Inspire us. Aid us. Bring us to a great consuming love and its perfection in Christ. You are the Queen of Saints. Be our Queen, too.*

QUEEN OF PEACE

How we long for the peace promised at Fatima. "There will be peace," I said. "If My requests are granted, Russia will be converted and peace will be restored to the world."

> *O Mary, hasten this restoration of peace is our plea.*

There was peace upon this earth. Adam and Eve enjoyed it in Eden. How long it lasted, no one knows, but it was destroyed by Satan.

But this power of the devil was not to last forever, for a Lady and Her Son were to crush his head. This event occurred with the birth and death of Christ. It is Christ Who made it possible to have peace again and that is why He is called the Prince of Peace. Consequently, the Mother of this Prince of Peace is called the Queen of Peace.

For any individual, the amount or intensity of personal peace depends upon sanctifying grace and conformity with the will of God.

Mary, who was and is full of grace, subjected Her will to God's will in all things. "Behold the Handmaid of the Lord." Whatever suffering She underwent did not disturb Her peace of soul, for Her will was in perfect conformity with God's will.

Is it possible to have peace of soul for us, to have peace among our neighbors and among nations? It is very possible, but there are conditions which must be fulfilled:

1. a state of Sanctifying Grace; sin must be avoided. Penances and self-denials must be practiced to pay for past sin and to fortify ourselves against the inroads of the devil
2. a complete submission to the will of God must be practiced

Our minds must be so disposed to accept His will and make it our own will. It is God's will that we love Him, ourselves, and our neighbor. "If you love Me, keep My Commandments," He says. "Love one another as I have loved you," said Jesus.

Fulfilling God's will is the answer for enjoying peace be it personal, social, national and international. Respect of each person is required and also justice among nations is needed for peace. Greed and abuse have no place among peoples if we are to have peace. Rights of individuals, of families, and of nations must be safeguarded according to God's will. We must respect everyone's life.

O Mary, Queen of Peace, obtain wisdom for all individuals and especially for rulers and big business people. Inspire us to share the world's wealth with the have-nots. Move our minds and hearts to live according to the two great commandments of love. O Mary, obtain peace for us.

If each individual fulfills these requests of Mary, we shall have personal peace, social peace, and international peace.

MARY, QUEEN OF THE HOLY ROSARY

So much has been said and written about praying the Rosary. Even with the Blessed Mother Herself begging for the daily recitation of the Rosary, we find people who complain of its recitation and refuse to pray it. Their reasons are:

1st objection: Men claim this prayer is for women. Also, some claim religion and church are for women. How wrong! In the Old Testament, men prayed. God chose men as patriarchs, prophets, and priests.

Women went along with men, who were the leaders in religion and devotion. Men are created by God to search for eternal happiness and so are women. The greatest joy on earth is contemplation which is needed to be shared by all mankind.

2nd objection: Rosary prayer is so childish. Are we not the children of God and is not Mary our Mother? How do we speak to our parents if not as children? Heaven is for those who become as children. Simplicity is a virtue while pride is the root of all evil and the cause of our ruination.

3rd objection: The Rosary is monotonous repetition. Lovers repeat their words and ideas of affection. We are or should be lovers of God and His Blessed Mother. So, as the loved one loves to hear endearing words, so do God and His Blessed Mother. They want our love and our love expressed in words and deeds.

Our thoughts while saying the "Hail Mary's" are not necessarily the same. The mind becomes full of thoughts as we consider the mysteries of the life of Our Lord and His Mother. Our distracted minds become concentrated as we relive the mysteries of faith.

Then there is a great satisfaction just being in the company of one's love without the necessity of speaking. Consolation and satisfaction is enjoyed by knowing we are with the ones we love. There is a sense of security and a good general overall feeling by being in the company of Our Lord and His Mother.

The recitation of the Rosary is not only for the month of October. It is a form of prayer to be used daily. It is a good family form of prayer and an excellent private form. It would be a plus credit for all of us to join in the recitation of the Rosary wherever and whenever it is said. We invite all to come to church early on Sundays and join in praying the Rosary.

O Mary, teach us how to pray the Rosary more fruitfully and through its recitation may we love Thee more and love Thy Son that much more.

You gave us the Rosary through St. Dominic. You recited the Rosary with St. Bernadette at Lourdes. You requested the children at Fatima and the people at Medjugorje to recite the Rosary. You ask all of us to say the Rosary daily. O Queen of the Rosary, teach us how to say the Rosary properly and to love reciting this form of prayer. May we fulfill Your requests and through You come to everlasting glory.

MARY, QUEEN OF POLAND

The title of Mary, Queen of Poland, was added to the many invocations in the Litany of Loreto for the Polish people. I know not of any other nation to have placed an invocation of their own into the Litany in honor of Our Blessed Mother.

How did this happen? History comes into play here. The army of Sweden, which had conquered most of Poland, was driven back from Czestochowa to the Baltic Sea. King John Casimir in 1665 in the Cathedral of Lwow dedicates Poland to Mary and declares Her to be the Queen of Poland. Ever since that dedication, no queen sat on the throne in Poland.

Poland has been dedicated to Our Lady and especially so to Our Lady of Czestochowa since Her miraculous icon came to Poland in 1382 and placed on "Bright Hill" in the city of Czestochowa where the Pauline Fathers have built a shrine to which millions come annually to honor the Blessed Mother, to place themselves under Her protection, and to beg for blessings.

Pilgrims on foot come from Warsaw and other cities to be with their Queen, especially on August 15th and/or August 26th, the feast of Our Lady of Czestochowa. Nine days on foot is not too great a sacrifice for the devotees of Our Lady. Practically every Pole resolves to visit Our Lady of Czestochowa some time in his/her life. So they come on foot, by train, by bus, and by car. It is nothing extraordinary for one million pilgrims to be at Her shrine on the Feast of the Assumption and, along with the people, is the Hierarchy. Usually the Primate of Poland concelebrates Mass with a large number of bishops and other prelates on that day.

It is a common practice for the newly ordained priests in Poland to offer their first Mass at the altar of the miraculous icon. Even when a seminarian is invested with cassock and surplice for the first time, he comes to Czestochowa to place himself into the hands of Mary as his Queen and Mother.

As Mary protected Poland during Her turbulent history, the Polish people pray today that She will help them and their country. A copy of the miraculous icon continuously visits home after home where the family and neighbors join in prayer and song. The hymn "Boze Cos Polskie" expresses the mind and hope of the whole Polish nation.

> *O Lady of Czestochowa, Queen of Poland, we approach You to safeguard Poland and all its people and also all people throughout the world. Save us from the power of the devil. Save us from the scourge of communism. Save us from all evil. Protect us now and obtain for us all the needed graces for a good moral life and eternal happiness with You and Your Son.*

— PART II —
THE MARIAN SHRINES

SHRINES OF OUR BLESSED LADY

A. Shrines Throughout the World

Most nations where there is some Catholic faith have a shrine or many shrines in honor of Our Blessed Lady. Some shrines have attained world recognition. All Marian Shrines are worth visiting, especially those where the Blessed Mother had appeared.

B. Shrines in the United States

There are many shrines of Our Lady in the United States. The National Shrine is the Immaculate Conception in Washington, D.C. A few are presented in this book. Perhaps a moment in our time will prompt us to visit these shrines.

Among the domestic shrines are those of parishes, schools, institutions and private residences. One grotto or roadside shrine may outrank another by its beauty and grandeur. Be as they may, all are signs of the love and devotions of and for the Blessed Mother.

SHRINES THROUGHOUT THE WORLD

OUR LADY OF SNOWS

The love of the faithful for the Blessed Mother has brought about one of the most beautiful churches in the whole world. No jewel or precious stone was too expensive for this church. The finest of all marble was used in its construction. The greatest of all artists and painters decorated its walls. This church, with its famous Sistine Chapel, is the great Basilica of St. Mary Major, or, as it is know in Rome, the Church of Our Lady of Snow.

The story of how this great church came to be built is most interesting. The property upon which the church stands belonged to a rich Roman nobleman by the name of John. Since he and his pious wife had no children, they resolved to will all their property to the Blessed Mother. They prayed for an answer of how to dispose of this property, which was on the Esquilline hill.

One night, in their sleep, they had a dream in which they were told to build a church on that part of the hill which would be covered with snow. Now this was August 5, in the year 358. Snow in Rome is very rare and, in the hottest month of the year, to have snow is a miracle. John hastened the next morning to the Holy Father, Pope Liberius, to tell him the message of the Blessed Lady, but was astonished to learn that the Pope, too, had a message from the Blessed Virgin to cooperate with the pious couple. The Holy Father, some clergy and a group of laity went to the Esquilline hill and there they found the ground white with snow and a plan of the future church clearly traced in the snow. The building of the church was started and finished in two years.

This first church proved too small for the crowds who flocked to it. Pope Sixtus III, in 432, enlarged it to its present size and thus erected a great memorial to the great Council of Ephesus which sanctioned and upheld our doctrine of the "Mother of God."

This church was beautified by many of the succeeding Popes. The Kings of Spain became the patrons of this church. The first gold brought from America to Europe was used to decorate it.

The bodies of Saint Mathias, the Apostle, St. Pius V and St. Jerome are buried in this church. The wood of the Holy Manger is in a chapel below the main altar, which is venerated especially during Christmas season. One of all the greatest treasures in the church is the Madonna di San Luca, the painting of Our Lady attributed to St. Luke. This miraculous picture is loved by all. Before it knelt some of the great saints of God. It was carried in procession throughout the streets of Rome in the time of a plague.

The Blessed Mother loves beauty, but there is no beauty that can compare to a loving heart. A soul which loves God and is devoted to Him is more beautiful than all churches. It is no wonder that the Blessed Mother appeared so often to saints and even placed Her Infant Son into their hands.

There is a shrine in the United States dedicated to Our Lady of Snows. Many make a pilgrimage there.

> *O Lady, under this special title, defend and perfect our souls making them most beautiful in the eyes of God. Help us in our trials Obtain for us the graces needed that we may always be most pleasing to You and to Your Son, Our Lord.*

BLESSED VIRGIN MARY - WALSINGHAM, ENGLAND 1061

Richeldis des Faverches, a pious widow of the town of Walsingham, England, had a vision in which the Blessed Mother showed her the holy house of Nazareth. Three times it was repeated and each time she was told to note the dimensions of the little house so that she could build a replica of it on her estate.

She had workmen build the small house but did not know where to place it. A heavy dew fell where she planned to put the house, but only two small rectangular spots were left dry. One of these was chosen and the men laid the stone foundation. They worked all day trying to place the house on this foundation, but to no avail. On the next morning, they found the house moved two hundred feet and sitting solidly on its stone foundation.

The monks of St Augustine took charge of the house, built a large church around it, and built many other buildings making this a large shrine to which many pilgrims came and, among them, kings and queens of England. Nobles contributed heavily to make the shrine beautiful. Even King Henry VIII made the pilgrimage to this new Nazareth, walking the last mile barefooted in the snow.

All this was destroyed by Henry VIII when he broke with the Church.

56

In the nineteenth century, excavating took place at Walsingham and Catholics yearned to return there, but this was impossible since all property was owned by Protestants.

A shrine to Our Lady was built at King's Lyorn a few miles away - a statue blessed by Leo XIII on August 19, 1897, was installed.

Of all the shrines, only one building survived, St. Catherine Chapel (28 feet, 6 inches long and 12 feet, 5 inches wide) known as the Slipper Chapel, which was the last stop just before the major shrine. Slippers were removed here and all walked barefoot to the shrine. Some of this shrine was restored by Anglican women and, in 1897, the first pilgrimage took place. Anglicans have devotions in this former Catholic shrine.

In 1945, American soldiers got permission from the Protestant owners to have services at the original spot. Now Benediction is given there regularly.

"When England goes back to Walsingham, Our Lady will come back to England."

> *O Blessed Lady, once England was devoted to You and Your Son. England needs Your protection and blessings. O Mary, help England to come to Jesus and to You. May England return to the Catholic Church as she was before the fire of King Henry VIII took You away from the great English people. Mother, take care of England and bring Her back to Rome. O Lady of Walsingham, pray for England and for all of us.*

THE BROWN SCAPULAR

An appearance of the Blessed Mother to an elderly man in the middle of the thirteenth century changed the dress of the people for many years and, even today, a Catholic will not consider himself fully dressed unless he has draped around his neck a scapular or the scapular medal.

In the year of 1247, the Carmelite Fathers chose St. Simon Stock as the General of their Order. The Order of Carmelites had its beginning in the Old Testament. Holy men dwelt alone in the caves in the sides of Mt. Carmel, a mountain in Palestine. Even Elias and Eliseus, the great prophets and their followers lived as hermits on that mountain. After the time of Christ, holy men lived there following the footsteps of Our Lord. In time, these hermits came to live under one rule of life and one superior. These Carmelites were dispersed throughout the world when the infidel Mohammedans took control of the Holy Land.

Some of these Carmelites came to live in England. Among them was Simon Stock, a man of great devotion to the Blessed Mother. For a time, this man lived in the trunk of a tree from which he gets his surname, Stock. This hermit formed the order as it was told to him to do by the Blessed Mother Herself. She told him that She had a special care of these religious.

It was while he was General of the Order and being laden with heavy burdens of the Order, he begged the Blessed Mother for help and pity. She came to help him. The Blessed Lady appeared to Simon Stock. The great brilliant light and the choir of angels surrounding the Virgin dazed St. Simon. She came to answer his prayer. She presented him with a garment to be worn on the breast and on the back suspended from the shoulders. She said, "This shall be a privilege for thee and all Carmelites; whosoever shall die wearing it shall not suffer everlasting fire."

Immediately after the vision, St. Simon let his Order know about this privilege granted by the Blessed Mother. The garment of the monks was changed to include the scapular. The lay people heard about this scapular and Confraternities were formed throughout the Church.

At first the lay people wore large scapulars, large brown pieces of cloth over their clothes. Later, for convenience, the cloth was made small and bound by cord to enable the people to wear the scapular on the breast and on the back. Within recent years, the Holy Father, Pope Pius X, granted the same spiritual privileges to those who could not wear the cloth scapulars, but if they wore a scapular medal. As a youth, each of us was invested in the scapular when we received our First Holy Communion. Some of us wore it only that day while others are still wearing it. It is the wish of the Blessed Mother that we all wear the scapular cloth or medal. If you are not wearing it, you should do so. Remember the words of the Blessed Virgin Mary, "Whosoever shall die wearing it shall not suffer everlasting fire."

THE CHURCH OF THE HOLY HOUSE - LORETO, ITALY

In Loreto, Italy, is located a most famous shrine of the Blessed Mother called the Church of the Holy House. The magnificent and large temple was built in the fourteenth century. All the greatest artists of the sixteenth century were used to decorate it. The paintings and sculpture work are of the finest in the world. Of all the beautiful and costly treasures there, the most important and the greatest item of attraction and veneration is the Holy House, the house in which the Blessed Mother was born, in which She heard the Archangel Gabriel speak to Her, in which She conceived and reared Our Lord and in which the Holy Family lived.

This Holy House is 31 feet long and 13 feet wide and made of rough, dark reddish stone. It has one square window on the west side. There is a crude chimney in its eastern wall. In front of this chimney is a cement stone upon which St. Peter, the Apostle, is believed to have said Mass. Over the altar is an image of the Virgin and Child blackened with age and smoke and believed to be carved in wood by the Evangelist, St. Luke. The statue appears as carved from a tree trunk.

How did this Holy House come to be located in Loreto?

It pleased the Blessed Mother that Her home should be located in Loreto. When the Holy Land was lost to the infidel Mohammedans in the thirteenth century, a legend has it that the house was moved by angels on May 10, 1291, to the city of Fiume in Dalmatia. This happened during the night. Upon morning, the people were astonished to see a strange house in their midst. No one could tell whence it came. When they looked inside, they were more amazed, for in it they saw an altar, the image of the Virgin carrying the Infant. There was a cupboard filled with domestic articles. While the people marveled at all this, their pastor came upon the scene. This added to the mystery because they all knew he was sick and in bed. He then explained to the people the reason for the house. He told them that the Blessed Mother appeared to him and asked him to explain how this house got to the city of Fiume. This house was Her house, She said. In this house She was born and lived, and conceived. The altar was made by St. Peter; the cedar image by St. Luke. The angels who loved the house transplanted it here for better security.

The governor of Dalmatia, upon hearing of this event, sent four men to Nazareth to investigate. They found the foundation of the exact dimensions of the house now located in Fiume. When the people heard about this house, they flocked to it from all localities.

Second Transference: On December 10, 1294, three and one-half years later, again the house is moved. Paul della Selva wrote to Charles II, King of Naples, the following: "On Saturday, December 10, 1294, at midnight, a great light from Heaven was observed on the banks of the Adriatic, and a celestial harmony was heard by many. Hundreds were aroused from sleep, and got up to gaze on the mysterious light and listen to the music. All of a sudden, they saw a house in the air, blazing in light, and supported by the hands of angels." The house was placed in a laurel grove, from this the name Loreto. The people from the vicinity came to see the house and prostrated before the sacred image. Eight months later, the house is moved again to a nearby hill; again it was moved four months later to a spot along a high road near the coast near the city of Recansti. Here the house still stands. But today it is enclosed by the large, beautiful church as described above.

O Blessed Mother, who takest care of all things, have care of us, too. You willed Your home be brought to Loreto and to have people come pray there. O Mary, thousands come to Loreto. They honor You and adore Your Son. They come with faith and hope and love. Many come beseeching You for graces, favors, and cures. Have pity on all. Grant all their requests. Give health to the sick. Obtain the needed graces for sanctity for all of Your children who come to You in faith, hope and love.

OUR LADY OF CZESTOCHOWA

There is an old tradition that St. Luke, the Evangelist, painted a picture of Our Lady and Infant Jesus on a part of the table on which Our Lord and Holy Family ate their daily meals. This picture, which is painted upon cypress wood, was held in great esteem by the Christians of Jerusalem.

In the fourth century, while St. Helena, the mother of Constantine the Great, was visiting the Holy Land and in particular searching for the True Cross, the inhabitants of Jerusalem presented her with that picture. When she returned to

Constantinople, she gave the picture to the emperor, who placed it in the chapel of his palace. As time passed, the picture passed through the hands of the Dukes of Kiev until, in 1383, it was given to Prince Ladislaus of Poland, the Duke of Opole.

This pious and noble Prince wanted a most deserving place for this painting. He entrusted it into the hands of the Pauline Fathers for whom he built a church and monastery on a hill, called Jasna Gora, overlooking the city of Czestochowa.

The Blessed Mother must have been pleased with the sanctuary of Her picture, for She showered many graces and favors to the faithful who prayed there. The word, "Miracle in Czestochowa," was heard throughout the country. This brought the faithful, the devotees of the Blessed Virgin, and the curious to the city. At times there were from fifty thousand to two million pilgrims at the shrine beseeching the Blessed Mother's aid in all their difficulty.

This painting today has three gashes on the right cheek of the Blessed Mother. This came about during the fifteenth century when a band of Hussites, the followers of John Huss of Bohemia, went about the country looting monasteries, burning churches and killing religious. It was in 1430 that they plundered the city of Czestochowa and the Monastery of the Pauline Fathers. These heretics broke the miraculous picture into three pieces, cutting the face of the Blessed Mother three times, and threw the picture into the mud.

When some of the monks returned to the monastery after the Hussites left, they were rent with grief at the destruction they found. But joy came into their hearts when they found the priceless painting, although it was broken and covered with mud.

When the king of Poland heard of this desecration, he engaged the most renowned painters to restore the picture to its original state. The artists easily succeeded in gluing the pieces together without leaving a trace of any cracks, but all their skill put together could not mend the saber cuts on the face of Our Lady.

This restored picture was carried in solemn procession through the streets of Czestochowa up to the rebuilt monastery. The King came to offer his prayers and gifts before this renewed painting. His example was followed by all succeeding kings and presidents of that nation.

Many miracles have been reported to have been wrought before this painting of the Blessed Mother in Czestochowa. There is one which is considered by Poland as the greatest and that occurred in the year 1655 when the whole country was overrun by the Swedes. Their armies were so strong that no opposition was thought possible. It was only at Czestochowa under the direction of the Prior of the monastery that the townsfolk gathered behind the walls of the monastery and from there they fought the enemy. After six months of siege, the Swedes retreated. Then the whole country arose up in arms and drove the Swedes out of Poland. The King, John Casimir II, came to Czestochowa. He solemnly dedicated his country to the Blessed Mother and proclaimed Her "Queen of the Crown of Poland" in a church in the city of Lwow.

Dear Mother, Our Lady of Czestochowa, You took Poland under Your protection and all its people. You have saved that nation from heresy and kept her faithful to Your Son. Continue to protect and obtain all favors and blessings for Poland and all of us wherever we may be. We are Your children who need You.

O Lady of Czestochowa, may we and our nation find favor in Your eyes and be protected from the common adversary, the devil, and from all dangers. Obtain graces and health for all. Keep us in the love of God. Safeguard us from the scourges of atheistic communism and from all infidelity. As You protect Poland and her people, may You protect all of us and keep us in the love of God. Your devoted children honor and love You. Be at our side in all our cares and woes. Obtain all the graces we need today for a peaceful and righteous living. May we see You when God calls us.

OUR LADY OF GOOD COUNSEL OF GENAZZANO

Upon reading or hearing of the astounding accounts of the wonders the Blessed Mother has performed during the course of history, our hearts have been moved to love Mary more intensely. Among the many favors the Blessed Virgin showed to Her children is the one at Genazzano, Italy.

In the fifteenth century in the city of Genazzano, there was an old church dedicated to the Madonna of Good Counsel. This church was rather small and not so beautiful. A devout elderly noble lady by the name of Petruccia da Janeo decided to build a beautiful, large church in honor of the Blessed Mother over this little chapel. She sold her large land holdings and had the work begin. The walls were very high already when the funds ran out. No one else would help with donations and the church prohibited soliciting of funds from the people. Here was the elderly, impoverished lady and now ridiculed and called a fool because she began a task which could not be completed and because now she is a pauper. In spite of the rebukes she received, she had great confidence that one day soon her Great Lady would come to her aid and take possession of the church.

On April 25, 1467, the feast of St. Mark, the Evangelist, which was for that city a day of festivity and celebration, a miracle happened in the sight of all present. It was toward evening when the people were enjoying themselves with the various amusements that they were astonished to see a thin cloud floating in the air and settling on one of the unfinished walls of the nearby building. They saw the cloud divide itself and disappear, and upon the wall they saw a picture of the Madonna and the Child. At this very moment, all of the bells of the church and of the other churches in town began to ring. People from neighboring towns and those who remained at home came running to learn the reason for the alarm announced by the bell ringing. Among those who came to the church was the lady Petruccia. When she saw the picture of the Blessed

Mother, she fell upon her knees and, with outstretched arms, she cried, "This is the long expected Grand Lady."

The people titled the picture "The Lady of Paradise" because they thought the angels painted it and brought it to them. The whole town came to pray before the Lady of Paradise. Soon people came from the nearby towns. But, upon hearing that miracles occurred in the unfinished church through the intercession of the Blessed Mother, people gathered there in great throngs. From April to August, 171 miracles were recorded by the special notary appointed to register all principal cases.

In a short time, the news of the miraculous picture reached Rome. Two men hurried from the Eternal City to Genazzano to identify the picture: one was a Slovinian, the other an Albanian. These men identified the picture as the one which was in the church in Scutari, Albania. One day, while these two men were praying before this picture in Scutari imploring the Blessed Mother to take care of them and their nation which was to be laid waste by the Turks, they saw the picture disappear from before their eyes and in its stead they saw a white cloud which passed through the door of the church. These men followed the cloud and, when outside, they were taken up by some mysterious force and carried in its company. This force brought them to Rome and there the cloud disappeared. For two days they searched for the painting in all the churches of Rome, but to no avail. On the third day, they heard of the miraculous appearance of a picture in Genazzano. They rushed there and identified it as the one from Scutari, Albania.

With all the gifts the people were leaving in honor of the Blessed Mother, the church was completed in three years into a most beautiful shrine.

This picture is very unusual, not only because it is claimed to be the best likeness of the Blessed Mother ever produced on earth, but also because of physical qualities. It is a fresco, a painting on a very thin plaster. Its age and origin are unknown. It is over 700 years old and the plaster is undamaged and the colors are startlingly bright and fresh. The way the picture hangs even causes more admiration because it defies the laws of gravity. The picture is not attached at all and it is not supported by the wall except for about two inches of the right hand corner which rests on a ledge of the wall. Baffled scientists have passed knives between the picture and the wall at all points except for that one corner.

This famous shrine of the Blessed Mother brought many people to love Her and Her Son. May this recounting of the history induce us to love and honor the Blessed Virgin more and to love Her Son.

OUR LADY OF THE OLIVES

There is a small city in France by the name of Murat where lightening never strikes - so it is reported. This unusual privilege by the grace of God is the work of Our Lady ever since 1493. Then the whole college of the city was destroyed by fire caused by lightening. Only one item was spared and that was a wooden statue of the Blessed Lady. The college was rebuilt and the statue enshrined. Ever since then, lightening has never struck in Murat

This particular statue is called Our Lady of the Olives. It is not known exactly why this title is given to this image of Mary. It could be because the wood used in the statue is that of olive wood; or named in memory of the passion of Mary as She shared the passion of Our Lord which He suffered in the Garden of Olives.

Another unusual occurrence in this rebuilt church is that the votive lamps which burn in Her honor must be of olive oil, otherwise the light dies out.

There is a medal stamped today of Our Lady of the Olives and the wearing of it or the use of this medal protects people and buildings from lightening. Regardless where the person may be during a storm, the marvelous medal beseeches the Blessed Lady for protection and safety is resulted.

A second privilege of this medal is to protect expectant mothers and to assist them in the hour of delivery. The Blessed Mother knows the difficulty a woman may have in giving birth to a child. She is willing to help and She does aid those who call upon Her.

Also, as any other medal, this medal of Our Lady of the Olives has a begging power for grace. This grace is given not only to mothers but also it brought sinners to receive the consolation of the Sacraments of the Church.

Our Lady of the Olives, protect us and our property in times of storms. Keep the flame of lightening away from us. Protect and aid all expectant mothers. Obtain for all of us grace that we may always be in the state of sanctifying grace. Help us to receive Your Son in Holy Communion now, and when we enter eternity present us to Your Son, our Lord Jesus Christ.

A VISIT TO GUADALUPE, MEXICO CITY

SEEING IS BELIEVING: In my wildest imagination I could not fantasize what my eyes beheld at Guadalupe, on December 12th. Already the Fiesta was in progress since last evening and lasted all night. At 6 A.M. from my hotel, a 20 minute drive, I could hear fireworks being exploded at Guadalupe.

The crowds were so huge our bus was forced to detour to a side street. Our walk for one block was through a crowded street, past vendors, some of whom had stands while others squatted on the sidewalk. Our headway was rather difficult as we passed varieties of food and merchandise. More people and more stands crowded the sidewalk and the grounds of the basilica of Our Lady of Guadalupe.

We forced our way through the mass of people, many of whom slept in these grounds all night. All color of skin was seen: the pure Indian, the pure Spaniard and the various mixtures of these and other bloods plus visitors from the United States and other countries. Their clothing matched the color of their flesh. Everything was seen from the modern American dress to the primitive garb of the Indian of the fifteenth century. Yes, ponchos and serapes were everywhere, and some of them were used by the pilgrims as blankets for we saw many who were still sleeping under them as they cuddled against this mammoth basilica built recently due to the old one sinking and cracking. An earthquake hastened its construction.

INDIAN FOLKLORE: The basilica was jammed when we got into it at 8:30 A.M. A rough estimate of the crowd was 30,000. As one crowd moved in, others moved out for Mass was said every hour. I did not see the number of worshippers diminish all morning and again, during the afternoon Masses, the shrine was still full.

We jumped at the suggestion to see the folk ceremonies which were in progress in front of the church, since we entered by the back door. The whole plaza was filled. Groups of Indians in native dress were performing ritualistic and acrobatic dances. Plumes of feathers, bright colored costumes, banners, flags, swords, and music furnished by violins, guitars, whistles, drums and other percussion instruments were seen. Six hours afterward, while in my hotel room, I still could hear these drumbeats or thumps in my head.

I watched about ten groups perform as I walked about the square. Even the approach to the square was crowded with people, stands, vendors and flowers. Oh, flowers were everywhere and large banks of flowers were on both sides of the main altar of the shrine.

Fascinating was my study of the people. The aged folk even crawled on their knees as they approached the shrine. Their faces demonstrated piety, humility, devotion and hope. Wrinkled faces, smooth faces, painted faces and even some of the dancers had masks over their faces. Innocence was seen in the eyes and faces of the infants in arms and in the children. The many teenagers showed faith while in church but frivolity and gaiety in the plaza. The older faces and eyes were looking for a better day. One could see a deep trust in these people in Our Lady of Guadalupe.

What was the faith of these people who came to the shrine of Our Lady? One person remarked, "They may not know much about the Blessed Trinity, nor be able to explain the Divinity and humanity of Jesus Christ, but don't tell them that the Blessed Mother of Jesus did not appear to Juan Diego in 1531 because they'll kill you."

The picture of the Virgin is framed above the main altar. An 18 karat gold crown tops the picture. This picture is what stunned the Bishop of Mexico City in 1531 when a newly baptized Indian came to him to tell him a beautiful young Lady wants a church built on that spot in Her honor. Shortly afterward, a church was built and served the people until larger churches were built.

Our group's thrill came at noon at the Mass of the Roses, which was concelebrated by 42 priests, six bishops and the Cardinal of Mexico City. The choir and organist were excellent, the Cardinal's homily brought applause twice, but don't ask me what he said because my Spanish is poquito poquito, which means, not so hot.

After the Mass, roses were blessed by the Cardinal who then presented a bouquet of six blooms to each of the bishops and us priests. By the way, the crowds responded well at this Mass as they did at all the other Masses of the day.

We were informed that the Knights of Malta, whose guests we were, invited us to a dinner to be held in the sacristy of the old basilica.

Cocktails and hors d'oeuvres were served in an anteroom. After the Cardinal entered the dining room, we all joined him. The tables were beautifully set up with three glasses at every setting and beautiful silver and flowers.

The dinner was fit for a king: soup, an "anti-pasto" of unknown ingredients, meat with peas, carrots and artichoke, and a fine dessert of a white custard garnished with orange sections and orange sauce. White and red wine were served in due time and then brandy to finish off the meal.

The waiters in white gloves stood with each new course at their starting place until the Cardinal was served. It was interesting to see the whole waiting crew of about twenty men start in precision when a portion was placed on the Cardinal's plate.

Guadalupe: I

The love the Blessed Mother had and has toward the Americas was expressed at Guadalupe, Mexico, where She appeared to Juan Diego requesting a church to be built in Her honor. Through Her intercession, graces and miracles have been extended to all people since Her appearance in 1531.

THE STORY OF GUADALUPE: Juan Diego had been visited four times by the Blessed Mother. It was on this fourth visit that She tells him to go up to the hill where She has been appearing to gather the flowers there, and carry them to the Bishop of Mexico City. He picked up the most beautiful roses in a stony spot where no flowers grew before. He filled his cloak, which the Indians call a tilma, with the roses and brought them to the Blessed Virgin Mary. She arranged them and said, "Behold here is the sign you must carry to the Bishop, and tell him to do what I command him. Do not show anyone what you carry and do not unfold your cloak except in the presence of the Bishop. Tell him what I have told you to do and you will thus encourage him to build My temple."

Juan left the Blessed Mother and, as he walked to Mexico City, he was very happy because he carried the sign the bishop wanted from the Blessed Virgin. He arrived at the Bishop's home and asked several times to be admitted to see the Bishop. Yet, each time the servants of the Bishop made little of him. Only after becoming annoyed at his continued requests, they attended to him. Seeing he carried something in his cloak, they ordered him to open it up. When he refused, they forced him. They saw these beautiful roses and three times they reached to take one, but each time the roses appeared to be unreal, painted, or interwoven in the material of the cloak. Finally, Juan Diego was admitted to the Bishop and repeated the message of the Lady. The sign requested was in the cloak. When Juan opened the tilma, the roses fell upon the floor and a picture of the Virgin Mary appeared painted in the cloth. The Bishop was astonished at the roses, which were out of season, but he was more surprised to see the picture of the Blessed Mother. He untied the cloak, venerated the picture before all, and placed it into his private chapel giving thanks to God and His glorious Mother. The Bishop kept Juan in his palace that day and, on the morrow, Juan lead the Bishop and his group to the place where he had seen the Blessed Mother.

Guadalupe: II

Juan Diego now requested permission to visit his uncle who was sick. The Bishop granted it and sent a company of Spaniards with him. When the uncle saw Juan with the Spaniards, he wondered what was the reason for all this. Juan told him of all the appearances of the Blessed Virgin Mary and Her assurance of his recovery from illness. The uncle, Juan Bernardino, who is completely well at this time, told Juan Diego that he, too, had seen the Lady as described at the same hour and minute and She restored him to health. She told him of Her desire to have a church built and told him that Her picture was to be called "Holy Mary of Guadalupe."

The Bishop's servants brought the two Indians to the Bishop and, upon cross-examination of his sickness, and appearance of the Lady, the Bishop was pleased with the truth.

Rumors of the miracle had spread throughout the city. Crowds gathered at the Bishop's palace to venerate the picture. Seeing the large gathering, the Bishop carried the picture in procession to the cathedral church and placed it upon the altar where all could see it and venerate it. There it stayed until the temple was built.

The picture on the Indian's cloak is one of perfect proportion of a maiden of fifteen years of age according to artists. The face and hands are dark, the mantle of the gown is blue-green, the flowered tunic is rose, and the rays and stars are deep gold.

The cloak upon which the picture appears is about six feet by three feet. It is made of very coarse material, as loosely woven as sack cloth. This cloth was not prepared for any painting and the artists are amazed at the colors and the different sorts of colors. In some parts, it looks like oil paint, other watercolor, and in others it appears like the tints in roses.

> *Our Lady of Guadalupe, You favored us by appearing in Mexico and by telling us You are the Mother of all America. Take care of us. Protect us from all evil. Keep us loyal to Jesus. Lead us all to eternal glory.*

Guadalupe: III

The love and devotion of the people of Mexico and especially of the Indians of that country of the Blessed Virgin has been very astonishing ever since the word got around of Her appearances and the miracles performed. This love and devotion has continued from 1531 until the present day.

The bishop's chapel was entirely too small to accommodate the crowds of people coming to venerate the miraculous picture of the Blessed Mother. The Bishop of Mexico City had to move the picture into the largest church in the city and this was the cathedral. Here the great crowds of people gathered until the church of Guadalupe was finished.

Large crews of Indians worked day and night in the building of this great Mexican shrine. When it was time to carry the holy picture into the newly completed church where there was a 1,500 pound gold frame, the Indians decorated the four miles from the cathedral to the new church with arches and bows. Flowers of all description were placed and strewn all along the road. In the long procession there were Indians of many tribes in their native costumes. They sang and danced and paraded in the honor of the Blessed Mother.

An incident occurred during the festivities of that day which was miraculous. In the festivity, the Indians had on their program a mock staged battle between two groups of warriors dressed in the costumes of the Chichimecs and Aztecs. During the excitement, an arrow accidentally flew from the bow of one of the Aztecs and lodged into the throat of a warrior in opposition. He fell dead. His colleagues carried him to Our Lady and begged Her to restore him to life. In an instant he got up. The arrow was removed and no wound remained except a slight scar was seen. The Indian thanked the Blessed Mother and, full of joy, he returned to his fellow soldiers and climbed into the canoe to continue the maneuvering.

From that day on, it was very common to see whole tribes and whole villages come to the Blessed Mother. When they came, they usually stayed and camped on the grounds near the church for about a week. They would crawl on their knees from the entrance of the church up to the Holy Picture. Here they thanked Her for the graces received and they begged for all kinds of cures and miracles. They came so abundantly that eight million were baptized within the six years after the apparitions.

Guadalupe: IV

The popes have heavily indulgenced the shrine and pictures of the Blessed Mother. Pope Leo XIII granted permission to have the picture crowned. This crowning of the picture took place on October 12, 1895, in the presence of 38 archbishops and bishops, hundreds of priests, and 50,000 laity. The crown stands two and one-half feet high and four feet in circumference. The special design of the crown has golden roses, diamond stars, 22 shields representing the 22 dioceses in Mexico and these are separated by sapphires and emeralds. The designs of angels and roses are all about the whole crown.

On the day of the coronation of the picture, the Archbishop of Mexico City blessed the crown, said a pontifical high Mass, and led a procession of all present through the church and all around it and back into the building. Two archbishops put the crown in place 30 feet above the floor of the church. As they fixed the crown over the Holy Picture, the whole congregation shouted: "Viva la Virgin de Guadalupe, viva nuestra Madre... viva Mexico." Then, in procession, each bishop present climbed the steps to the picture and laid his crosier and miter at the feet of the Blessed Mother as an act of homage. At the same time, all the church bells in Mexico rang out.

Since then the church of Guadalupe has been raised to the dignity of a basilica. Every church in Mexico has been ordered to have an altar dedicated to the Blessed Mother.

When the atheistic government took over all the affairs of Mexico, one thing it wanted to do was to close and suppress the Shrine of Guadalupe. The orders were given to the army to close the shrine. The people of Mexico heard about the orders. When the soldiers came to the shrine, they were dumbfounded. There were a million Indians camped about the shrine. They dared not close the doors of the shrine.

The shrine doors of Our Lady of Guadalupe are open at all times, for the crowds of Mexicans fill the church daily, for the Mexicans know that the Blessed Mother takes care of them and loves them. They love Her in return.

O Lady, may our hearts be open always for You and Your Son, Our Lord. Help us to love You and Jesus properly. May our devotion to You increase daily. May You be at our side now and especially when God calls us from this world.

OUR LADY OF THE PILLAR

The love of the Blessed Mother for Her children and the Catholics for the Blessed Mother has caused some of the most beautiful churches to be built. One of these large temples is called "Our Lady of the Pillar" which is in the city of Saragossa, Spain.

It is a Spanish tradition that the Blessed Mother visited St. James, the Apostle, in the year 40. While St. James, who came to Spain to Christianize the people, prayed one night on the shore of the river Ebro in Saragossa, the Virgin Mary appeared to him. St. James saw Her standing upon a column of marble. She encouraged him in his work and gave him a statue of Herself. The Blessed Mother requested a chapel be built in Her honor. In a short time, St. James fulfilled Her desire. The chapel became too small for the crowds that gathered under its roof. Consequently, a large basilica, which is still standing, was built.

It is impossible to know what happened to that statue which the Blessed Mother gave St. James. But, there is a most beautiful image of the Blessed Virgin in that church today. The statue is only fifteen inches high and is made of wood and richly decorated in gold. It is a statue of the Blessed Mother holding the Infant Jesus. The crown which the Blessed Mother wears is beautiful, costly, and intricate. Thirty-three jewelers worked 44 days to make it. In it there are 2,835 diamonds, 2,725 roses, 125 pearls, 74 emeralds, 62 rubies and 46 sapphires. The crown of the Infant is identical with that of the Blessed Virgin's except it is smaller.

Pilgrims came to this shrine from time immemorial. People throughout Spain came to honor the Blessed Mother because of the countless miracles She was performing. While at this shrine, hymns were sung and processions were made in Her honor and everyone would kiss the marble pedestal upon which Her statue stood. The marble column has been kissed so many times throughout the centuries that the lips of the faithful have worn out a space in the pillar.

Since the year 1642, when a man named Juan Pillar was cured from an ailing limb, the city of Saragossa vowed to keep October 12th sacred in the memory of the apparition of the Blessed Mother. In that year, She was proclaimed the Patroness of the City. The whole nation of Spain observes this feast day and it is a special day of rejoicing, especially for the people of Aragon.

During the Napoleonic wars in Spain, the city of Saragossa was laid siege. A large French army fought for two months to take the city, which was defended by a very small group of men and women. Although the French took and ransacked the city, including the shrine, they did not dare touch the statue of the Virgin. One general did cut a jewel from the crown to give as a present to his wife. In its place he offered a valuable gift in exchange. This general lost his leg in battle shortly after.

> *O Mary, You are honored in many cities of the world. You have appeared to a number of the faithful. Inspire us to honor You no matter where we may be. Make our hearts love You for You are good and merciful. May it be our joy and honor to see You and be led by You to Our Savior.*

THE MIRACULOUS MEDAL - 1830

Since we started our discourses on the Blessed Mother, little has been written about how She took special interest in a few particular persons. Today, let us consider Her appearances to St. Catherine Laboure. It is interesting to know a little about this St. Catherine and the favors She received from God.

Catherine Laboure entered the convent of the Daughters of Charity in 1830. While in this convent in Paris, She was chosen by God for many favors. She saw the charitable heart of St. Vincent de Paul in one of her visions. Then, Our Lord would show Himself to her in the Blessed Sacrament.

Her childlike faith was most simple. With this love of God and great devotion to the Blessed Mother, she begged the favor of seeing the Blessed Mother. This favor was granted on July 18, 1830.

It was later that evening, after an evening conference on devotion to the saints and to the Blessed Mother, that Catherine woke up from her sleep. It was 11:30. Three times someone called her. She looked to the spot from where the voice came and saw a child of about four or five years of age, who said, "Come to the chapel, the Blessed Virgin awaits you." She hastily dressed and followed the child. Once on the corridors, she was amazed to see all the lights burning. The doors would open at the instant of touch by the child. When they got to the chapel, the church was lit up with brilliant light. The child led her through the sanctuary to a chair used by the Director of the convent. Here Catherine knelt down and waited The child said, "Behold the Blessed Virgin." The Virgin Mary came down the steps of the altar and sat down on the chair. Catherine threw her arms around the Blessed Virgin's knees. The Heavenly Queen then told Catherine that God had chosen her for a special mission. When the Blessed Mother left, the child and Catherine returned to the bedroom It was 2:00 A.M.

Needless to say, she slept no more. St Catherine believed that the child was her guardian angel.

The most famous appearance of the Blessed Mother to Catherine Laboure occurred on November 27, 1830, at 5:30 P.M. during her meditation. She heard a rustling of a dress and then she saw near the picture of St. Joseph a person, the Blessed Mother. She was standing. She was most beautiful, of medium height, a brilliant bright robe and a white veil which came down to Her feet was Her raiment and She stood upon the globe of the world. In Her hand was another globe. "This globe represents the entire world, and each person in particular," She said. "The rays are symbolic of the graces the Blessed Virgin obtains for those who ask for them. Have a statue made."

The globe then disappeared and an oval frame appeared about the Blessed Mother, and on it appeared these words: "O Mary, conceived without sin, pray for us who have recourse to Thee." Here the Blessed Mother requests a medal to be made upon this model and promised to all who wore it graces and especially graces to those who ask for them. Then the reverse side was shown to Catherine. On it was a large letter "M" surmounted by a cross having a bar at its base. Under the letter "M" were two hearts; one of Christ surrounded by a crown of thorns and the other Mary's pierced with a sword. This was surmounted by a ring of twelve stars.

The Archbishop of Paris in 1832 gave formal permission to have the medal made according to the vision. Immediately, miraculous cures were seen and the people made a great demand for the medals. Millions have been made and millions are worn by the faithful.

The Blessed Mother told St. Catherine that there are graces for all who ask and pray for them. She requests that the people pray for them. Let us in our love and devotion to the Blessed Mother pray for the graces we need and for the graces others need, too. Let us pray for all who have left the Church to come back so that all may have the consolation of the love of Mary and of having Jesus in their own hearts.

> "O Mary, conceived without sin, pray for us who have recourse to Thee." May we receive the graces we need for a life of love and for a happy death.

GREEN BADGE OF THE IMMACULATE HEART - BLANGY, 1840

Today we see a Green Scapular. What is it and how did it come into use?

The Blessed Mother wanted Her Immaculate Heart to be known and devotion to it started. First, Our Lady revealed Her heart to St. Catherine Laboure in 1830. In 1832, after Our Lady requested a parish priest, Father Des Gennettes, to consecrate his parish to the Most Holy and Immaculate Heart of Mary, his parish, which was practically dead spiritually (only ten came to Mass on Sunday), the church became overcrowded.

Now in 1840, the Blessed Mother revealed Her heart five times to a young Sister Justine Bisqueburu in the Novitiate of the Daughters of Charity in Paris, and again at the town of Blangy, September 8, 1848, where Sister Justine was sent to teach school. In Her right hand, Our Lady held Her heart surrounded by flames and in Her left a sort of scapular - a green scapular. One side had a picture of the just described apparition and on the other side a heart in brilliant light, pierced by a sword and surmounted by a cross. An oval inscription surrounded the heart which read, "Immaculate Heart of Mary, pray for us now and at the hour of our death."

A voice told her such scapulars were to be made and distributed. They were for the conversions of the unfaithful and to procure a happy death.

Sister Justine contacted her Mother Superior and notified the Chaplain of the convent, but nothing was done. The Blessed Mother appeared again one year later and complained that no scapulars were made. Five years later, scapulars were made. The chaplain requested Sister Justine to ask the Blessed Virgin what the requirements for wearing the badge were. On September 8, 1846, the Blessed Virgin Mary appeared and stated: No formal imposition required, to be blessed by a priest, wear or place it near the person and recite only the prayer on the scapular daily; graces will be received in proportion to the confidence of the giver of the scapular.

Since 1942, when Pope Pius XII consecrated the world to the Immaculate Heart of Mary, the Sisters of Charity have taken upon themselves the task of having this scapular manufactured in large quantities and distributed.

Many favors and graces were obtained through the use of this Green Scapular.

> *O Immaculate Heart of Mary, pray for us now and at the hour of our death. Defend us from the loss of faith and the loss of hope. Keep us faithful to Your Son. Obtain the graces we need to live a holy life and be blessed with a happy death.*

OUR LADY OF LA SALETTE - 1846

The nation of France has been favored by the Blessed Mother for one reason or another. Her love for the French has brought Her down from Heaven more than once. She has brought grace, miracles, and warnings to that country.

A miraculous shrine with a beautiful church now stands in the village of La Salette, France, near the Alp Mountains where the Blessed Mother appeared in the year 1846 on September 19th.

On that day, two children, Maximin Giraurd, age 11, and Malanie Mathieu, age 14, were tending cows in the mountains when they saw a brilliant light, and out of the light appeared the Blessed Mother. She appeared sitting upon stones and weeping. Her elbows rested upon Her knees and Her face was in Her hands. Immediately She rose and came toward the boy and girl. "Come to me, do not be afraid. I am here to tell you great news." She said.

When the children came near, they saw the Beautiful Lady as they called Her, dressed as follows: the shoes were a sparkling white with a square golden buckle. Encircling the shoes were tiny roses. Her apron was golden and it came to the bottom of Her full white robe. Her arms were folded concealing the hands in the folds of the garment. She was crowned with roses and She wore dazzling chains about Her neck and shoulder.

This Lady of Light had a most beautiful face, but it was pale white as one burdened with suffering and sorrow. Upon Her bosom rest a golden crucifix with pincers and a hammer of the Passion.

In explaining the manner of the Blessed Mother's dress, the following interpretations are given: the three garlands of red, white and violet roses stood for the glorious, joyful and sorrowful mysteries of the Rosary; the glistening chains were symbols of penance and good works; the crucifix represented the sign of consecration to Jesus through Mary; the hammer signified the punishments from God if the world refused the Blessed Virgin's messages; the pincers were a symbol of reparation.

The Blessed Lady had a message to give to the children and who, in turn, were to publicize it. The message was "A Turning to God." She told them that She was holding back the Hand of justice of Her Son. The abuses of God's Holy Name, the non-attendance of Mass, and the working on Sundays were calling for justice from Christ. The non-observance of Sunday and the taking of God's Name in vain were the two crimes the people were committing and this was calling on the wrath of God for justice. God ruined the crop of potatoes last year because of these sins and, if the people don't pray and quit committing those sins, then the whole wheat crop will be destroyed. It will turn to dust.

Speaking in French, Our Lady said, "Well, My children, you will make this known to all My people." With this She became very bright and, rising a little off of the high spot of ground, She disappeared. A miraculous spring appeared where the Weeping Mother of God had rested Her feet.

France was not converted to God immediately and had to suffer many misfortunes, even with the warnings of the Blessed Mother. May She also give us warnings when we fall away from God. Better still, may we pray that these warnings given are seen as pertaining to us and are heeded by us. Even if we do suffer a little, it is better to turn to God as soon as possible than to suffer now and be damned forever.

> *O Mary, warn us of all dangers and turn us to God now and keep us near Him at all times. Dear Mother, You want us to be faithful and loving children. You want us to keep all the Commandments. You want us to be blessed here and hereafter. Dear Virgin, help us to be wise and to know what is best for us. We beg You to stop crying because of our past unfaithfulness and sinfulness. We now resolve to heed Your words and we promise to live according to the Will of God and the command to love God and fellow man.*

OUR LADY OF LOURDES

To the happenings at Lourdes in France in the year 1858, this can be said what prefaced the movie "Song of Bernadette": "to those who do not believe there is no explanation, to those who believe, they need no explanation."

The attention of all of France and then all of the Christian world became centered upon the town of Lourdes when the news like wildfire spread throughout the nation and world. The news was: The Blessed Virgin appeared to Bernadette Soubirous at the grotto outside Lourdes. The curious, the religious, the pious, the sick began to crowd the space about the cave and until this day crowds still gather there to honor the Blessed Mother, to beg for miraculous cures and above all to adore Her Blessed Son, and venerate Her.

In the year 1858, the town of Lourdes had a population of about five thousand. It rested in the foothills of the Pyrenees mountains in southern France. It was not much different from other towns of France, except that this town was once a fortress protecting France from Spain.

In this town there lived a poor family by the name of Soubirous. This family lacking business ability, could not make their flour mill bring in the necessary monies to pay the bills. It was necessary for the family to find cheap quarters in a garret room which at one time was a prison. Both Francis and Louise Soubirous were forced to go out searching for work. Although they were poor, they never begged. They saw to it that the children learned their prayers, went to school whenever possible and were neat.

The oldest child of this family was Bernadette. She knew what it was to be hungry and cold from her earliest days. She had to tend the younger children while mother went out to earn a penny. She was even sickly, weak, asthmatic, and even smaller than other girls of her age.

Our Lady of Lourdes pray for us sinners and develop in us a spirit of love of God and His Commandments.

Thinking that life in the country on the farm would do Bernadette some good, the parents sent her to a friend of the family, about two miles from Lourdes. There she worked partly in the house and partly tending the sheep. It was out in the fields that she showed her love of God by building altars and decorating them with flowers and frequently saying the Rosary. As to book knowledge and formal religious instruction, she had none. The lady of the house tried to teach her, but had to give up. When the lady of the farm would get disgusted, Bernadette would put her arms around the lady's neck and whisper, "At least I shall always know how to love the good God".

Bernadette did not stay on the farm too long, for in about six months she was back in Lourdes where now at fourteen she was being prepared to make her first Holy Communion.

It was on Thursday February 11, 1858 Bernadette, her sister Marie, and a companion Jeanne Abadie went one morning to gather some twigs for firewood. They walked out of town down to where the little river of the Gave passes a large stone hill called the Massabielle. While the sister Marie and her companion took off their shoes and dashed across the cold waters to pick the twigs on the other side, Bernadette took her time in taking off her shoes. Suddenly she heard a strong wind. She looked around and found nothing. The sound came again. This time Bernadette looked at the cave in the rocks and there saw the vegetation move. Then to her utter amazement she saw a most beautiful young Lady of about fifteen years of age surrounded by a light. She was dressed all in white. The gown came to Her feet. Yellow roses were at Her feet. A blue sash was at the waist. A white veil covered Her head and fell at Her feet. She held a Rosary of white beads on a gold chain.

The Lady beckoned to Bernadette. She said nothing. She made the sign of the cross and Bernadette followed suit. When Bernadette finished the Rosary, the Lady disappeared.

When the sister and companion returned, they found Bernadette kneeling. They scolded her for being lazy. On the way home, Bernadette told her sister of the vision. This could not be kept secret as it was promised. The whole world learned of it in good time.

Our Lady of Lourdes, as You protected France now protect that nation and all of us sinners now and at the hour of temptation of deflection. Be at our side when God calls us.

Continuing the story of the appearances of the Blessed Virgin at Lourdes, we all become stricken with awe as was the whole town of Lourdes and the nation of France. The beautiful Lady was seen many times, She conveyed Her message and finally told Bernadette who She was.

During the first apparition, the Blessed Mother did not speak. Nor did She talk during the second appearance which occurred on Sunday, February 14th. On this day, Bernadette after the High Mass, obtained permission from her parents to visit the Grotto. When the Vision was seen, Bernadette cast some holy water towards Our Lady saying, "If You come from God, step forward". The Lady smiled and advanced. During this apparition, Bernadette fell in to a state of ecstasy during which her face became most beautiful.

Bernadette and her family suffered ridicule from the townsfolk because of these visions. She was threatened with imprisonment. Yet the girl always kept to her story no matter who interrogated her or how she was threatened.

On Thursday of that week, February 18th, Bernadette had paper and pen with her to have the Lady write down Her wishes. When the Blessed Mother came, She spoke Her first words, "It is not necessary for Me to write what I have to say to you". She continued, "Will you be gracious enough to come here everyday for a fortnight?" When Bernadette said she would seek permission from her parents to comply with the Lady's desire, the Blessed Mother said, "I do not promise to make you happy in this world, but in the other".

All in total the Blessed Mother appeared to Bernadette eighteen times. It was during the sixth apparition that She asked Bernadette to pray for sinners. Frequent prayer and penance was Her message to be conveyed to the people by Bernadette.

Secret messages were given to Bernadette during the seventh apparition, but during the eighth appearance at which about five hundred people were present, the spectators saw tears streaming down her checks and heard this message, "Repentance, Repentance, Repentance".

> *Our Lady obtain for us the grace of being sorry for our sins and develop in us a firm purpose of amendment and reparation for our sins.*

During the ninth appearance came the command to drink out of the spring and to wash in it. The crowd gathered there were surprised to see her eat by command the herbs that grew in the grotto. Then she dug a little and found some water. She tried to wash her face in the water and did take a drink. This was the beginning for the famous Lourdes water which brought so much happiness to the sick. This water is sought by all pilgrims and many want to bathe in this curative water.

In the apparitions that followed again the Blessed Mother asked for prayer and repentance. Also, She asked Bernadette to bring a lighted candle with her and to leave it in the grotto. That practice is kept up to this day by all the faithful pilgrims who visit the Grotto. During the thirteenth and fourteenth apparitions She requests Bernadette to let the priest know that She wants a chapel built on the sight of the apparitions.

A large crowd gather at the grotto on the last day of the two weeks hoping to see a miracle and find out the identity of the Apparition. But they were disappointed because as always only Bernadette saw the Blessed Mother and there were no miracles.

It was on March 25th, the sixteenth apparition that after repeated petitions as to Her identity, the Blessed mother conceded and said, "I am the Immaculate Conception". Although Bernadette did not know what these words meant, nevertheless the whole world did for just four years before the Holy Father, Pope Pius IX defined the doctrine of the Immaculate Conception.

Two more times did the Blessed Mother appear to Bernadette and showed Her beauty to the girl. The sight of the Blessed Mother caused Bernadette to fall into an unearthly ecstasy. Her heart was filled with Joy.

> *Our Lady of Lourdes fill our hearts with Joy. May we experience Your love and protection. May we live as God wills. When God calls, O Lady, graciously smile to us and lead us to Your Son, Our Lord Jesus.*

We need not ask the question today whether' the Blessed Mother really appeared at Lourdes or not, for the history of Lourdes proves conclusively that She did. But there were those who denied the supernatural and remain in their unbelief.

First of all, there were those who claimed that Bernadette suffered from hallucinations; that she was mentally unsound. The doctors examined her and found her completely and <u>wholly</u> sane.

Then they claimed this was a hoax, a scheme to make money. The more these critics voiced their claim, the more the Soubirous family refused to profit by the events. Refusing gifts the family remained poor lest they fall into traps and bribes for which they could be condemned.

Lastly, seeing that these skeptics were defeated, they argued that the water from the spring was a special mineral water with curative powers just like many of the spas and mineral springs in the vicinity. This argument of theirs too was completely refuted when water experts came and analyzed the water and declared it to be pure natural mountains water possessing no therapeutic value whatsoever.

The authorities of the town gave opposition to the devotion at the Grotto. They put up barricades and only with the consent of Napoleon III in the Fall of 1858 did the people get free access to the grotto to venerate the Blessed Virgin Mary and to leave their lighted candles as tokens of their love.

> *Our Lady, as we place a lighted Candle at Your Shrine or before Your image, accept it as our prayer and act of love, veneration, and devotion.*

The clergy did not get overly enthusiastic about these appearances at Lourdes. Many visionaries were frauds and frauds were suspected in all cases, even in this. It was only after Bernadette had her eighteenth vision that the bishop of the place ordered a complete investigation which took three years to complete.

During these three years Bernadette was subject to all kinds of questions. She had no rest. Friends and foes interrogated her trying to trap her in contradiction of her story. This continual singling at and questioning of Bernadette began to tell on her health. To safeguard her from any ill effect, the pastor of the town, Father Payramale had her put into a boarding school with the Sisters of Charity. There she had some peace and made some progress with her studies.

O how happy was Bernadette and the Blessed Mother too, when on January 18, 1862, the Bishop Laurence decreed: "It is our judgement that Mary Immaculate, Mother of God, did really appear to Bernadette Soubirous on February 11, 1858, and on subsequent days, eighteen times in all, in the Grotto of Massabielle, close to the town of Lourdes."

With the approval of the bishop and of the church, Lourdes became a source of blessing to millions of pilgrims who visit the Shrine every year. Many Americans travel to Lourdes to honor Mary and to be inspired by Her. Some come for cures.

> *Our Lady of Lourdes, You have cured many sick and have restored faith to the doubtful and unbelievers. Cure our souls of sin and the inclinations to sin. Also strengthen our faith. May we be true believers of God and true children of God and You.*

It would take a long time to tell all the wonders which took place at Lourdes and still take place there. All of the miracles are astounding and each has its own beautiful story which can motivate us only to love the Blessed Virgin Mary more and more.

But now let us see what happened to Bernadette and to the request of the Blessed Mother.

Bernadette went to school in the convent of the Sisters of Charity at Nevers. Here she progressed spiritually and intellectually. She was permitted to receive Holy Communion twice a month and after Confirmation, each Sunday. She then sought to enter that congregation but her health delayed her entrance for two years. Only in July of 1866 did she bid her final farewell to her "Heaven at Lourdes,' and become Sister Marie-Bernard.

Her life was not so easy in the convent. Her health was poor, and her superiors and especially the Mistress of the Novices gave her many a heartache. Thus she was protected against pride and developed the great virtues of obedience and humility. As to her work, she was infirmarian and later sacristan - rather easy and agreeable work and this she did well. She was loved by the members of her community.

Bernadette did not stay long on the job, for she was called to see the Blessed Virgin Mary and Her Son this time again and forever in 1879. She died at the age of thirty-five. Her body can be seen and venerated at Nevers where it lays intact - incorrupt. Her final earthly glory came in 1933 when she was canonized a saint by the church.

From Her place in Heaven she watches what goes on at Lourdes. She sees how the shrine has grown to many buildings including the beautiful Basilica church. The request of the Blessed Virgin to have a chapel built there has been fulfilled. The Popes heavily indulgenced the Shrine and have shown their love for the Blessed Virgin by approving of the Shrine, granting a special Mass and office of the apparitions at Lourdes.

Today one can see the Grotto at Lourdes much different than what St. Bemadette saw it. The beautiful church with its processional ground, the hospitals, the baths bring admiration to all pilgrims and to all of the curious.

Although Lourdes is especially dedicated to the Blessed Virgin Mary, yet the whole setup, the processions with all its singing of the praises of the Blessed Virgin Mary, the blessing of all the sick with the Blessed Sacrament lead up to one individual Christ, Our Lord, Our God, the Son of Mary. And that is the way She wants it. Through Mary to Jesus.

> *Oh Mary, may our love for Thee increase daily so that through Thee we may live with Jesus. As we think of Lourdes, may we keep in mind Your love for all mankind, Your desire to keep us away from sin, and Your requests that we love Your Son, Our Lord, with all our hearts. Protect us. Keep us loyal to Jesus. Fire our hearts with a great devotion to Jesus and You.*

A DAY AT LOURDES

At 7:00 a.m. a short walk from our hotel took our group to the Shrine of Our Lady at Lourdes. As we entered the shrine compound, the Basilica dominated the area.

We walked briskly through the courtyard to get to an altar for Mass. We decided to walk up the ramp to the second floor where we said Mass. Masses were being said on altars on each of the three floor levels of the Basilica.

Behind the Basilica our group came upon the Grotto where Our Blessed Mother appeared to Bernadette Soubirous. Mass was being celebrated there, people were placing lighted candles on a stand nearby, and others were filling containers with the famous Lourdes Water.

After brunch, we were back at the shrine to take part in the afternoon procession. Many people Joined the procession in which were laity, women religious, priests, and bishops. One bishop carried a large monstrance in which was a Consecrated Host. As he walked passed the sick on both sides of the square, he blessed them. It is said about half of the miraculous cures that occur at Lourdes, happen at this benediction service. These sick were brought to the shrine complex by attendants who wore halter belts. The other half of the miracles at Lourdes occur in the Baths. After general benediction the crowd dispersed only to meet again for the evening devotions.

Again the square in front of the Basilica is filled for the evening procession which is formed at the Grotto. Lighted candles are carried by everyone. When the devotees of the Blessed Virgin Mary arrive at the front of the Basilica, hymns and prayers are recited.

During the singing of the "Lourdes" hymn, which hymn is known and sung throughout the whole Catholic world, every pilgrim sings at the top of his voice. What a chorus! One hundred thousand people sang their praises of Mary.

Curiosity took its hold of us. What are the Baths like? We must enter the miraculous Waters of Lourdes.

The women entered their section of the large building while we men passed through the doors designated for men. Once inside attendants took command. "Undress and cover your body with this denim cloth." It was dripping wet and cold.

We moved up to the shallow pool and watched others receive their bath. Two men lead me into the water about stomach high. A prayer was recited. The Blessed Mother's name was invoked in French. A tender nudge put my head under water for a brief moment.

Once back in the dressing area, we wet, without the pleasure of a towel, redressed. There were smiles on all our faces. We felt refreshed and holier.

As we walked into the open air, we remarked, "We had no towel and look how dry we are." "This must be a Lourdes miracle," I responded.

Once again we were on our knees at the grotto thanking God and Mary for the privilege of being in this holy place. Another look at Mary's statue and then filling our containers with the Lourdes Water, we came to the square in front of the Basilica.

Here another large statue of Our Lady attracted our attention and so did the many bouquets of flowers placed on the iron picket fence which surrounded the statue.

In front of us were the medical buildings and the Church of Pope Pius V which has its seating area underground.

Miracles do occur at Lourdes. But miracles have to be verified. That is the purpose for the medical buildings and hospital. Each patient is examined upon coming to and leaving Lourdes. His records are compared to see any change in the sick. Definite medical proof must be established before the officials at Lourdes declare any cure a miracle. Many cures do happen at Lourdes.

It is reported that an atheist brought a crippled boy to Lourdes. He promised he would become a Catholic if the boy were cured. The boy returned home lame as he came, but the atheist after experiencing the devotion at Lourdes returned home a baptized Catholic.

PELLEVOISIN 1876

The nation of France is dear to the heart of Mary. Our Lady appeared time and time again in that country and there gave messages for the world. Yet, France is not too loyal to the church.

After Lourdes, again the Blessed Mother appeared in France and now in a town of Pellevoisin in 1876, to a maid by the name of Estelle Faguette.

Estelle was dying from consumption. She also had a large tumor. She was moved from Paris to Pellevoisin in September of 1875. She was at this time thirty-two years old. Her first devotion to Our Lady is shown by writing a letter to the Blessed Mary and having it hidden in the stones of a new shrine which was being erected in that town in honor of Our Lady of Lourdes.

Once Estelle was so weak that doctors gave up all hope. She only then resigned herself to God's will after fighting and complaining about her sickness and saying it's a pain for her to die since her family depends upon her for a livelihood.

One day as the priest came to see her, she told him she saw the Blessed Mother. Although in extreme danger of death, she didn't want to go to confession and be anointed. She said she would be well. On that Saturday she was completely cured.

The Blessed Virgin appeared, fifteen times to Estelle Faguette. In one of the appearances Our Blessed Mother held a Sacred Heart badge and asked her to spread devotion to the Sacred Heart.

She appeared dressed in white and with hands extended. From Her hands drops of water fell as rain. These are the graces Mary bestows upon us people. Mary said, "Jesus loves me so that He refuses no request of mine." Mary warned France will suffer because of her unfaithfulness to God.

These appearances were approved by the church in 1894; and the Scapular approved in 1900. It is reported that Our Lady said, "I'm all merciful and Mediatrix of all Grace."

> *O Mary, all merciful and Mediatrix of all Grace, obtain mercy for our sins and forgiveness. We beseech You to obtain all graces for us personally, for the church universally and for our beloved country so that we may do the Will of God and enjoy peace and prosperity.*

OUR LADY OF THE JAIL

Here is an unusual story for a Catholic country of the Philippines. The townsfolk of Navotas were having a fiesta one day. They formed a procession in which they carried a statue of the Blessed Mother. Their singing and shouting annoyed the local government which was in session. The politicians became so incensed that they wanted to arrest all for disturbing the peace. But when they saw a very long throng of faithful, they changed their mind. Knowing the jail could not hold all of the fiesta celebrators, the officials arrested the Statue of the Blessed Mother as the disturber of peace and placed Her in jail. To this day the Blessed Mother in that community is referred to as Our Lady of the Jail.

In recent times other faithful and devoted children of Mary were put into jail because they too were disturbing the peace, the Communistic peace.

In China it is a crime to belong to the Legion of Mary. Thousands of the Legionaires are in jail. Their organization is outlawed and disbanded.

The legionaires of Mary and the faithful of Christ behind the Iron Curtain are persecuted, imprisoned, and put to death. They, too, are the disturbers of peace.

Peace in the communist language means a slavish submission to authority. No freedom of thought and action is permitted. There is reasonable cause for revolt, to revolution for freedom, peace, and prosperity. Man has a sacred right and obligation to keep himself free from enslavement of sin and tyranny.

> O Mary, "Our Lady of the Jail," help all Thy children who are in jail and restore freedom of worship and peace under God to the world. Help those in prison to think of God and of everlasting freedom and peace in Heaven. Instill in them a holy hope of liberation and eternal joy

A VISIT TO FATIMA

Thousands witnessed the Miracle of the Sun at Fatima. Thousands came to Fatima to honor Mary, the Mother of Jesus, and to experience an awesome feeling of holiness for here in 1917 the Blessed Mother appeared to three children: Lucy, Jacinta, and Marco.

The holm oak is no longer there, but in its place is an altar under a roof but open on three sides. Behind the altar stands a statue of Our Lady of Fatima and beyond that is a shelter or sacristy where the Statue is protected when not exposed.

This spot of the apparition is about midpoint in the huge area, but to the left beyond this sacred shrine on a hill is the huge Basilica. Many steps lead to the doors of that church.

Definitely our group visited that basilica and prayed there. Therein are interred the bodies of Jacinta and Marco. Sister Lucy is still alive and resides in a convent some distance away.

We priests joined the local bishop and about eighty priests in a concelebrated Mass on an altar on the steps of the basilica. In front of us were about twenty thousand people in the plaza which was about the length of two football fields. The Mass was said in Latin and Portuguese, but the invocations in the prayers of the faithful were in about ten languages.

A point of interest to me was the construction of the ciboriums. The cap or top was fixed/welded to the cup. A turn of the cross on top made an opening large enough for the fingers to get hosts for distribution to the people receiving Holy Communion. Experience taught the clergy to construct the ciboriums in that manner because of the wind. At one time I have seen wind blow communion particles out of the conventional constructed ciboriums.

In the afternoon our tour took us to the village of Fatima where we visited the home of Sister Lucy, the community parish church, and the stations of the cross. While walking along the route of the stations, we came upon a statue of an angel holding a ciborium. The explanation of the statue was: "Here the angel gave Holy Communion to the three children." There was another statue of an angel near a water font where again it appeared to the children.

During the evening a large crowd was gathered at the site of the apparitions. Immediately after mass a procession was formed in which the a most beautiful Statue of Our Lady of Fatima was carried. All Joined this devotion praying the Rosary and singing hymns.

Leaving the shrine area to return to our hotel, a group of people caught my eye. One person was walking on her knees the whole length of the plaza, over a hundred yards. I was told many people traverse the length of the plaza on their knees. To ease the penance a rubber strip was laid down.

Upon turning to the shrine, we saw that the crowd had dispersed. Only a few remained to perform private devotions.

A satisfying and humble feeling came upon me. I'm glad to be fortunate to visit and pray in a privileged location where Our Blessed Lady appeared and gave a message to the world.

Rosary, Brown Scapular and Tennis Shoes

What a combination: Rosary, Brown Scapular, and Tennis Shoes! Who in the world ever heard of this expression? I have and so did a number of Pilgrims at the Shrine of Our Lady in Fatima, Portugal.

At the Domus Pacis a Byzantine Priest, Father Skurla, remarked, my "What the world needs is Catholics of deep faith who will possess a Rosary, a Brown Scapular, and Tennis Shoes".

Our Lady in Her appearances at Fatima requested the daily recitation of the Rosary. She also is Our Lady of the Scapular. "I can see the Rosary and the Scapular, but where do you fit in the Tennis Shoes?" I asked. This was in 1976.

"We are slow," replied Father Skurla, "while the enemies of God and the church are working hard in tearing the church apart and converting many to communism. The errors of atheistic communism of Russia is spreading rapidly. When Sister Lucy was asked, "Will communism come to the United States?", She remarked "yes".

"Look how Russian influence is on the rapid move - in Asia, - in Africa, in Europe, in South and Central America. Don't fool yourself and say 'There are no communists in the United States'! Besides we do have many who are atheists. You can dial an atheist in practically every large city."

"In spite of the Ecumenical Movement as begun with the Vatican Council II, little progress has been made although the work moves on too slowly. We need to run. We need to move faster. We need tennis shoes instead of clodhoppers."

Everyone knows the dedication of the Mormons and Jehovah Witnesses. Two by two they knock on doors seeking converts. Their fire and zeal urges them on and on. They are moving perhaps not as fast as communism, but they are moving.

From Utah, the Mormons have invaded every state. They continue to knock on doors. The youth spend two years at their own cost in the missionary work of their church.

The Jehovah Witnesses do not stop after two years of their house to house campaign. In spite of rebuffs, slamming of doors in their face, and rejection, they continue. How many so called Catholics have joined them? Much to my surprise was the remark of a new arrival from western Poland that 7% of the people are Jehovah Witnesses. Only 90% of Poland are now Catholics.

Say what you will about the proselytizing of the communists, atheists, Mormons, and Jehovah Witnesses, there is one thing certain: they are making giant steps forward. Many are being taken into their ranks. The Devil is succeeding in snatching souls and ripping the Mystical Body soul by soul.

In spite of Our Lady's prophecy of the spread of these errors, we Catholics are complacent, we remain uninformed of the truths of our faith, we fail to truly love God and man, and we refuse to share our greatest possession - our faith - with others.

We heard of the Fatima promise that the Immaculate Heart of Mary will triumph. So why should we worry?

Look at the dissension in the world and look at the misery caused by communism! Look how many nations are deprived of their freedom! Look how many are sent to labor camps, or just disappear, or are killed by Russian authorities! Count how many families are torn apart! Count how many souls are lost for all eternity!

We need the Rosary. We need the Scapular. We need tennis shoes. But possession is not enough. All three must be used.

To promote the Rosary, the use of the Scapular, and the hurrying of spreading the true faith is to be the work of each and every true Catholic.

Our Lord ordered the Apostles to go and teach all nations. True, we do have missionaries who do just that. But how about us? Aren't we members of the Mystical Body? Don't we possess the true faith and the love of God which by their nature want to spread? Don't we have an obligation from the Command of Christ to love our neighbor, to help him to know the Truth, to love the Truth, and to Possess the Truth?

We need our Tennis Shoes. We need to move. We need to spread our faith, our love, and our joy. We need speed to do all of this.

May the Blessed Mother of Fatima help us to save our souls and the souls of others. May Her graces move us to work tirelessly and rapidly in preserving the faith in the believers and in giving the faith to the unbelievers.

Our Lord prayed that all may be one. We too are to pray and work for the unity of the Mystical Body of Christ.

The Servant Of Jacinta

Should the children who witnessed the apparition at Fatima be canonized? Yes, say some. No, say others. Those who say "No" claim the children exhibited no heroic virtues although they were told by Our Lady they would go to Heaven. Those who say "Yes" claimed there were heroic virtues.

Among the promoters of the canonization is an American by the name of Robert Lesnick. "What do you mean, no heroic virtues," he asks. "Didn't The Blessed Mother not say to Jacinta "You will suffer much". And did not Our Lady tell her she would die away from her family and alone? How about her sickness? How about the operation without proper anesthesia?

Robert kept us entranced for hours as he related the story of Jacinta from the time of the apparitions unto the present day: How her body remains intact in spite of the lime placed on her corpse; how the church bells rang by themselves during her funeral; how miracles occur through her intercession.

Bob fights strongly when skeptics deny the unusual occurrences associated with Jacinta.

"Bob, how is it that you have spent thirteen years here at Fatima?" I asked.

"I wanted to leave after being here for a short visit. I thought my mission was completed after making a retreat here. I was determined to return to the states. The morning I was to depart I broke my leg. The doctor ordered me to stay five months. During this time, I prayed and studied the whole Fatima apparition story.

My leg was strong enough for me to return home. I was packed ready to leave. I became horrified. I lost my American passport. It took three months before the government issued me a new one.

Once again I determined to return to the United States. My apartment was ready for the next lessee and my bags were packed. The night before my departure, my apartment burst into flames. Even to this day the cause of the fire is unknown.

What was Our Lady and Jacinta trying to tell me? Did they want me to stay in Fatima? As I tried to reason the three deterrents, I came to the conclusion that the Blessed Virgin Mary and Jacinta want me here in Fatima.

Consequently I have labored for the past thirteen years on the cause of spreading the devotion to Our Lady and of Jacinta whom I know is a saint and who should be canonized."

Fatima Stories

Two young men from Geneva, Switzerland came to Fatima for Christmas: one was a Catholic, the other a Calvinist, who insisted on coming to Fatima although he was prevailed upon to go to Lourdes. Their first day at Fatima was on Christmas Eve.

It was at 10:30 P.M. when they came to the cova. It was cold that evening. Only a small group of pilgrims was present. Each prayed and each had his own intention.

As the hour to twelve approached, the attention of all shifted to a woman who held a bundle in her arms. She was praying loudly, "O Blessed Mother, on Christmas You gave birth to a wonderful Son. He was healthy and had beautiful blue eyes. Help my child to see".

The two Swiss and the others came near the woman and child. She pulled the blanket off the baby's head. One peek made everyone turn their heads to the statue of Our Lady. They saw a baby with a forehead that extended to the nose. There were no eyes.

Twenty-four persons forgot their own reasons for praying and concentrated upon the baby. Again they heard "O Blessed Mother, don't let my baby go through life without eyes. Your Son has such beautiful eyes. Give my baby sight". Although the baby whimpered and stirred a few times, the mother and all the pilgrims continued to pray. Something moved the woman to look at the baby. She screamed. All came to her. Now they saw a normal head. Two slits were evident. As they watch the opening became larger and larger until they reached the normal size for baby's eyes. It open its eyes. There all saw blue eyes where there were only skin and flesh before.

When the two Swiss returned home, both were convinced in the power of Our Lady and of faith. It was not long afterward the Calvinist took instructions and became a Catholic. A couple years later he entered a seminary and was ordained a priest.

I Don't Believe In Miracles

A group of Pilgrims left New York to come to Fatima. These people convinced a friend of theirs to come along. This man was a wheelchair patient for the past thirty-five years. In the conversations before leaving New York and while on the plane, much of the discourses were on the miracles of Fatima. With each recounting of a cure, the patient remarked, "I don't believe in miracles".

Upon arriving at the Shrine, John was wheeled before the Statue of Our Lady. After the group finished their veneration, John arose from his chair and standing on his feet for the first time in thirty-five years, shouted, "I don't believe in...miracles".

Now I Can Speak

John Brown had a thriving restaurant in Brooklyn. Although he was pleased with his business and his wife, he was saddened because his nine year old daughter could not speak. No doctor nor hospital could help her to talk.

At one visit to his regular doctor, John heard, "Why don't you take your daughter to Fatima. I hear many miracles come about through the Blessed Mother."

John made arrangements for his family to make the trip to Fatima. Prayers were said at the cova and petitions were made.

Mrs. Brown caught sight of a priest who was walking up to the Basilica. "Father, will you say a Mass for our intention. You see our daughter cannot speak."

"I'll be glad to oblige. I'll say the Mass in your intention tomorrow morning at 10."

"We shall be there," John and Agnes Brown answered in unison. Immediately after Mass, Father Michael came to the Brown family and took them to the tomb of the incorrupt body of Jacinta. They all knelt down. Father Michael took the hand of Elice and placed it on the tomb. "Now repeat after me," he said. "Jesus, Mary, and Jacinta."

John and Agnes burst into tears. They heard the words "Jesus, Mary, and Jacinta" come out of the mouth of their mute daughter.

It took some time before Elice spoke perfectly, but she continued to speak. Her speech improved daily. Today she speaks English, good Portuguese, and is studying French.

In appreciation for the miraculous favor obtained at Fatima, John and Agnes sold their business in Brooklyn and moved to Fatima. They managed to acquire the rights to operate a restaurant in the nearby two thousand year old castle at Ourem where many of the kings and queens of Portugal resided. This castle became Portuguese property only after the Moors were defeated and driven out.

A Moor princess by the name of Fatima who lived in that castle married a Portuguese prince. From her comes the name of the village of Fatima. She was buried where the parish church is located. In this church the three children of Fatima were baptized.

Buses took our party of 180 pilgrims up the mountain to a parking landing. Here we waited for vans which carried about ten passengers. From the towers of the fortress two individuals dressed in medieval garments greeted us with trumpet acclamations. We were told a prince on horseback was to meet us, but none came. Instead four vans came racing down the steep narrow incline at the end of the trumpet fanfare.

Once in the entrance of the palace, Mr. Brown dressed in medieval garments greeted us and had teenage girls also dressed in royal clothing present us with an exclusive formula cocktail.

About a dozen of us were sent into the wine cellar where huge empty vats were stored while the others were ushered into a large dining hall. These few were given garments of dukes, duchesses, princes and princesses, etc. At last the two remaining were made king and queen of the day, The royal party sat at the head table. Crowns were placed on the heads of the king and queen. This caused a hilarious moment. Flash bulbs blinded us as photos were taken.

The dinner was served in regular Portuguese style - a fish plate first and then meat. Plenty of wine and fruit accompanied the meal. There were songs and much laughter. The reigning king dubbed all present knights and dames.

During all banquets at the castle, John Brown stages a pageant of the history of the castle. The decor of the dining hall remains as it was when royalty lived there. He brings back "Seven Ghosts" to life on the stage.

The actors and actresses were the ones who served the meal. The youth were dressed in costumes of the 11th or 13th century if there is a difference. Among these was the formerly mute daughter of the proprietors. She was pointed out privately. She and the other servers, now actors, did well in both functions.

The scenes of history were tableaus augmented by a movie narrated by John Haffert, the co-founder of the Blue Army of Mary. They were in good taste.

It is this John Haffert who promotes the message of Fatima and who sponsors pilgrimages to Fatima, Lourdes, and other Marian Shrines. John is a strong advocate of the Rosary and Reparation which the Blessed Mother requested at Fatima.

An enjoyable evening is experienced by all who venture to climb the mountain of the Castle of Ourem.

Fatima At Night

"Get your candles. We shall take part in the Candle Procession at 9:30 tonight." Our guide led us from our hotel to the cova. Already about ten thousand candles were in the hands of the Pilgrims. Prayers were being recited. I was told I would lead the Third Mystery in English.

Father Santos and I hurried to get vested, but we were the last to join the clergy at the altar of the Shrine. A priest in charge looked us over. He called two young people to read the meditation before each decade.The young man and young lady read in Portuguese.

The master of ceremonies came to Bishop Luna, a pilgrim from Guatemala to the microphone. My heart fell two feet when I hear Bishop Luna, the Papal appointee as the head of the Blue Army recite the prayers in English. "Darn it, why was I late getting to the Shrine?" I missed my chance.

The Rosary was finished and the hymns ended. Directions were given and we moved into the open for the procession. First a cross and candles moved into the square. Priests and people followed. The Fatima Hymn was sung. We were supported by an organ and a choir. The amplification was perfect.

About ten thousand people moved along with the Blessed Mother of Fatima whose statue was carried by four strong men. This was a sight to behold. The carriage on which the statue stood was bedecked with a solid bed of flowers.

When we returned to the Shrine, the statue was taken away after we all sang "Salve Regina". Handkerchiefs were waved in farewell.

Shortly afterward the crowd thinned out. I lingered at the Shrine to say some of my private prayers. From the corner of my eye I saw a woman putting on knee pads. I wondered if she would walk on her knees from a starting point to the Shrine.

As I walked up the grade to the beginning of the smooth runner path, I counted fifteen individuals crawling on their knees coming to the cova and to Our Lady.

One day a bishop observed a young man walking on his knees. His knees were bare and bleeding. He was not using the runner but the blacktop rough pavement.

"Why are you walking on your knees and bleeding so much? Surely Our Blessed Mother doesn't demand that penance and devotion," asked the bishop.

The youth remarked, "Jesus spilt His last drop of blood for our salvation. Why can't I shed some blood for my salvation and for the salvation of others."

It was a satisfaction to see teenagers and younger take an active part in the devotions at Fatima. May God bless us all through the intercession of Our Lady of Fatima.

Sunday At Fatima

A hot dry July Sunday was given to us at Fatima. Although we were glad there was no rain, we did hope for more moderate temperature.

Buses came to our hotel and drove us to the village of the visionaries, the three children who were graced to see the Blessed Mother.

Our first stop was at the ancient village parish church where Lucy, Francesco, and Jacinta were baptized. Since Mass was in progress, Fernanda, our guide, took us across the street to the village parish cemetery. She stopped at the Marco family plot and revealed that the bodies of both Jacinta and Francesco are now interred in the Basilica, one on the left and Jacinta on the right up near the main altar. Later we saw these tombs.

After Mass we entered the parish church to say a short prayer and observe the appointments.

The buses took our group to the homes of the children. Now each home in the village is a religious article or artifact store. This was not so when I visited here in 1964. Tourists and pilgrims give a good opportunity for these poor farmer families to make money. We did go through the home of Sister Lucy.

A short walk took us over rough terrain to the hillside stations of the cross and to the spot where an angel appeared to the three children and gave them Holy Communion.

Time was running short. I asked our guide to get me to the Basilica for the eleven o'clock Mass. She hailed a passing automobile. I got a ride since the hour of eleven was near. I rushed into the sacristy. Already the procession to the outdoor altar in front of the Basilica was in progress. Hurriedly a Spanish priest and I vested and joined the tail end of the procession as it climbed the many steps to the altar.

The bishop of the area was the principal celebrant. About fifty priests were on the altar. These priests distributed Holy Communion at the proper time to about twenty thousand people. I was among them.

The Mass was in Portuguese except the "Canon" which was in Latin since we had clergy from many nations. The prayers of petition were in seven languages. The homily was delivered by the bishop and it was over twenty minutes long making a long meditation for all who knew not the language.

The rest of the day was on our own except for the meals. Time was had for more prayers and shopping. This last function was most popular with many of our group. In fact they craved to shop everywhere. I think some spent more time shopping than praying. I'm glad their purses were stuffed. By the way so were their luggage by the time we were ready to return home, but still purses were not empty of money.

FATIMA AND THE BLESSED VIRGIN MARY

The brutal World War I continued into its third year. France in particular was being devastated. With this useless destruction and killing of youth, people prayed for peace.

A message of peace came from Heaven. On May 13, 1917 the Blessed Virgin Mary intervened with human affairs and promised peace through three children in Portugal.

Francesco and Jacinta Marto with Lucy were diverting their attention from watching sheep by praying and frolicking. Their activity brought them to a valley in this hilly countryside.

They were startled to see Our Blessed Mother dressed in a long garment standing on top of a small holm oak tree. As Francesco and Jacinta looked on in utter amazement, Lucy achieving self-composure began to speak with the Mother of Jesus.

During this conversation Mary makes some requests and promises, Her first petition was: "Come back here on the 13th of each month," She would tell them Who She was later. She wanted them to be devoted to the Rosary and requested the Rosary be recited. Our Lady asks them to be ready to suffer anything for the reparation of sin and the conversion of sinners.

The Blessed Mother foretold the end of the war, but warned all people to return to God. If people would not, another war more terrible would befall mankind. During the next war, She warned, much martyrdom would occur, great errors would arise, nations would be destroyed and the Holy Father would suffer much.

As we look back at what happened during and after World War II, we see how true were Our Lady's predictions: the concentration and extermination camps; the killing at random plus inhuman experimentation by the Nazis; the killing and sending innocent people to Siberia by the communist Russians, and the taking over of all "Eastern" Europe into Russian domination and subjection.

But there is salvation and help for mankind, the Blessed Mother promised, Peace will return and Russia will be converted if man will be consecrated to the

Immaculate Heart of Mary, the Rosary recited daily, make five first Saturdays of consecutive months for reparation and Russia to be consecrated to the Immaculate Heart of Mary.

> *O Mary, Our Mother, we long for peace, people in satellite countries cry for independence. We faithful Join our hands, hearts, and voices in supplication begging You to obtain mercy for all peoples, obtain peace, obtain freedom, obtain liberation from the inundating forces of materialists which are attempting to flood the whole world. We need You and Your assistance now. O Mary, pray for us.*

FATIMA AND MIRACLES

What reactions did the appearances of the Blessed Virgin Mary bring about in Portugal? Surely the general public was agitated. The civil government was antagonistic and with that ridiculed the whole notion of Mary appearing to the three children. The children were even imprisoned. Also the clergy of the Catholic church kept themselves aloof.

As more pressures by the civil authorities were enforced upon the visionaries, more and more people gathered at the cove, the site of the appearances. Seventy thousand were there on October 13, 1917 to see the Miracle of the Sun.

That day started off as a miserable one. It rained all day. Mud was everywhere. It was time for the foretold miracle, The rains stopped. The sun appeared as a silver globe. Everyone could look upon the sun with naked eye. As the thousands watched, the sun began to spin like a fiery wheel. All hues of the rainbow were seen. This spinning started and stopped a number of times.

While the sun spun, various scenes were presented to the people. They saw Our Lord Blessing them, Our Lady as the Lady of Sorrows, and Our Lady of Mt. Carmel with a scapular in Her Hand. The spinning stopped and then the sun began to fall. Screams of terror. People fell to their knees and prayed, The Act of Contrition was heard. Suddenly the sun stopped falling and returned to its place in the Heaven. Added to the peoples' amazement was "everything was dry", their clothing and the ground were completely dry.

The miracle of the sun seemed to be enough proof for the Church and people that Our Blessed Mother really and truly appeared at Fatima. Faith was restored in the hearts of not only the villagers of Fatima but also in all of Portugal and the Christian Catholic World. Hope began to grow that the Immaculate Heart of Mary would triumph.

What happened to Fatima since the Miracle of the Sun? Fatima became a center of pilgrimages. A shrine was built on the spot of the holm oak. A large church and other building were erected. The government cooperated in fostering Fatima as a shrine where millions of people come to pray. A new town with moderm building and hotels arose. A hospital was erected. Offices of the church were constructed and persons were assigned to manage the affairs and transactions pertaining to the shrine. Over one thousand miracles were recorded.

The attraction of Fatima and its message lives on. Each year large groups of pilgrims arrive at Fatima to be with Mary, Our Mother. Many come with the hope of seeing a miracle or being the subject of a miraculous cure.

O Mary, Our Mother, You inspire hope in all of us. We hope for Your protection. We hope You will obtain miracles for us. We hope for peace. We hope Your words will come true concerning Russia and communism. May peace reign in this world. May Russia become a nation of faith and love. O Lady of Fatima, pray for us.

FATIMA'S MESSAGE: REPARATION

During the apparitions of the Blessed Mother at Fatima, She gave the world and to each one of us the plan for peace among nations and peace with ourselves. In Her first appearance to the three children on May 13,1917, She requested the first of the four point plan for peace. She asked, "Will you accept all of the sacrifices that God will send you in reparation for sin and the conversion of sinners?"

On the subsequent apparitions, the Blessed Mother showed the children the penalty of sin and begged them to tell the men and woman not to sin again.

It was during the July apparition that She permitted the children to get a glimpse of hell where they saw the souls being tossed about in the fiery furnaces. They saw the ugly and hideous devils tormenting the condemned souls. What a horrible impression this must to have made upon the minds of these youths. No doubt they were frightened. It was in the plan of the Blessed Mother that they should see these horrors so that they would pray for the conversion of sinners, and tell others not to sin.

Our Lady told the three child shepherds to tell the world that "more souls go to hell for sins of the flesh than any other". Surely, the Blessed Mother doesn't mean by that that those are sins which a person may commit rarely and being sorrowful for them, goes to confession and has them remitted. It is those sins of the flesh which people continue to commit and defy God and are unconfessed and unrepented.

Our Lady begged through the children "Men must cease to offend My Divine Son" and "tell the mothers of the world to stop committing ugly sins". Among the ugly sins is the sinful crime of abortion.

How far we must have gone from the straight and narrow path to have the Mother of God Herself come down to reprimand us for our sins. Seeing so many sins being committed. She who loves us so much had to do something. She had to remind us. She saw it fit to do this by telling us through the three children at Fatima not to sin.

O Mary, thank You for revealing yourself and Your mind. Thank You for reminding us of the gravity of sin and the horrors of hell. Thank You for warning us NOT to sin. Please Mary obtain the graces for me to avoid all sin and especially the sins of sex and murder or of condoning the idea of free choice and that I am the boss of my own body and all its actions by which I can do anything I want in violation of the Commandments of God and respect of life and the means to propagate life.

FATIMA'S MESSAGE: REPARATION II

An ugly and strange thing has befallen us and that is the loss of the sense of sin. Sin at one time was considered by all as a serious wrong. One would rather die than commit a mortal sin. Virgins suffered martyrdom rather than submit to man.

A mortal sin is so serious that it cuts us off from the love of God, drives God out of our soul, fills us with the ugliness of vice and makes us subject to eternal hell fire. Mortal sin is tuning ones back on God and attaching self to a creature.

But somehow that sense of sin our fathers and mothers had is no longer with us. Sin to means little anymore. We have killed our consciences.

What if we do wrong. What is sin anyway? What is killing another? What is stealing, defrauding the laborer of his just wage, destroying another's property or good name? It is nothing to miss Mass on Sunday. It is most common to hear of divorce, birth control, and abortion. Second and third marriages mean nothing. Civil marriages mean nothing. These people take their place in society as if they were most righteous. It is natural, they say, to do these things. The answer to all who think thus is, "It is natural for such a soul to burn in hell fire".

Let all of us here and in the world learn and know forever that sin is the most horrible thing on earth. Let all of us here cooperate with the grace of God and fly away from sin and the occasions to it. Let us come back to a good certain true conscience of what is sin. Let God's Law direct our actions.

That is not enough. The Blessed mother asked more from the three children. She said, "Will you accept all of the sacrifices that God will send you in reparation for sin and the conversion of sinners?" That is the will of God for us too and the teaching of the church. If you never did this before, then let each and everyone of us resolve to accept all the sacrifices, crosses, hardships of our state of life as a penance for our sins and for the conversion of sinners. Your work, your duties, your cares, pains, self-denial and the careful and conscientious fulfillment of your station in life are all such sacrifices if you offer them as such.

O Blessed Lady accept all our sacrifices as a reparation for our sins and the sins of others and use the merit they gain for the conversions of sinners. The children of Fatima suffered as You requested. We too, can do the same with Thy help. Present to Jesus our morning offering in which we offer ourselves and everything we think, say, do, enjoy, and suffer for the honor of God and our salvation and the salvation of others.

FATIMA'S MESSAGE III: PREPARING FOR THE COMING OF CHRIST AND THE DEFEAT OF COMMUNISM

When Our Lord was to come upon this earth, God prepared for this event by choosing a most pure Lady, one who would love Him above all. Also the Virgin Mary prepared Herself for the Divine Child by prayer, retirement and a complete resignation to the will of God. Her mind was at perfect peace and Her heart was in perfect love for She submitted Herself and Her will completely to the Will of God. It was after this love and purity blended with the perfect cooperation with the will of God, that Christ came to Her.

It seems that this co-operation is the exact way Christ wants everyone to have before He comes into one's heart. Each individual is to prepare for the Coming of Christ into his heart by prayer, penance, sacrifice, and a total submission to the will of God. This is also true for the redemption of a nation and the world.

For a while it seems man forgot this truth. It took an apparition of the Blessed Mother to have man recall this truth. It was at Fatima that the Blessed Mother spoke concerning this. She told the three little children how the people were to prepare for the Coming of the Reign of Her Son. She told them how peace can come into the world.

The first request of the Blessed Mother in Her plan for peace and the overcoming of Communism which threatens the whole world with misery and war was: "Tell the people to stop of offending My Son with sins."

Since 1917 the human race did not stop committing sins. We have lived through the most terrible war the world ever knew, and communism is continuing to reign in many parts of the world. This Mary predicted at Fatima would happen if we did not stop sinning. Individual persons and whole nations are guilty of bringing these miseries upon people. The shooting war was horrible, but this spreading of the Communists perhaps was worse. Hundreds of millions of people are made slaves, millions are put in jails, millions are deprived of their freedom, of their home, of their families, and millions are put to death. Property and wealth are confiscated. The greatest lies are told. Families are broken and one is made to hate and betray one another. It seems that hell has let loose with its fury and Satan himself was ruling in the Kremlin.

O Mary, Our Mother, help us to understand the curse of atheistic communism, help us to flee from its power, and help us to remain free to love and serve God and to venerate You. Our hearts are created to Love, but we need Your help to direct our power to love to the Greatest Good. May our Mother lead us to true love and to God. May the Bamboo Curtain fall to give freedom to all.

FATIMA'S MESSAGE: IV

We all can see how horrible Communism is a yet we all are responsible in a way for its triumph, for we have not heeded the words of the Blessed Virgin.

She has begged us to quit committing sin, She has begged us to do penances. She begged us to sacrifice for the love of God. She begged us to recite the Rosary daily. She begged the families to recite the Rosary together. How many of us have heeded Her words and requests?

Suffer we must because of the sins of the world. The church is in a great crisis in the countries beyond the Iron Curtain. This persecution is called even greater than the persecutions of the early christian martyrs in the times of Nero and Diocletian.

The love of God for the faithful and care of the Blessed Mother for us all gives us the hope we need for victory over sin and over Communism. She told us that Her Immaculate Heart would triumph in the end. We are not to delay this triumph, but prepare our heart for Christ by stopping committing sin, doing penance, and by completely surrendering our wills to God's will. Thus will the Prince of Peace reign in our hearts, in our families, and among nations.

> *O Mary, You have taught us in Your appearances at Fatima what we are to do to please Your Son. Help us by obtaining all the graces we need to fulfill God's will and to be pure and sinless. Without Your help we shall drown in evil. Save us now and at the hour of our death.*
>
> *Mother, it is not necessary for You to appear again upon this earth. We have Your messages. Your instructions to the children of Fatima were not only for them, but also for us and the whole world. Because we did not heed You and Your words, the world suffered the most horrible of wars, World War II. Even the evils of Hitler and the atomic bomb have not soberized us to heed Your plea. Even the threat of communism conquering the world has not brought us to penance and reform of life.*
>
> *O Mother, in Your power bring us to our senses, to our knees, and to a true love of God. Spare us firm the ravages of communism and war. O Lady of Peace, obtain that peace and love of mankind for all of us that this world and all its people should have and enjoy. May Jesus, the Prince of Peace, through Your intercession grant us peace and love.*

OUR LADY OF KNOCK 1879

As tourists and pilgrims come to Ireland, they find their way to the Shrine of Our Lady of Knock, in the County of Mayo. Here they humbly kneel at the shrine of Our Lady, a most popular shrine in Ireland.

Our Blessed Mother appeared at Knock on the 21st of August 1879. It was at 7 pm on a rainy day when an unusual bright light was seen over the church building. This attracted the priest's housekeeper, Mary McLaughlin, who was on her way to visit some friends. As she passed the church, she saw a strange light near the church and in the light she saw three figures which she identified later as the Blessed Virgin Mary, St. Joseph, and a bishop.

Thinking the pastor purchased some new statues, she paid little attention to what she saw. On her way back home about 8 pm, she and her companion, Mary Beirne, saw the same scene. Mary Beirne remarked, "Why didn't you tell me that Father got new statues for the chapel?"

When they came closer they saw the figures move. They recognized the Blessed Virgin. With joy and excitement they called other people to see the vision. Fourteen people came and beheld the apparition.

Since that day Knock has become a mecca for Catholics and non-Catholics. People from many parts of the world come to see this spot favored by The Virgin Mother and pray there. Among the famous pilgrims to kneel in prayer at this shrine was Pope John Paul II.

It is said the Virgin smiled here, but did not say anything. In LaSalette She cried. In other apparitions She spoke and warned people and requested prayer and penance, but not so in Ireland. Was Our Lady pleased with the love and devotion of the people of Ireland?

> *O Mary, You favored the Irish by appearing in Knock. Not that we ask You to appear to us, but we do need Your help. Obtain the graces we need to be faithful to Your Son, Our Lord. May we be cheerful all the days of our life because You are our Protectress and beloved Mother. As You smiled at Knock, may You smile at us now and especially when Our Lord calls us to Himself. Keep us in the grace of our God. Safeguard us from all harm. Keep us steadfast in our faith and love. Protect us from all error and from sin. Keep us loyal to God and to You. Be our Mother always and lead us to life everlasting.*

MARY AND ROME IN 1944

The Nazi Army conquered much of Europe by 1944. Country after country had fallen and so did Italy. Rome was occupied by Hitler's army which was determined to keep Rome or leave it in utter ruin.

Opposition came to the Nazis as the allied forces acquired a stronghold in Italy. Salerno, Anzio Beach, Monte Casino were taken and the allies were nearing Rome. To hold Rome the Nazis had the city barricaded, guns placed in church steeples, and ammunition placed to blow up the bridges.

Ten miles from Rome a pilgrimage was started at the Shrine of Our Lady of Divine Love. The people carried Our Lady's statue into Rome to the church of St. Ignatius. There a solemn octave of prayer began. Masses were celebrated every half hour in the morning; Devotions begging Our Lady for help continued in the afternoon and evening. The church was filled all the time. "Spare Rome. " The people promised to amend their ways. Hope was fading away as the sounds of big guns boomed nearer and nearer.

As people were leaving the church one day, news came: "The allies have entered Rome.... The Nazis left the city....There is no fighting. 0, thank God, Rome is spared."

The next day thousands of Romans flooded St. Peter's Square to hear the Pope and to thank God and Mary. Pope Pius XII remarked, "The Mother of the Roman People has saved the city."

A week later the Holy Father goes to St. Ignatius Church. During his sermon he tells everyone that Our Lady saved Rome. All the people in jubilation joined the Holy Father in thanking Mary for deliverance from the Nazis.

O Mary, as You saved Rome, save Your church today from all her enemies and errors. Keep all the faithful close to the Holy Father. Bring all fallen-aways back to the church so that as one family of faith, hope, and love we all may please Jesus, Your Son and Our Lord.

FONTANELLE MYSTICAL ROSE

Who knows how many times Our Blessed Mother appeared on this earth to reveal one of Her titles or honors bestowed upon Her by God? We know at Guadalupe She revealed Herself as the "MOTHER OF THE AMERICAS". At Lourdes, Our Lady tells us She is the IMMACULATE CONCEPTION. At Fontanelle, a small suburb of Montichiari in the northern section of Italy, in 1966 Our Mother told Pierina Gilli She wants to be known as MYSTICAL ROSE.

Since 1947 the Blessed Mother has appeared a number of times to Pierina Gilli of Montichiari. On Easter Sunday 1966, Our Lady spoke with Pierina telling her "My Divine Son sent Me here to bestow healing power on this water. I want the sick and all My children to come to this miraculous well. A basin is to be built here to immerse the sick and to provide water for drinking. My children must first ask pardon for their sins and then draw water lovingly from the well".

A basin was constructed to immerse the sick and to provide drinking water as Our Mother requested. Pilgrims arrive at, Fontanelle especially on the first Saturdays of the month, to honor Mary, to partake in the processions and Masses and to be healed. Healing comes to many favored.

Here at Fontanelle, Our Lady warned of the ruin of the world. "Because the world is on the verge of ruin, Our Lord demands prayer, sacrifices and penance". "Pray the Rosary" is requested here as in other places. Our Mother assures that all who pray the Rosary will receive many blessings from Her. She also requested a Holy Hour of reparation to be held annually on December 8th at noon and world wide reception of Holy Communion of reparation on October 13th. Strange, these requests have not been publicized. We need to know and to fulfill the requests of Our Heavenly Mother.

At the request of Mary, a medal of the Mystical Rose was stamped and statues according to the Pierina's description were made and sent to various countries. Our Lady said, "I invoke a blessing on these statues which represent Me. Wherever I go, I shall bring joy, peace and grace for many souls".

Written reports from many have been recorded of blessings, cures, peace and health received from Our Lady, the Mystical Rose.

O Mary, Mystical Rose, take care of us, Your children, and obtain graces and blessings for us. Spare us from the calamities of this world. Stimulate us to be sorry for our sins. Bring us to a greater love of Jesus and You. O Mystical Rose, obtain for us the joy, peace and grace needed to be loyal and faithful to You and to Our Lord, Jesus. May we, because of our love and devotion, be fortunate to be with You for all eternity.

SHRINES IN THE UNITED STATES:

Among the various Shrines dedicated to the Blessed Mother in the United States there are those established by the Spaniards. Our Lady of Leche in St. Augustine Florida is one of the oldest. The missions in California established by Father Junipera Serra would be next. Mission of Our Lady of the Angels (Los Angeles) and Mission Dolores in San Francisco are a must for Catholics visiting in the far West.

In recent years a number of religious orders have built Marian Shrines. Circulars are received inviting people to Illinois, Ohio, and New York. Also a group of Pauline Fathers from Poland built an American Shrine to Our Lady of Czestochowa in Doylestown near Philadelphia.

The National Marian Shrine in the United States is that of the Immaculate Conception in Washington, D.C. where more visitors come than to the Capitol. The pilgrims come from everywhere to honor the Mother of Jesus and our Mother.

It was in the year of 1846 when the Bishops of our country dedicated the United States to Mary Immaculate and it was decided that a shrine befitting the honor of the Blessed Mother should be built in the Capital. Real action on the Shrine only took its impetus from Bishop Shahan, rector of the Catholic University in 1913. Popes Pius X, Benedict XV, and Pius XI not only approved of the plans for the shrine, but sent their blessings and expressed their hope that the people of the United States would contribute in amounts large enough to pay for the shrine.

It seems that the Blessed Mother desires all the faithful of the United States to pay for the shrine for it could have been completed long ago. An elderly rich couple wanted to pay for the complete shrine. They made their intention known and asked Bishop Shahan to visit them. A few days before the appointed time for the visit, the elderly man died and the will had no provisions for any bequests for the Shrine. Consequently a nationwide fund raising campaign was organized. Thus the Shrine was completed.

As one visits our National Shrine he can see work continues and more work has to be done. As each side chapel is visited, everyone must admire their beauty and dedication. Religious orders and groups of faithful have altars of their own dedication.

Of special interest for people of Polish heritage are the Chapel of Our Lady of Czestochowa with its painting, the mosaic ceiling decorations in the dome, and the huge mosaic of Christ the King, executed by the famous Polish artist, John DeRosen. (By the way DeRosen paintings may be seen at St. Bernard's in Mt. Lebanon and in the Holy Family Church in Lawrenceville, Pittsburgh, Pennsylvania.)

> *0 Mary Immaculate, protect our nation and all its people. We are under Your wings. In Particular protect and defend our youth from the poison of impurity and pornography. May we all have the grace to remain faithful in our love of You, Your Son, and Our Father. May the Holy Spirit sanctify us and strengthen us in our stand for purity and chastity.*

OUR LADY OF LECHE

When the Spaniards landed in Florida and founded the city of St. Augustine, one of the first thing they did was to build a chapel in honor of the Blessed Mother.

On the first day of their landing, Mass was said in thanksgiving and they placed the new colony under the protection of Our Lady of Leche, Our Lady of Milk. A statue of the Nursing Madonna was placed upon the altar. To this very day a statue of the Nursing Madonna stands in the chapel of the Shrine of Our Lady of Leche in St. Augustine. Everyday of the year, people kneel before this statue and give thanks to Mary for the favors She granted them and beg Her for more graces. If ever near St. Augustine, stop and visit this edifying shrine.

The Spaniards had and have a great devotion to the Nursing Madonna. Their artists have painted and sculptured many likenesses of Our Lady giving suck to the Infant.

Looking upon the image of Our Lady feeding the Child Jesus strikes a most tender chord in our hearts. Love and devotion are portrayed by this. The attachment of Mary to Jesus must have increased with each nursing and each suck. Here, She a pure mortal not only giving humanity to the Son of God but also keeping Him alive by something which is a part of Herself. It is no wonder such a nursing mother has a profound love for her child.

When considering these modern times of the bottle baby, it is little wonder why there is little attachment of mother to offspring and offspring to mother. Affection is gone, tenderness is absent and missing are the kiss, the embrace, and the nurse. The child becomes to many a mother as a stranger and many a mother really becomes a stranger and is treated so by her child later in life.

> *Our Lady of Leche, obtain the nourishment needed for our soul's health and strength. Inspire us to receive the Holy Eucharist and obtain all the graces to fill our souls with love for God and our fellow man. May we be sated with Your Love.*

"OUR LADY OF PROMPT SUCCOR" NEW ORLEANS, U.S.A.

It is unusual how the Shrine of Our Lady of Prompt Succor in New Orleans began. The strangeness started in the year 1809 when Mother Michel Gensoul, a French Ursuline nun wrote to Pope Pius VII for permission to leave with a group of exiled nuns to the Ursuline convent in New Orleans. She prayed for a favorable answer and promised to honor Our Lady by the title of "Prompt Succor".

Five weeks later in April she received the requested answer from the Pope who was at this time a prisoner of Napoleon.

Mother Michel had a statue carved and placed in the chapel of the convent. The War of 1812 was then started and for two years dragged on without any decisive battles. Now that England defeated Napoleon, she was going to concentrate on the young United States.

Therefore England sent a fleet of fifty ships and twenty thousand men to take New Orleans and capture Louisiana. Against this force General Andrew Jackson had six thousand poorly trained, armed, and clad men.

The British were sure of victory. They even brought a civil government to rule the city.

When the people saw the large force coming, they fled to the Church and begged God for help. The Ursuline Nuns also prayed in their chapel and beseeched the Blessed Virgin for help promising a Solemn High Mass to be said in Her honor yearly on January 8 th.

The battle began and lasted only twenty-five minutes. The British fell like leaves. They were forced to withdraw and thus New Orleans was saved.

General Jackson visited the Sisters after the battle and acknowledged the help of God in his victory.

In 1895 Pope Leo XIII ordered the statue to be crowned. Mass has been celebrated there yearly as the Sisters promised.

Today many people visit the shrine. And if by chance you are in New Orleans, please visit the Blessed Mother of Prompt Succor.

> *Blessed Mother, we are assured of Your prompt help for those who invoke Your aid. Blessed Mother, protect us now and forever. Obtain graces for our nation. Keep it loyal to Jesus and His laws. Never permit us to be swallowed up by atheism or immorality. Protect our women. Protect the church. Obtain more vocations to the priesthood and religious life. We are confident of Your prompt succor. O Mary, help us.*

OUR LADY OF VICTORY - LACKAWANNA, NEW YORK

In the early 1900s a convert to the faith who also became a priest was appointed to take care of the charities at Lackawanna. He is known throughout the country as just plain Father Baker. His love for the Blessed Mother was shown in a particular way: in the building of the Shrine of Our Lady of Victory.

Really, this striking Basilica is a museum in itself. The many beautiful statues, the life-size stations of the cross, the expensive marble altars, the many paintings of the Litany of the Blessed Mother, the marvelous work of architecture all go into making a magnificent expression of the love of the Blessed Mother.

To appreciate this church in its fullest, it would be best to visit it and to have a map or booklet of the church. Then as the pilgrims go about the church, they can see and appreciate every article and painting.

The whole church took $3,800,000 to complete and the paintings in it are valued at $300,000. This is a lot of money. But this money was gladly given so that the Blessed Virgin Mary could be honored as She should be honored.

Father Baker's special charity was toward orphans whom he placed under the care of Our Lady. On the Shrine's property is a large orphanage where hundreds of children found protection and love. Especially noted here is the baby section.

When Father Baker lived, orphanages were common throughout the United States. Even in the Pittsburgh Diocese there were orphanages for ethnic groups as St. Paul's for the Irish, St. Anthony's for the Italians, Holy Family for the Polish, and Good Shepherd on Troy Hill for the Germans. Not one of these exists as an orphanage. Only two of these four charities are in operation: St. Anthony's in Oakmont for exceptional children and Holy family Institution in Emsworth for wards of court. Recently, St. Anthony's was closed.

A visit to Father Baker's Shrine of Our Lady of Victory is most rewarding. Definitely a visit there can foster a greater love of Our Lady.

O Mary, Our Lady of Victory, pray for us that we may be successful in all our undertaking and struggles. Obtain victory for us over our weakness and our battle against vice and the devil.

OUR LADY AND GREEN BAY, WIS.

Adele Brisse was born in Belgium in 1831. In her teenage years she wanted to be a nun. This pious girl was devoted to Our Blessed Mother and she desired to spread the faith and devotion to Our Lady in the missions.

When she was nineteen her parents moved to the State of Wisconsin. She refused to go along with her parents, but upon the counsel of her confessor she went. The confessor assured her that she would be rewarded for her obedience.

At this time in Belgium there was a shortage of priests and many people were losing their faith.

It was in 1858 that Our Lady appeared twice to Adele Brisse. When she told her confessor of the apparitions, he instructed her to ask, "In God's name, who are you and what do you desire of me?" Our Lady said, "I am the Queen of Heaven, who prays for the conversion of sinners and I wish you to do the same. Pray for conversion. If there is no conversion, there will be punishment. Teach catechism to the children."

This apparition has not been given approval by the church. Who knows if it will ever be recognized as a supernatural event? At times approval takes a long time and at other times private visions of Mary or even Jesus have remained as private without the church's sanction.

A strange fire broke out in Wisconsin destroying all the buildings except the convent of Sister Adele's community. Today a brick chapel stands where the apparitions occurred.

Sure there were opposition to the truth of Mary appearing to Adele Brisse. There were opposition at Lourdes and Fatima, too. Opposition will continue since many do not believe in the supernatural. Also, there is this human element that comes into play: "Why her and not me to be favored by a visit from Our Lady."

> *O Mary, favor all of us by Your protection and grace. May we heed You and be converted to Jesus. May we also teach others to love You and Your Son. Grant us the favor of seeing You forever in Heaven.*

THE SEVEN DOLORS OF THE BLESSED VIRGIN

On Friday when we celebrate the Feast of Our Blessed Lady, let us recall the seven swords which pierced Her heart with anguish:

1. The prophecy of Simeon that a sword would pierce Her heart.
2. The flight into Egypt.
3. The loss of Her Son in the temple for three days.
4. Meeting Her Son on the steep climb to Calvary.
5. His awful Crucifixion.
6. Removing the Body of Christ from the Cross.
7. Seeing Him sealed in the tomb.

The devotion to Our Lady's Sorrows was fostered by the Servite Fathers who kept the feast of the Seven Dolors most solemnly as early as the seventeenth century. The feast was extended to the whole Church in 1817 by Pope Pius VII.

MARY AND THE MISSIONS

From the beginning of the Church, our faith became known and was embraced through the prayers, intercession and actual intervention of Our Lady.

All the Apostles received encouragement from the Mother of God. The Apostles looked up to Her, loved Her and sought Her advice. As they returned to Jerusalem from their Missions, She was pleased to hear their stories.

As Our lady prayed for the Apostles, so too, She continues to pray through all time and unto today. The work of the missionary is bringing Christ to the unbelieving world - this was and is Her task. She wants all to know Jesus and to love Him.

When the missionaries arrived into a new land, they placed the land, its people and their work under the protection of Our Lady and besought Her intercession. They brought Her images and statues along with them and received encouragement to carry on even though the opposition was so strong.

We have one account where the Blessed Mother wanted a faster conversion of the Indian. This happened in Mexico. Shortly after the country was conquered by the Spaniards, the Blessed Mother appeared at Guadalupe to an Indian. In a short time afterward, the whole nation became Catholic.

This interest shown by the Blessed Mother for the welfare of the missionaries and for the spread of the faith is Her grave concern in hoping to have the whole world believe in Her Son and worship Him. She continues to aid all in the work of spreading the faith and establishing the Kingdom of God upon the world.

We have another actual personal intervention in the missionary work by the Blessed Mother. This at Fatima. From a nearly anti-clerical country and one almost dead in religious practice, Portugal became a virile Catholic Nation.

At Fatima Her missionary activity continues in prophecy - Russia will be converted if we pray.

O Mary, pray for the missions and bring all people to the feet of Thy Son. Make one sheepfold - one flock at the command of the One Shepherd, Our Lord, Thy Son.

OUR LADY OF THE HIGHWAY

A comparatively new devotion in honor of the Blessed Mother has started in the United States under the title of Our Lady of the Highways. This new devotion is increasing rapidly since there are so many deaths upon our highways. A new medal has been designed for travelers and the protective care of the Blessed Mother is invoked.

The Blessed Mother knows what it is to travel and She knows the dangers of leaving home. Seven times the Gospels record Her journeys:
1. Journey to Visit Elizabeth, (The Visitation)
2. Journey to Bethlehem, (The Nativity)
3. Journey to the Temple to be Purified, (The Presentation)
4. Flight to Egypt and back, (To save Jesus from King Herod)
5. Journey to Jerusalem when Christ was twelve years old, (The finding of Jesus in the Temple)
6. Journey to Cana, wedding feast, (First Miracle of Jesus)
7. Journey to Jerusalem and Calvary, (The Sorrows of Mary)

Also there was Her journey with Saint John to the city of Ephesus where She lived for some time and then back to Jerusalem where She "fell asleep".

Because of Her journeys, the Blessed Mother is truly a patroness of travelers. Because She is interested in everything we do, She is very much concerned when we travel for in traveling we are in danger of our lives. She wants us to attain our perfect happiness. And we pray that She will take care of us "at the hour of death" and take us into Heaven - our last journey.

Since we do take our lives into our hands when we enter an automobile or airplane, it will be well for each and everyone of us to place ourselves under the protection of Our Lady of the Highways. May She obtain the prudence for us to drive care fully, safely, and considerately.

> *O Lady of the Highways, pray for us as we journey through life and particularly pray for us while we are on journey on the highways. Protect us from accidents, from injury and a sudden death, but most of all direct us in our last journey as we travel from earth to Heaven.*

THE WEEPING MADONNA MIRACLES

How many times has the Blessed Mother cried? No one will be able to say. But She has cried and often. From time to time we read of a crying Madonna picture here in the United States, a miracle?

During Her life upon this earth, the heart of Mary was full of grief. Her heart was broken to see how Her Divine Son was treated, abused, disbelieved, and killed.

It will be impossible to know definitely how many times Our Lady appeared upon this earth in tears after Her assumption.

She appeared at LaSalete, France in tears.

Again in Syracuse, Italy Mary shed tears. This happened from August 28th to September 1, 1953 in the home of a pious worker. At this time, She uses a terra cotta Madonna statue for this purpose. These tears were real tears as chemical analysis proved. The Bishops of Sicily verified this miraculous happening. Thousands flock to this home to witness the statue where the manifestations occurred. Here the wonders of God are wrought, Grace fills the hearts of men and broken bodies are healed.

Why does She cry? She cries for you and me because we do not love God, Her Son, our souls and our fellow man as we ought. There is so much abuse of Her Son by us. Look how many deny Him and sin against Him. He loved us totally and still loves us, but we prefer passing pleasures and sin. Communists and many men don't go to church and curse, blaspheme and commit all kinds of sins. She cries for the souls which are lost and are headed for perdition. She as a loving mother cries for Her bad children. She cries for Her people who were swallowed up by the Reds. Look how much people suffer in the countries behind the Iron and Bamboo curtains!

She also cries because of lack of devotion. Where is there love? Where is there true love? Where is there devotions held in Her honor?

Oh, may we so live as not to hurt Our Lady and bring tears into Her eyes.

> *Oh, Lady, strengthen us to love Thy Son and live upright lives. Keep us from sin and lead us through Love to be obedient to Your Son with Whom we want to live forever.*

— PART III —

OUR BLESSED MOTHER'S PREROGATIVES AND LOVE FOR US

OUR BLESSED MOTHER'S CONCERN FOR US

From the Gospels we read of the solicitude of Our Lady for people. From the LIVES OF SAINTS we read how the Blessed Mother came to the aid of these holy persons and how She helped them in their ministry for the good of all people.

In this section of this book we shall see HOW MARY'S PERFECTIONS came to bring grace and succor to the needy. This account is not exhaustive.

Thanksgiving should be our form of appreciation for all Our Blessed Mother did and does for Her children.

OUR LADY OF PROVIDENCE AND CANA

After the Holy Family's experience of losing Jesus and finding Him in the temple, they returned to Nazareth. Nothing is heard of them again until Christ began His public life with His Baptism by St. John the Baptist. St. Joseph is no more mentioned and it is presumed he died a happy death since he expired in the company of Jesus and Mary. For this reason he is the Patron of the dying. The next recorded event in which the Blessed Virgin Mary appears is at the Marriage Feast at Cana.

Sacred Scripture tells us that Mary was with Jesus and His disciples. We can picture this happy social event and how the people enjoyed themselves. A social disgrace was about to happen. The Blessed Virgin observed the wine was running short. She came to Jesus and said, "They have no wine." (Jn.2, 1-13).

Jesus said, "Woman, what is that to Me and to Thee? My hour is not yet come." (This word "woman" is not a sign of disrespect as some think. This was the usual way of address in the oriental language and here already Christ is extending His Mother to all.)

Mary immediately said to the waiters, "Whatsoever He shall say to you, do ye." Here one can surmise that the Blessed Virgin Mary knew of the miracle to be performed and made provisions for it.

The Gospel Story continues with Our Lord changing the water into wine which was exceptionally good wine for which the bridegroom was praised.

After this first miracle, Our Lord went down to the city of Capernaum and with Him went His Mother and disciples, but they did not stay there for any length of time.

The Blessed Mother came upon the scene at the Marriage Feast in Cana for a special reason and that to intercede for a miracle and to witness that miracle. The Blessed Virgin knew the power of Her Son and She knew and still knows what He can do and does. As She interceded for the first miracle, She still intercedes for Her children to Her Son. Lourdes, Fatima, LaSalette, Guadalupe, Czestochowa, and other shrines are proof of Her begging Her Son for us.

One thought to take home with us today is this: When you find it hard to get something from a certain man, see his mother. When some find it rather difficult to request a favor from Christ, or find Him terrifying in His response, ask His Mother. Who can refuse the requests of his mother? No, not you nor I nor even Christ.

O Mary, beseech Your Son for and obtain the graces we need. You knew at Cana the situation of that young couple. We beg You to help us in our dire situations, but above all help the newly married couples to love each other and to persevere in their mutual life until death takes them to Heaven. Keep them loyal and faithful to God and to each other.

THE FLIGHT INTO EGYPT - SORROW OF THE BLESSED VIRGIN MARY

King Herod became furious when the Three Wise Men refused to obey him. He ordered them to come back to Jerusalem to tell him about the newly born King of the Jews. His jealousy was aroused from the first moment when he was asked about the newborn King. His mind was already made up. But since he was rebuked by the Magi, he ordered an edict to have all male children to be killed from two years and younger in and about the city of Bethlehem.

But as the Magi were warned by an angel not to return to King Herod so too the Holy Family were visited by an angel and ordered to leave the city and flee to Egypt. (Matt.2, 13).

Immediately they arose and fled. The journey was done on donkey and on foot. There is a legend told about this flight in reference to the good thief who was crucified with Christ.

The legend tells us a story of the Holy Family stopping at an inn for the night. The Blessed Mother obtained a basin of some sort and warm water to bathe the Infant Jesus. As She was about to spill the water into a ditch, a woman begged "Let me wash my infant in this water". The request was granted.

As the woman placed her sick son into the water, his leprosy was cured. Surely, the woman was grateful to Our Lady.

When this cured boy grew up, he became the thief who was crucified with Jesus. Did he recall his miraculous cure? Perhaps he remembered what his mother told him. Now Dismas turns to Jesus. Again he is cured and now taken into Heaven.

How long the Holy Family lived in Egypt is not known, but as soon as they heard from an angel that King Herod was dead, they returned.

It seemed that Joseph had intentions of making his home in Bethlehem, but hearing that Archelaus was King, succeeding his father in Judea, Joseph was afraid to go to Bethlehem. He was warned in his sleep to go to Galilee. They journeyed to Nazareth and made Their home in that town.

Surely, we can see why sorrow fill the most pure heart of Mary. What had Her Son done? What had She or St. Joseph done that they had to flee for safety? Here He is the Savior of mankind and already He is hated.

Many a mother's heart is broken when She sees Her child abused, hated, sick and crippled. What has the child done to be so afflicted? Many a child suffers for the sin of its parents and grandparents. God did say He will punish the evil unto the third and fourth generation.

O Sorrowful Mary, help us in our sorrows. Be our consolation and bear us up in our misery.

THE LAST FOUR SORROWS OF THE BLESSED MOTHER

The Gospels do not contain much about the life of the Blessed Virgin Mary. The purpose of the New Testament was to show to all that Christ, the Son of Mary, is the true Son of God, the Messiah, the Redeemer and Savior of Mankind. All that is recorded in the Gospels about Mary is there to show us how She loved God and served Him by accomplishing and fulfilling His Will.

During the public ministry of Christ, very little is heard of the Blessed Virgin after the Feast at Cana. We can presume that Mary did witness some of the miracles and saw some of the triumphs of Christ. But we know definitely She was with Christ during His Passion and death.

The four last sorrows of the Blessed Virgin occurred in fast succession on that Good Friday. During that death march up to Mt. Calvary, the two Holy Persons met. This is the fourth station of the Stations of the Cross. Much has been written about this meeting and much can be said about it. Surely during your meditations upon this event, your hearts can be moved. The Mother beholds Her condemned innocent Son. Her heart breaks; Her eyes fill up. She now knows the price of sin as She sees the heavy cross crushing Jesus to the ground.

In a short time Her heart was pierced again. She saw Her Son being raised upon the gibbet of the cross. No one except a mother knows the suffering a woman goes through in mind and heart at the sight of the suffering of Her child. The pain and anguish of Mary was far greater than that of any other mother, for She knew Her Son was God-man who loves all so much to die for man's salvation.

This three hour long agony was a continuous piercing thrust of a sword through Mary's heart. Each gaze upon the face and body of Jesus added painful sorrow and so did His final seven words. Could there be any consolation in the exchange of sons? Jesus bequeaths Mary to John and John to Mary. In this Last Testament all mankind receives Mary as its Mother.

The Pietà of Michelangelo captures the piety of Mary as She embraces the body of Her Son and Lord. She who brought Jesus into this world, now holds on to Him as never to give Him up. Hugs, kisses, and tears continue.

The time had come for the sad parting. The dead must be buried. With the assistance of a few faithful, the anointing and other preparations were completed: the Body is carried into the tomb. The stone slowly rolled in place. The broken hearted Mother of Jesus stands there in utter silence. Was She stunned? How could She act any other way than She did? Her heart was pierced through and through.

O sorrowful Mary, help us in our sorrow. You know what sorrow is. Help us and especially all mothers, who must bear the pains caused by their children and especially in early death.

MARY, TABERNACLE OF CHRIST

To the unbeliever of spiritual life this discourse is sheer nonsense. To the believer in the doctrine of Grace, this article will show to what dignity God called us when He entered our soul, a dignity akin to that of Our Lady in a sort of way,

From the very beginning of Our Lady's life, She was the temple of the Holy Spirit for She was full of Grace. In proper time, She became the ciborium of Christ carrying Christ in Her own body. All this while Her whole body and soul were the sanctuary, the Holy of Holies, in which the Blessed Trinity lived. The inhabitation of God in Mary kept Her full of Grace. Although She was a future resident of Heaven, yet She lived in the anteroom of Heaven upon this earth. All She needed was to have the material veil lifted from Her eyes and She would see God as She sees Him now in His full Glory and Power.

In a way all Catholics who live in sanctifying Grace are "other Marys". We are temples of the Holy Spirit for once we are in love with God the Holy Spirit, the whole Blessed Trinity, in fact, lives in us. "If you love Me, We will come and build our mansion in you". After Confirmation, we become the Temples of the Holy Spirit in a special manner.

We are a ciborium carrying Christ: momentarily carrying His humanity and divinity as our Blessed Mother did when we receive Holy Communion. This Christ is the very same who walked upon this earth and is in Heaven. Think of the honor and dignity conferred upon us! Our bodies carry Christ.

We are the sanctuaries of the Most High God Omnipotent. We are tabernacles. Our bodies become the place in which God dwells. The Jews of old had the greatest of respect for the Holy of Holies. We, too, should have the greatest of respect for our own bodies and bodies of others, for God, the most Holy, deigned to be present in them in a special manner when we are in sanctifying grace.

Living in sanctifying grace continuously, we too only need the material veil removed from our eyes in order to see God face to face as we shall see Him in Heaven.

O Mary, the Tabernacle of God, make us pure, true, and perpetual tabernacles, mansions, ciboriums of God. O Mother, You always remain with God, intercede for us that we may love God always and be with Him forever.

COURSE OF LIFE ENDS FOR THE BLESSED VIRGIN MARY

After the Holy Spirit descended upon the Apostles on Pentecost Sunday, the Disciples went forth throughout the world teaching all things Christ had ordered them to teach. Along with one of them, St. John, went the Blessed Mother. St. John was to take care of Her and this he did.

It is impossible to know exactly all the places and towns visited by Our Blessed Mother while with St. John. We know that She lived for a time in the city of Ephesus in Asia Minor in the country we call Turkey today. How long She lived there is impossible to determine, for there are no written records concerning this.

Tradition tells us that the Blessed Mother after a time returned from Ephesus to Jerusalem and lived near the house called the Cenacle, the house where the Last Supper was held.

She longed to be with Her Son and with God. This lonesomeness for Her Son caused Mary to see Him, for it was not too long after She moved to Jerusalem that She "fell asleep" and was buried in the family tomb where already Her parents, SS. Joachim and Anna, and Her husband St. Joseph were buried. This family tomb is located across the Kedron River towards the Garden of Gethsemane.

It is a definite fact that the Blessed Mother ended Her course of life. Her grave is venerated by the Armenians, Mascovites, Moslems as well as Christians as the resting place of "The Lady Mary". There was no reason which would excuse Mary from death and it was fitting that She should be like Her Son in accepting death. This death though was not a consequence or penalty of sin, since Mary was without all sin. Pope Pius XII in defining the Assumption did not use the word death but "course of life ended".

The cause of Her death was not sickness or old age. Most probably the cause of Her death was the great love and great desire of being with God and Her Son.

From the death of Our Lord and Our Blessed Mother we are to learn how to accept death. We too are to subject ourselves willingly to the Will of God. We too are to long to be with God, to see Him face to face, to live with the Blessed Trinity and enjoy forever the joys, beauty, and life with God.

> *O Mary, obtain for us the grace to die in the love of God, in sanctifying grace. When our time comes to have completed our course on earth, be at our side to give us consolation, strength, and assurance of victory. O Mary, Mother of God, pray for us now and at the hour of our death.*

ASSUMPTION

My being proclaims the greatness of the Lord, my spirit finds joy in God my Savior.

Lk 1, 46 - 47.

As the angles of God shouted with joy when Our Blessed Mother was taken up into Heaven, we too can shout with joy for Our Blessed Mother has received the crown of glory from God Himself upon Her being taken up to Heaven.

As our Mother found joy in God Her savior, we too find joy in Our Savior and in His Mother who is our helper in our struggle to attain glory. We pray for help from Her as we say the "Hail Mary".

We rejoice that God chose Mary to be the Mother of Jesus, to be Our Mother, to be our help in this life of ours.

While upon this earth, Our Blessed Lady was concerned for the welfare of the people. It was at Her insistence that Our Lord performed the first miracle. She wanted Our Lord to bless, to cure, and to feed the people. She wanted the people to listen to Her Son, to follow Him and to come to Him.

Ever since She was assumed into Heaven, She has been most interested in all people. Who knows how many times She has appeared upon this earth? In recent years we have reports of the Blessed Mother appearing in the U.S.A., Mexico, Argentina, Africa, Europe, Ireland...There are reports She is giving messages for our welfare and for our sanctity. She asks us to reform our lives, to pray...especially the Rosary and that daily...to receive the sacraments often. She wants everyone to know Her Son, to love Him, and to live according to the will of God so that all will be with God forever.

You and I are the children of Mary. Let us rejoice that Our Mother wants us to live with Her, with Jesus, and with God almighty forever in glory. Let us rejoice that She prays for us. She comes upon this earth to warn us and to encourage us to live a good life. Let us rejoice for Mary will be at our side to help us to rise in glory.

Mary Our Mother, pray for us now and at the hour of our death
— Amen.

BLESSED MARY, GABRIEL, JESUS

The Gospels and history admit Mary was a real Jewish woman upon Whom special favors were bestowed by God. All interested in knowing more of the Blessed Virgin can read many a book on Mariology,

The Gospels and history verify that Jesus was a real Person Who was born of a Woman, performed human acts and died. Also the Gospels and history ascertain that Jesus is not only true man but also True God. His resurrection is the greatest proof of His Divinity.

There are questions concerning the Archangel Gabriel. Did he appear in a visible human form? Was he a ray of light as one movie portrayed him? Was he an inspiration only? Did he speak as we speak? Upon whose authority did he convey the message to Mary that She would be the Mother of Jesus, the Messiah? How could Mary know Her child would be a Son and called Jesus?

If angels appeared in body form to convey lesser messages, surely Gabriel would appear in a physical assumed human form to speak to Mary about this greatest event in the history of mankind.

The Archangel Raphael not only appeared to Tobias but also accompanied and defended him. Jacob wrestled with an angel. Zachary sees an angel. An angel appears to the three children at Fatima and even gives them Holy Communion. Then why should the angel in physical form not appear to Mary?

The whole account of the Annunciation of the Savior to be born of Mary is written in St, Luke's Gospel beginning with Chapter 1 verse 26-38. It is therein stated that the Angel Gabriel was sent by God to Mary and upon coming to Her, he revealed God's design.

Should Mary believe the words of the Angel? Wouldn't you? Sure She was frightened, but also She listened, questioned the possibility of conception, and once assured of Her position, She agreed to fulfill the Will of God. Only after She gave a positive answer, the Angel left Her.

Do mothers know the sex of their conceived child? Mary knew because the Angel told Her She would have a Son.

Do mothers know what name to give the expected baby? They may have selected a number of names for a boy and for a girl. Mary knew the name of Her conceived Child. The Angel told Her His name is Jesus.

Do mothers know what vocation or work in which their child/children will be engaged? Mary knew because the Angel told Her. (v,31-33).

Was Mary puzzled by the words of the Angel? Definitely She was. She knew how children were begotten. She was only betrothed to Joseph and not married, "How shall this happen," She asked.

The Angel gave the answer. "The Holy Spirit shall come upon You and the power of the Most High shall overshadow You and therefore the Holy One to be born shall be called the Son of God."

By Divine providence Mary and Joseph were married so Mary would have a protector and breadwinner, to confuse the devil, and to safeguard Mary from being accused of adultery,

The Angel appeared to Joseph with messages, too. Surely Joseph and Mary spoke to each other about their experiences and their position in the history of the Salvation of mankind.

Because of Mary's exulted position, She had all needed consolation and assurance from God, from the Angel, and from Joseph. The plenitude of grace bestowed upon Her made Her the most exceptional human being who ever lived upon this earth.

O Mary, Mother of God, pray for us to have a deep and living faith so that we too will fulfill the Will of God.

MARY OUR MODEL

Why should we have the Blessed Virgin as our Model in life since we have Jesus a Model to follow and imitate? The answer is simply this: Jesus is our Perfect Model and Mary is the perfect imitator of Jesus in all things. Thus She also is a Model for us and for our way of life.

The more models we have the better for us. There are certain virtues others have that we can easily learn and accept to our advantage and our correction.

Our Blessed Mother and Her virtues can be of advantage to all and for our wholesome good living and eternal salvation.

Mary is a Model for virgins. She who while upon the earth was a pure chaste inviolate virgin before, during, and after the birth of Jesus knows the honor of a virgin. Definitely She can aid all who respect their bodies and its integrity.

Mary is a Model for all married couples. She who was a true Wife led a sinless life in Her relationship to Joseph. Because of Their vocation They lived as brother and sister. They had the greatest respect for each other. They knew the vocation of each other and They honored each other as the special chosen of God to bring salvation to mankind. They knew they were to help bring sanctification to all. All husbands and wives are to help each other to attain Heaven by doing the will of God, by living without committing sin, and by assisting each other to attain perfect happiness.

Mary is a Model for all parents in that all parents are to educate their children to fulfill the will of God and attain Heaven. Mary was anxious for Jesus to bring about His mission and salvation for all of us.

Mary is a Model for all the rich and also for the poor. She lived as the poor people did in Nazareth. She was devoid of luxuries. Although She was and is Queen of Angels and Saints, yet Her home was that of a poor woman. Nonetheless She was most rich because She was full of grace and the Mother of Jesus. Her wealth was grace and Her glory was being with God. May all who have material wealth prefer spiritual wealth to any other. Wealthy indeed is the person who is with God now by living in grace and the wealthiest is he/she who attains Heaven.

Mary is a model for all of us in this that Her virtues shine forth in beauty and glory. We who possess Her virtues can rejoice and also shine in glory before God and man. Can we pattern ourselves to attain and possess Mary's virtues of humility, purity, faith, hope, charity, piety, patience, and resignation? Who of us can say we love our fellow man as Mary loved Her neighbors?

> *O Mary, may we model ourselves after You and may we imitate Your virtues so that we may attain the perfection of spirit You possess. Mary, pray for us to acquire Your virtues so that we may bring glory and praise to God.*

MARY, OUR ADVOCATE

The Blessed Virgin Mary is compared to a rainbow by St. Antonius. A rainbow appeared in the sky after the Deluge as a promise from God that there would never be another flood to destroy all mankind. He called Our Lady a rainbow because Our Blessed Mother is that protection before God to save mankind from total destruction. Mary speaks for us. Mary is our Advocate.

It is our faith that Jesus Christ is the only one and necessary advocate and Mediator in salvation economy. It is also our Christian Catholic doctrine that Mary is a secondary Advocate and is the "Co-Redemptrix" in our salvation since

She cooperated with Jesus. Mary continues in Her functions in our salvation. Mary appears upon earth from time to time to assure mankind of Her interest in us and in our salvation.

Mary is a most merciful advocate. She speaks to Jesus for us because She knows of our trials and miseries and because of Her love for us who are Her children.

Our Blessed Mother is compared to Queen Esther who appeared before King Assuerus and pleaded for the people. Because of her petitions the Jews were saved from Haman. May Mary intercede for us too, for our salvation.

An advocate is a "lawyer" who pleads another's cause. Mary is a powerful Advocate. If Moses by his prayers had God change His mind and thus the Hebrews were spared of punishment, Mary who is greater in dignity had and has greater power with God. By common admission we say, "the dearer the intercessor, the greater mercy and favor he obtains". Is it possible for Jesus to refuse Mary's petitions? How could Jesus refuse Mary's petitions because of Her great love and also because of Her suffering for all people?

Our Lady is a most efficacious Advocate. She does obtain help for all who ask for it. She has the power to stay the hand of God's justice.

We see how Mary's power saves souls from hell and also liberates souls from purgatory. In Her appearances to St. Simon Stock, Mary gave him the Brown Scapular and promised to save souls from purgatory. At Fatima, Mary asked us when reciting the Rosary to add after each decade, "O my Jesus, forgive us our sins. Save us from the fire of hell and lead all souls to Heaven who have most need of Thy mercy".

> *In the consoling prayer "Hail Holy Queen" we pray, "Turn then, most gracious Advocate, Your eyes of mercy toward us, and after this exile show to us the blessed fruit of Your womb Jesus". Mary, plead my cause before Jesus, my Judge.*

MARY'S OBEDIENCE

The first occasion of Mary's obedience in the Gospels is at the Annunciation when She says, "Behold the Handmaid (servant) of the Lord, be it done to Me according to Thy Word." (Luke 1,38). Here the scene and conversation of Mary and the Archangel Gabriel is described.

Only after Mary knew the necessary details, did She completely submit Herself to the Will of God. Surely She knew what the message of the Angel meant for Her and for all of mankind. Nonetheless, She willingly accepted the responsibility, the onus, the duties, and the privilege of being the Mother of Jesus.

Obedience is the acceptance of the will of another and fulfilling that will. It is not necessarily an involuntary or compulsory slavery or a total negation of one's own will, but rather the virtue of obedience is a voluntary realization of cooperating with another's will and executing his/her desire.

Even before the Annunciation, Mary as every Jewish girl lived according to the family lifestyle of Her parents and community. If the Proto-Gospel of St. James has any credulity, then we see Mary in complete obedience to Her mother St. Anne, who had Her take residence in the temple where She learned the necessary rudiments of a Jewish woman's life.

At a tender age She was betrothed to St. Joseph, married him and lived with him according to God's will and the custom of the people. She had to fulfill the functions of a housekeeper and mother. Natural laws had to be followed in this regard.

We see Mary's obedience to God and St. Joseph during the childhood of Jesus in the circumcision and presentation in the teryle, the flight to Egypt, the return to the Holy Land, and the quiet life in Nazareth. Mary required obedience also from the waiters at the Marriage Feast at Cana.

As Mary's Son taught the Father's will is to be done, Mary as the Mirror of God followed Jesus in fulfilling the Will of God. As Jesus completely and faithfully fulfilled His Father's Will, Mary in imitation of Jesus did the same. It would be well for all of us to follow Mary's footsteps in this manner of fulfilling God's will.

> *O Mary, once You knew the will of God, You executed it. Be that will made manifest to You by the Archangel, Your parents, the clergy, natural and church law and by the natural life of wife with a husband (we must understand Mary and Joseph lived a most pure, chaste and continent life). You accepted it and functioned accordingly. Help us to be obedient to God's will no matter how or where it may be manifested to us. O Mary, Most Obedient, obtain the graces necessary for us to be obedient.*

MARY'S PATIENCE

"In your patience you shall possess your souls."
Luke 21, 19

In our life's experiences we have seen many kinds of patience: a child awaits the correction of an abusive parent; a wife awaits the correction of an errant husband; a husband awaits the correction of an arrogant and spendthrift wife: a prisoner awaits his liberation; a sick person bears suffering with the hope of recovery, an expectant mother awaits the birth of her child.

To the virtue of patience belong corresponding virtues of fortitude, long suffering, meekness, perseverance, resignation and the strength to bear trials and crosses especially inflicted upon us by others, nature, or ourselves.

The Christian patience is not stoical, that is, "I can take it," but rather it is a resignation to God's will with the motive of offering everything for the honor and glory of God and for one's own salvation.

How are we disposed to suffering? Do we have the willingness to "take up thy cross and follow Me," as Jesus said.

Two men were dying from cancer. One cursed and damned everything because as he said, "I have everything to live for. I have a position, money, wife and family. And now I have to die." The other thanked God for all His blessings of position, money, wife and friends. "Father, let me die in peace and come to You."

How was Our Blessed Mother patient? She awaited the birth of Christ. She waited for Christ to start His Mission. In fact we can say She hastened it at Cana when She told the waiters to do whatever Jesus said. We see how She bore the pain and anguish during the Seven Sorrows, the death of Joseph, and the death of Jesus. In quiet endurance She longed for the reunion with Jesus.

"All right God, I'm the Mother of God and I'll stay true to My assignment and to My Son." "I'll share in My Son's work: (therefore, Co-Redeemer). This is Thy Holy Will: I submit to it. I'll not get angry, criticize, murmur, complain, nor try to get out of My job."

O Mary, teach us how to be submissive to God's will and be patient with our trials and crosses. Help us to offer ourselves and everything we think, say, do, enjoy, and suffer for the honor and glory of God and for our high place in Heaven.

CRUSHING THE HEAD OF THE SERPENT

In the garden of Paradise, immediately after the fall of Adam and Eve, God appeared on the scene and held a court trial, so to speak. In the trial God pronounced punishment upon the serpent, Adam and Eve. But here also God gave mankind a ray of hope that the power of the devil will be crushed when He said, "I will put enmities between thee and the woman, etc.".

Ever since then there has been warfare between Christ, Mary, and the righteous on one side and the devil and all his helpers of evildoers on the other.

Our Lord completely crushed the head of the devil when He died for us. Our Blessed Lady crushed the head of the serpent, too, by Her immaculate conception, by Her sinlessness, and by Her cooperation in our redemption. The saints crush the head of the serpent likewise by refusing to subject themselves to evil and the temptations of Satan.

The warfare continues in each of our lives. The temptations to sin are many and strong. Yet each time the serpent raises its head in poise to strike us, we can crush that head with the help of grace begged for us by Mary.

First of all, we must choose sides in the battle between goodness and wickedness. Since we desire salvation we automatically place ourselves on the side of Christ, Mary and the saints. Knowing our side of the battle, openly and bravely we are to fight iniquity in every form it may appear. The battle attack must commence with the fortitude of God's grace, with assurance of victory for the head will be crushed.

The serpent's head rises again and again in the form of occasions of sin be they a person, place or thing which may lead us to sin. All occasions are to be avoided or our disposition changed that no longer is our salvation jeopardized.

115

O Mary, be ever at my side to crush the devil of temptations and all occasions of sin and bring me to eternal victory. May I have the peace of mind because of deliverance from temptation and evil. May I have the joy of victory over the devil and evil. With Your aid I am confident I shall conquer for You are at my side. I shall live with You and God forever because You, O Mary, are my Protectress, my Advocate and Mother.

A SPECIAL LOVE - LOVE OF MARY

Along with the Love of God, there is a singular love which true believers of Christ possess and that special love is for and of the Mother of Our Lord Jesus Christ.

A little review of Who Our Blessed Mother is, may stimulate our hearts to beat stronger love toward Her Whom God singled out in His plan for our salvation and designated as "Our Mother".

God knew Mary inside out and saw that She was good. To fit Her properly for His task, God gives Her a special privilege which no one has ever had nor will have. Because of the merits of Jesus Christ, Mary from the first instant of Her conception was protected and preserved from every stain of original sin and all sin. She alone is the Immaculate Conception. She is full of grace.

This Mother of God and your and my Mother loved God so much that nothing else counted. Sin did not enter into Her. Pride was most foreign to Her. In all humbleness She accepts the great privilege of being the Mother of God by saying, "Behold Thy Handmaid; be it done to me according to Thy will". Who amounted to something? Who counted? Mary? No. Love was everything. She had the great secret of sanctity self-abandonment. It is God and God alone that counts. "Let Thy will be done."

Mary is a Person worthy of our recognition...more...our love. If She is so beautiful to be loved by God Himself, then we too should love Her.

We have come to the knowledge that Mary does truly love us. A true mother and a good mother cannot but love her children. This Mary does, for She is truly Our Mother and we Her children. A true mother takes care of her children. How does Mary take care of us? Mary is the Almoner of grace, that is, all grace flows through Her. We receive grace when we are baptized and receive the other sacraments. It was through Mary that we received that grace. Mary is the refuge of sinners. Where are we to flee when we are in trouble, to whom should we turn? To our mother and Mary is that Mother Who can help us. Mary is the comfort of the afflicted. When you are down and out, turn to Mary for She knows what it is to be down and out...She experienced that when Her Son was crucified. She is the Help of Christians as a true mother takes care of her children. Her loving care for all Her children is pictured in painting by a large mantle or cloak under which we all gather to be protected from any wrong and to be taken in to Heaven. The title of this painting is "Under Your Protection". "Pod Twoja Obrone" (ln Polish).

This is the Mother of God whom God gave us as our Mother. What a privilege it is for you and me to have the Mother of God as our Mother. Our LOVE of Her should prompt us to imitate Her, to follow Her requests, to express our love of Her, to be devoted to Her, and to have Her in our mind and heart most frequently. May "our" love of Mary bring us to Jesus and eternal joy. Honor Her during the month of May.

DEVOTION TO THE BLESSED VIRGIN MARY IN GENERAL

The year from June 7, 1987 to August 15, 1988 was dedicated to Our Lady in a singular manner and throughout all Christendom special devotions were held in Her honor: litanies, rosaries, processions, May Crownings, and the beautiful hymns. All of these surely will please Our Lady and bring many benefits to our soul. May every year bring us close to God and Mary.

To obtain many great favors and graces from Our Lady two things are necessary: first, we offer Her homage from a pure heart free from sin; second, we persevere in our devotion to Mary.

On the first point Saint Peter Celestine relates the following story. A certain French legionaire stationed in Algiers, a man of great vice, offered a Rosary to Our Lady daily. One day while lost in the Sahara he suffered great hunger. Our Lady appeared to him and presented him some delicious food. But this food was on such a filthy dish that he turned from the plate. I am the Mother of God who has come to relieve your hunger," said Our Lady. "But I cannot eat from that vase," he replied. "And do you wish that I should accept your devotions offered me from a soul so polluted." Needless too say, the soldier abandoned his evil life. He became a hermit and lived thirty years in the desert. Upon his death Our Lady appeared to him again and conducted him to Heaven.

As to the second point of perseverance in devotions, Thomas a'Kempis relates this following story about himself.

As a young man he prayed daily to the Blessed Virgin. One day he omitted this devotion and after some time he left it out completely. One night in his dreams he saw the Blessed Virgin embrace his companions, but upon coming to him She said, "What do you expect, who have given up My devotion? Depart, for you are unworthy of My favors. These words shocked Thomas. He awoke terrified and immediately resumed his practice of daily venerating Mary.

In our veneration of Our Mother let us fulfill Her requests of "a pure heart and a constant prayer". A pure heart is pleasing even to all of us and more so to Mary and Her Son. But perseverance in our good works and attachment to our ideals and prayers shall obtain for us the protection of Mary, Her favors and graces and finally everlasting Joy in Heaven.

O Mary, my Mother, strengthen and inspire me to venerate You daily. Keep me faithful in my devotion of You. May I too be visited by You upon my deathbed and lead me to the Throne of Your Divine Son Our Lord.

DEVOTIONS TO MARY, THE MOTHER
OF GOD AND MY MOTHER

From the earliest days of Christianity, the believers in Jesus had a great respect and honor for His Mother which was and is expressed in the various forms of devotions which we may call LOVE or VENERATION.

The words of the Archangel's greeting became the first part of the prayer we know as "Hail Mary". The living church added the second part to that prayer. This form of honor was learned by the young and the illiterate as well as by the adults and the educated. While the monks and religious recited the Divine Office, the laity recited 150 "Hail Mary's". It can be assumed from the many "Hail Mary's" came the Rosary. A beloved form of prayer and devotion.

To bring the image of Our Blessed Mother to the mind of the faithful and to stimulate reverence of Her, pictures were painted and statues were carved. It is reputed that St. Luke painted a number of pictures of Our Lady among which are the ones titled "Our Lady of Perpetual Help and Our Lady of Czestochowa".

Today there are many pictures and statues of Our Lady. Every artist wants to paint or carve an image of the Blessed Mother. Some of these pictures are very famous as are the statues. The statue of Michelangelo entitled the Pietà is most renowned. Practically every church throughout the world has a painting and/or statue of the Blessed Virgin.

A multitude of pictures and statues have resulted from Our Mother's appearances on this earth. And wherever She appeared there are shrines in which a picture is held in devotion. For example, the picture of Our Lady of Guadalupe, a picture no one knows how it was executed, what paints were used, who the artist was, and how and why it is in the perfect state of preservation, is loved and honored by all the Americans and especially by the Mexicans.

Be it a picture, a statue (in the image of Mary), a shrine, a church, dedicated to our Blessed Mother, Catholics everywhere express their devotion and love to the Mother of God and to the Mother of us all, for Jesus bequeathed Her to us as our Mother.

Devotion to the Mother of God is called HYPERDULIA, which means the highest honor and devotion one can give to a saint. Dulia or veneration, is the honor and respect given to all other saints. But because Mary is the Mother of Jesus, She receives the greatest of reverence.

All forms of Hyperdulia are used by us faithful. Among these are the Rosary, the Litany, the various devotions, May Crowning, songs, the Divine Office, various prayers, pilgrimages to Her shrines, accepting Her name, joining congregations and societies dedicated to Her honor and the Angelus.

Jesus honored His Mother. We are to honor Her, love Her and to have devotions to Her. May our love of Her bring us to Her in Heaven where She will present us to Her Son, Our Lord Jesus.

DEVOTIONS TO THE BLESSED MOTHER

"The Blessed Virgin means something to me now," said a pilgrim after visiting Her shrines in Europe. "0, I knew She was the Mother of Christ and the

Great lover of God, but little did I know that She was and is extremely interested in the people of this world." These sentiments are expressed more and more in modem times and especially lately since there are so many Christians visiting the holy places and shrines. Nearly every country has a great Shrine in Mary's honor.

During the 1950 Holy Year, thousands upon thousands of the faithful made it their business either on the way to or from Rome to pay homage to the Mother of God. It was and is not enough for the devout to say a few "Hail Mary's" in the four famous basilicas of Rome, Fitted in the beauty and grandeur of St. Peter's, of St. Paul's outside of the walls, of St. John Lateran's, and of St. Mary Major's are altars and little shrines dedicated to the Virgin Mary, but somehow no one is satisfied to pray to the Blessed Virgin there. There is a restless craving to say the "Hail Mary" in the spots which were so graciously blessed by Her own appearance.

Lourdes, Fatima, and LaSalette are being crowded by the faithful. Here in these places they know the Blessed Virgin appeared and here She is still working Her wonders for the children of God. An awe inspiring feeling overcomes the pilgrims. It is hard to explain why one is automatically moved to a greater love of the Blessed Mother of Jesus at these shrines. Graces of all kind abound in these holy places. Thousands are seen upon their knees. Thousands crowd the confessionals and Communion rails. The Stations of the Cross are visited most frequently by a continuous stream of devotees. All the statues and paintings of the Blessed Mother are admired. Upon their knees the pilgrims present themselves, their causes and troubles to the Queen of Heaven. Be in Guadalupe and see the number of pilgrims for yourself.

Here where the Blessed Mother once appeared, She still does profoundly influence all. The Rosary is no longer a strange thing or a burden to these people. The Blessed Mother has become their beloved Mother. To recite the Litany of the Blessed Virgin is a satisfying and consoling pleasure as the most intimate conversation with one's best friend. To speak of the Virgin Mary or to say the "Hail Mary" brings to one's mind vivid pictures of Her as if we were living with Her in Palestine or in Heaven. Statues and paintings of Mary do the same for our mind.

> *O Mother, it is good for me to think of You, to venerate You, to visit Your shrines, to recite Your Rosary and Litany, to have an image of You. As I pray daily I am in Your company. You are my companion and intimate friend. Please walk with me always and lead me by Your hand to Your Son*

SPIRITUAL PERFECTION AIDED BY MARY

In the course of our life we need many encouragements to attain our goal. A word from parents, superiors or friends, a pat on the back, and some form of approval gives us heart and strength to carry on even though the difficulties are numerous or almost insurmountable.

In our spiritual life we also need encouragements and grace if we are to attain perfection in our love of God and man. Man left alone to his own powers and abilities withers away by the wayside.

Our spiritual life began with baptism when God came into our hearts in sanctifying grace. This was only the beginning of supernatural life. This seed must grow and develop into full maturity of Faith, Hope, and Love.

In the course of life we were encouraged to attain this maturity by the reception of the sacraments, prayer, examples of the saints, and accepting the graces God gives us. With these means of encouragements in us, there exists in us elements fighting for the good, the noble, the pure, and the divine. "If you love Me, keep My Commandments," says Our Lord. But we all know how difficult they are to keep. Also there is the weariness and weakness of our flesh and will. Therefore we cry out for help.

Our will places selfish love and interest before our eyes while the body craves to be satisfied with pleasure. To overcome our weaknesses of our fallen nature, there is the grace of God. "Sufficient is My Grace for thee." "I will be Your sanctification." Our goal is established by God and He gives us the means to attain it.

Our heart takes courage to know God comes to our aid with this grace to overcome all weakness, to do good and avoid evil. It is also most heartening to know others attained a perfect love of God. The saints are our ideals. They too wish our sanctification and intercede for us that we may attain a great love of God.

Needless to say, the Queen of all Saints is most interested in our sanctification. Our Blessed Mother sets many examples for us of how to love God. She intercedes for us. She obtains the needed graces for us. She inspires us to overcome the world, the flesh, and the devil. Her appearances upon this earth have brought about the conversions of nations, the holiness of many and their elevation on the altars. Wherever there was enkindle a spark of love of God in man's heart, Mary feed oxygen to it producing a bursting flame of love. Through Her love of souls, She brought man to the perfection of love.

> *O Mary, Thou who knowest how to love God best, teach us how to love Our Lord. Lead us along the road of love. Encourage us. Inspire us. Aid us. Bring us to a great consuming love and its perfection in Christ.*

HOPE OF VICTORY WITH MARY

From time to time the world seems to turn against God. A vast number of people begin to hate God, His Church, and its members. This happened in the first century of Christianity, in the fourth and fifth century with its heresies concerning Christ, in the sixteenth century with the Protestant Revolt and now today in the form of communism and Neo-paganism.

Not only does it look bad for Christianity, but it is bad for everyone. More and more people are falling under the yoke of communism. Nearly half of the world is engulfed by it. Untold suffering are being endured. Many martyrs are being made. Also, there is a world campaign against private schools. Here the Catholic Church is attacked because she has the greatest number of such schools. Even in some of the so called Catholic countries, the government is giving the Church a hard time because of its schools.

There is a campaign on right now against God, against the Catholic Church which is His great defender and against moral law. The devil, his followers, and communism are making an all out drive for success.

This confusion in the world cannot last too much longer. God and His Church will triumph. This has happened before and it will happen again.

Pagan Rome hated Christ but through the intercession of Mary, Rome was converted.

All the heresies were defeated through Mary. The whole living Church turned to Her for help. Prayers and mortifications were offered to God through Mary's hands.

Today our Blessed Mother asks us to pray, to pray continuously for victory, and victory shall be ours! For She gives us hope, as Christ gave us hope, of final victory when He said, "There shall be one Shepherd and one flock". "My heart shall triumph", Mary said at Fatima.

Neither God nor Our Mother will stand for such persecution of the Church, the denial of truth, the mockery of Moral Law. The blood of the faithful has moved the heart of God. Mary's heart has been broken by these events. Pity has stirred Her. Surely our prayers must be as intense today as they were in the first centuries of the Church.

The Holy Father begs us to turn to Mary in this present crisis. We are to ask for help. We are to pray for help. We are to stop sinning. We are to spread the faith. We are to sanctify ourselves and the souls of others. We are to become real lovers of God and zealous for the honor and glory of God. Others are to see the sincerity of our love and faith and thus be converted to God by our example.

This present day success of communism and the devil is only a short lived one. Soon the Queen of Victory shall conquer. Russia is crumbling.

O Mary, Our Mother, tarry no longer. Please end this confusion. Bring the world to its knees before Christ. Stop this persecution. Grant us peace, O Lady of Peace. We join You in prayer before the throne of God that Your Immaculate Heart will have a speedy triumph.

MARY AND THE MISSIONS

From the beginning of the Church, our faith became known and was embraced through the prayers, intercession and actual intervention of Our Lady.

All the Apostles received encouragement from the Mother of God. The Apostles looked up to Her, loved Her and sought Her advice. As they returned to Jerusalem from their Missions, She was pleased to hear their stories.

As Our Lady prayed for the Apostles, so too, She continues to pray through all time and unto today. The work of the missionary is bringing Christ to the unbelieving world - this was and is Her task. She wants all to know Jesus and to love Him.

When the missionaries arrived into a new land, they placed the land, its people and their work under the protection of Our Lady and besought Her intercession. They brought Her images and statues along with them and received encouragement to carry on even though the opposition was so strong.

We have one account where the Blessed Mother wanted a faster conversion of the Indian. This happened in Mexico. Shortly after the country was conquered by the Spaniards, the Blessed Mother appeared at Guadalupe to an Indian. In a short time afterward, the whole nation became Catholic.

This interest shown by the Blessed Mother for the welfare of the missionaries and for the spread of the faith is Her grave concern in hoping to have the whole world believe in Her Son and worship Him. She continues to aid all in the work of spreading the faith and establishing the Kingdom of God upon the world.

We have another actual personal intervention in the missionary work by the Blessed Mother. This at Fatima. From a nearly anti-clerical country and one almost dead in religious practice, Portugal became a virile Catholic country.

At Fatima Her missionary activity continues in prophecy - Russia will be converted if we Pray.

> O Mary, pray for the missions and bring all people to the feet of Thy Son. Make one sheepfold - one flock at the command of the One Shepherd, Our Lord, Thy Son.

WILLINGNESS TO HELP OTHERS

How often have we heard or even used the following expressions? "Don't bother me with your troubles; I've got too many of my own." Or, "This is a too happy of an occasion to think about other people's needs. Let's celebrate."

There were occasions of great joy and ecstasy and of extreme sorrow in the life of Our Lady, and yet She found time for others.

At the time of the Annunciation, Our Lady was filled with ecstasy and joy. Frightening was the visit from the Angel, but more awe inspiring was the overshadowing by the Holy Spirit. Stunning was Her choice as the Mother of God, but completely elating was the fact Christ now lived in Her. Her heart had reason to rejoice for She was chosen from among all the women of the world. Her mind had food aplenty for meditation upon this great mystery of the Incarnation.

But yet in spite of Her glory and joy, Mary hastens out into the hills of Judea to give a helping hand to our elderly lady who was to give birth to her first child. St. Elizabeth was old and she would need help. How would she do her work? How would she fare in the delivery? Our Lady's love for a relative in distress urged Her to temper Her joy and to help one in need.

Then when Her heart was filled and pierced with grief on Mount Calvary to see Her Son nailed to the cross and abused, Our Lady did not just fold up. Her heart was broken to the extent where She could fall into shock, or complete uselessness. But yet, that was not so. Her love of God and of Her Son sustains Her to give comfort to Him. Her thoughts are not of Herself, but of Him and of His disciples. Her presence strengthens Christ and encourages the Apostles and the faithful.

O Mary, teach us to be considerate at all times, to be full of charity, to expend ourselves and our energies for the good of our fellow man. Teach us to share our good fortunes. Teach us to see the great misfortunes of others and inspire us to give a helping hand even though we're in trouble, sick, and miserable ourselves. Help us to practice the spiritual and corporal work of mercy to all peoples.

MARY INSPIRES US TO BE GREAT

Franz Jozef Haydn, the Austrian composer, remarked that if he ever lacked any idea or melody for one of his numerous compositions, he would say a "Hail Mary". Immediately his mind was filled with song and his pen wrote at high speed.

Papa Haydn was not the only person to be inspired by the Blessed Mary. Many musicians, painters, sculptors, and writers worked under Her inspiration. After invoking Her aid, they did masters' work.

But the example of Our Lady's life and Her intercession can be and should be an inspiration to all people on this earth. Her courage to accept the Will of God and all the consequences of being the Mother of Christ did and will always inspire mankind for all times.

It takes courage to fulfill the Will of God. It takes great strength to live according to the Will of God in any and all the vocations of life. The strength of God's grace is needed to venture into a new phase of life. The young girl entering the convent for the first time needs inspiration and much bravery. The undaunted fearlessness of the missionaries causes us all to pause in wonderment. Whence came their strength, their courage, their self-sacrifice?

This same self-sacrifice and determination is needed in married life. It is not easy to be pure in courtship when the fires of passion engulf the whole body. But dedication to God's Will, co-operation with His grace, and inspired by Mary, chastity can be enjoyed. Conjugal chastity can be exercised by both the husband and wife under Mary's inspiration and God's grace. It does take great courage to have children. It takes greater courage to have a large family. But it takes an undaunted courage to live according to God's Will in all phases of married life for the whole duration of the marriage.

O Mary, inspire us to do great work for the honor and glory of God. Keep us in courage and in a resolute will to do whatever God demands of us no matter what our station of life may be. Inspire the youth to be loyal and chaste. Inspire the young to dedicate their lives to the service of others. Inflame the hearts of the young to dedicate their lives to the service of others. Inflame the young to be priests, brothers, and sisters. Obtain the graces needed in our vocation and station in life to live as God wants us to live.

0, Mary, You appeared in many areas of the world and You continue to reveal Yourself and Your messages. You want all of us to know Jesus, to love Jesus, and to fulfill His Will. Mary, help us. My we become more and more like unto Your Son. We do love You and we do want to listen to You. Obtain the grace needed for our salvation.

Blessed Mother, as often as I see Your icon or statue, as often as I sing a Marian hymn, and as often as I say the Rosary, Litany of Loreto, or the various prayers in Your honor, and as often as I say a simple "Hail Mary", I place myself into Your arms and await Your caress. I am Your child who needs Your embrace, Your smile, Your consolation and assurance. Mary, may my devotions be my sign of my love for You. Mother, take me under Your protection, take me by my hand and present me to Your Son, my Lord and my God. Then I shall rejoice forever.

As I visit Your shrines and churches dedicated to You, ignite a greater fire of love in my heart for You and Your Son. Surely You want us to know You and to love You, but definitely You want us to know Jesus and love Him. Keep on directing us to Jesus. Keep on directing our lives to fulfill the Will of God. Mary inspire me to be ever close to You.

HOW THE MAY DEVOTIONS BEGAN

In the Catholic Church today, one month is especially dedicated to the Blessed Mother. This is the month of May.

The May devotions are really the work of one man, a certain John Martin, who was born in Switzerland in 1636.

The life story of John Martin is very interesting. He had no formal education. As a youth he tended sheep and played upon a flute. His ability as a musician brought invitations from everywhere. At Strasbourg he joined the choir and read avariciously in the Cathedral library. His ability as an actor, poet, and musician gave him the directorship of the court theater of the Holy Roman Empire.

As fame and honors came to him, he found little time for prayer, Mass, and the Sacraments. Soon the handsome brilliant director had the ladies of the court play for his heart. He became engaged to one and wrote to another who was passionately in love with him. But when she read between the lines of John

Martin's letters, she learned he ridiculed her. Being humiliated, she spread lies and detractions to defame him.

This experience changed John. His jolly personality changed. Soon he became sick. During his serious illness, even his fiancee did not come to visit him. Where were his many friends?

He now turns to God and the Blessed Mother and is cured, attributing his cure to Mary. After gaining his strength, he enters a seminary and becomes a secular priest. At the age of thirty-three he joins the Capuchin Fathers, as Father Lawrence.

His unusual talents were not buried, but he used them in preaching. After ten years of extensive, hard parish work, his superiors retired him from active labor because of his bad heart. From active pastoral work, he turned to writing. Among his many books is the one entitled "May Flute", or "Praises of Mary" in which he wrote hymns, prayers, and meditations for everyday in May. They were introduced in the Realm of Emperor Leopold to all the people.

Twenty-five years after his death, these devotions were suppressed because of a current heresy, but they were revived later by the Italian Jesuits and have been accepted by the whole Catholic Church. Through one man's ability and efforts, May is now dedicated to Mary.

> *O Mary, guide our talents, no matter what they may be that we too, may use them to the best of our ability to honor God and to praise Thee.*

VENERATION OF MARY
AND PERSONAL SANCTIFICATION

The Blessed Virgin Mary can and does aid us in our personal sanctification. Veneration of Mary does lead us to Jesus, to the Holy Spirit, and to God, the Father.

Our Lady leads us to Her Son Whom She wants us to know, love and follow. She directs us to Him.

Mary wants us to be filled with the Holy Spirit. As holiness was Hers, She wants us to be holy also, Union with God, the Father, is Mary's triumph. She wants us to share this glory in which all of us as Her children will rejoice forever making all one holy, happy family.

To aid us to attain the Beatific Vision, the Blessed Mother stands at our sides. As God wants us to love Him totally - with our whole heart, soul, mind, and strength - Mary wants to aid us in this consecration. Read and recite the next few lines, a prayer:

> *"I venerate Thee with all my heart, O virgin most holy, above all angels and saints in Paradise, as the Daughter of the Eternal Father, and to Thee I consecrate my soul with all its powers."*
> *"Hail Mary"...*

Our body and soul in union make us what we are. It is through our bodies that we perform acts which were conceived in mind. Our acts are the external expressions of our intellect and will. Our body with all its senses to bring glory to God. Read and recite the next few lines, a prayer:

> *"I venerate Thee with all my heart, O Virgin most holy, above all angels and saints in Paradise, as the Mother of the only begotten Son, and to Thee I consecrate my body with all its senses." "Hail Mary"...*

Although it is with the will that we love, nonetheless in a common expression we say, "I love You with all my heart." It is this heart (willpower) that moves mankind's senses. All human acts done while in sanctifying grace and offered to God become meritorious gaining a high place in Heaven for us. Therefore it is important for us to live in the state of grace, to offer everything to God, and to express our desire to gain all merit possible.

While making this intention of gaining merit, it is profitable to have an intention of gaining all the indulgences possible. It is not necessary to know what indulgences one will gain by his prayers or good acts. They will be gained if one is in the state of grace, wants to gain them, and performs acts to which they are attached.

Our Lady will help us in this regard and helps us to direct our affections properly. Read and recite the following, a prayer:

> *"I venerate Thee with all my heart, O Virgin most holy, above all angels and saints in Paradise, as the beloved Spouse of the Spirit of God, and to Thee I consecrate my heart and all its affections, imploring Thee to obtain for me from the Most Holy Trinity all the means of Salvation." "Hail Mary"...*

> *O Mary, we are Your children. Inspire us to live according to God's will and lead us to Your Son, our Lord. May we rejoice with You and all the saints in union with God forever.*

MAY CROWNING

During the month of May, we read of many May Crownings. This form of devotion has become very popular and most striking in attractiveness. We all love to see a procession, a parade, a spectacle, a demonstration. These move our spirits to love Mary more each time we participate in such an act of veneration.

Surely, these forms of venerating the Blessed Mother are most pleasing to Her and especially if they are made in sincerity and love. For truly they have as their aim the sanctification of all who partake in them.

Sanctification is motivated by the act of dedication to the Blessed Mother as Our Queen. By this dedication there is to be an acceptance of Her as the Reigning Queen of our hearts and minds.

To accept Our Lady as Queen of each and everyone of us, means to accept Her as our lawgiver and ruler, to pay Her homage, to imitate Her in all Her virtues. Surely no one can have Mary as his Queen without becoming a great lover of God.

The acceptance of Our Lady as the lawgiver is to accept the laws of God and fulfill them. Time and time again Our Lady warned us not to sin, not to transgress the Commandments, to love Her Son. She wants us to follow Her wishes and also to fulfill Her desires. And when we fulfill requests, Mary is truly ruling us in a special sense. May we love Her most dearly.

Every Queen receives homage from her subjects. Mary's homage consists primarily in devotions of various forms offered to Her honor, v.g., Rosary, Litany, hymns, processions, novenas, scapulars and medals, prayers, etc.

But the greatest honor which anyone can give to another is to imitate him/her. The greatest honor we can give Our Lady is to imitate Her in all Her virtues. We know how in Her humility She fulfilled the will of God in all things. Her one aim in life was to serve God in obedience and love. "Behold Thy Handmaid, be it done to Me according to Thy word." She was most fond of speaking to God. She denied Herself everything to be the most pure lover of God. She kept Her body intact as a tabernacle of God. Obtain the grace for us to accept God's will in everything.

0, Mary, be our Queen. Reign over our hearts and minds. Fill us with a devotion to Thee and a readiness to follow in Your footsteps. Keep us pure. Keep us as a tabernacle in which God lives now and shall live for the rest of our earthly life.

MARY FILLS EMPTY HEARTS

In this troubled world we find people with disturbed minds and empty hearts seeking peace and love. This peace and love can be had and often times it is the Blessed Virgin Who shows the way to that peace and love.

In such a manner peace of soul and love of heart came to Douglas Hyde, the London editor of the Communist Daily Worker.

While a Communist, Douglas Hyde realized a great abyss in his heart. He yearned for something which would satisfy his inquisitiveness of mind and fill his emptiness of heart. At times he would stop in a Catholic Church hoping to find the answer to his problems. He was searching for Faith and peace.

One day while in church he saw a little servant woman kneeling before the Statue of the Blessed Virgin Mary. Her face was very troubled. But as her fingers glided over the Rosary, her whole countenance changed to one of peace, of joy, and of radiance.

This was a miracle he judged and he hoped a similar miracle would occur to him. He hurried to the statue and knelt before Our Lady. As he knelt there, he thought of some special prayer. As he reviewed prayer after prayer, none he knew seemed to fit the occasion and idea which he would like to express. Then as he racked his mind for a fitting prayer, the lines of a popular dance tune flooded his mind and forced him to say, "O sweet and lovely lady be good, O lady be good to me".

These words of a dance tune pleased the Blessed Mother and She obtained the grace of conversion for Douglas Hyde. From that moment, his progress into the Church was certain and he did become a Catholic. Now as he fought to spread communism, Douglas Hyde fights to further the Church.

> *O, Blessed Mary, I too need peace and love. Obtain the grace to open my heart very wide to love You. Then with the grace I shall love God totally and I shall love my neighbor. Surely this blessing obtained by You will give me that peace for which my mind yearns. O, Queen of Peace, pray for me and for all people. Also pray for peace in the troubled world. May all people enjoy Our Father's blessings, salvation wrought by Christ, sanctification of the Holy Spirit and the protection of You, Our Lady.*

> *Remember, O most loving Virgin Mary, that never was it known that anyone who fled to Your protection, implored Your help, or sought Your intercession was left unaided. Inspired with this confidence, we turn to You, O Virgin of virgins, our Mother. To You we come, before You we kneel, sinful and sorrowful. O Mother of the Word Incarnate, do not despise our petitions, but in Your mercy hear and answer us. Amen.*

CHRISTMAS, A FEAST OF THE BLESSED MOTHER

Of the many scenes presented to us by our faith, literature, and art at Christmas time, there is one in particular which moves my heart to tenderness. My heart is effected unto sweetness every time I see a mother hold an infant and especially so of a newborn child, but somehow my heart beats differently when I behold Mary and Joseph in complete ecstatic adoration of the newborn Jesus.

In your mind's eye see a picture of Mary and Joseph in adoration of the Infant. Or if it is easier, look at a painting of the Nativity of Jesus or at a manger with Jesus in a crib. See the improvised crib. Look at the long promised God man. Observe Mary and Joseph as they behold Jesus.

Turn your eyes to Joseph for a moment. His face is radiant and yet one can see it is spellbound. We let him remain in his ecstasy and silent adoration as we turn to Mary.

Mother Mary, how fortunate You are to give birth to Your Lord. As You behold Your Child, You cannot believe - but it is true - You, yes You gave birth to Your Creator, Your Redeemer, Your God now made flesh. Look at Your Son, the true God and true man for Whom all creation groaned and awaited.

What can one read in or from Your face and eyes as You behold Your Son? I read joy, love, and submission to God's Will. I read gratitude for the honor God had bestowed upon You by selecting You to be the Mother of His Son. I see

128

peaceful astonishment, a deep reverence, a spellbinding awe, an admiration beyond description. I see You in sweet love and devotion. Your face is so mild and lovely while Your eyes radiate happiness and softness.

In Your whole demeanor I see a willingness to be of assistance to others. You who were submissive and cooperative to the Will of God are now ready to bear anything and everything to accomplish Your sublime mission as the Mother of God, the protector of Christ, and the Mother of all mankind.

Your mind is in deep thought as to what will be the course of Your Son, what will be His future, how will You fulfill Your dutiful task as His mother, how will You raise Him, and will all the people recognize Him and accept Him as the Son of God? Definitely You are concerned about His future and Your own.

As You gaze upon Your Infant, Your loving heart beams love for all who accept Your Son. Oh, how You wish all mankind will accept Him, recognize Him, love Him and obey Him and His requests of "Come follow Me".

Another question comes across Your face; Will mankind accept Me as its Mother? Oh, Mary, we do see in Your love an all embracing love for the whole Mystical Body of Christ of which each of us is a member.

O Mary, as You adore Your Son, we join in that adoration and we express our love of You and we venerate You as the Mother of God and our Mother. May our hearts glow with some of the love You possess. Open our hearts with love for Jesus, with love for You, with love for our immortal soul, and with love for everyone of our human family for we all make up the Mystical Body of Christ. Your beloved Son.

CHRISTMAS, A FEAST OF OUR LADY

Christmas is rarely thought of as the Feast of Our Lady but it is on this day She becomes the Mother of God.

True, as in everything the Blessed Mother does to lead all to Christ, so too at Christmas She remains in the background properly giving Her Son the place of honor and directing all attention to Her Son. This is very evident from all the paintings and statues of the Madonna and Child. Her head and eyes direct all who look upon Her to the Child.

Yet, this feast fills Her heart with great joy. First of all Her Son is born. The gratification of seeing Her own flesh and blood filled Her heart. But the knowledge that Her Son is also the Son of God, the long awaited Messiah, makes Her heart overflow with happiness. As She looks upon Him, She adores Him as Her God.

The joy of Her heart increases as the shepherds come to adore Christ. She listens diligently to their words of how the angels told them to find the Child. She reads the gladness in their faces as they behold their Redeemer. Her joy increases as the Magi come to adore Him. Her Son will be known throughout the world for all times. Her heart glows with proper delight to know that all men, the whole human race, will be able to live in love with God again.

As Mary looks upon the newly born Son of God, She could not help it but be pleased with His appearance, His strong body and comely face. She was pleased as all mothers are pleased to see their offspring. She was pleased to know She fulfilled the purpose of Her creation. She was pleased to give the Son of God a human body and soul. She was honored to be chosen by God to be the Mother of His Son.

Our hearts fill with joy as we behold the manger or reflect upon the Nativity. Our eyes shift from the Babe to His Mother and back again. We are spellbound in wonderment of this great mystery. We adore Our Lord and we smile with reverence and thanksgiving to Mary. And words are formed upon our lips.

> *"O Mary, Mother of God, show me Thy Son and lead me to Him. You brought Him into the world for my salvation and the salvation of all mankind. Obtain the Grace of enlightenment to know Jesus as my Lord and Savior. Obtain the favor to Love Jesus, my God. Through Your aid bring me to see Jesus and You forever.*

THE ANNUNCIATION

There is the beautiful Church of the Annunciation in Nazareth. When a pilgrim is in the Holy Land, this church is on the must list.

Here, in this church, long before it was a church, is where the beginning of the history of Jesus Christ began.

On the first floor of the church is the indicated spot where the Archangel Gabriel spoke to Mary.

This place, the home of Mary, must have had a cave attached to it or the house was attached to the cave.

This cave is behind the altar. Over the cave are the letters FIAT. The letters also are on the priest's vestments.

It is here that the Angel presented the will of God that God wanted Mary to be the Mother of His Son. Mary's response was, "How can this happen to me? I know not man."

With that, the Archangel Gabriel reveals to Her the mind of God. God has selected Her for the maternity of His Son.

In a movie on the Annunciation, a ray of light is shown coming through a window and resting on Our Lady. The Gospel tells us definitely it is an angel.

If an angel in human form appeared to the patriarchs, to Tobit, to St. Peter, and even to the three children at Fatima, surely this most important event in our salvation history demanded far more than a ray of light.

Following the Gospel, we must say Gabriel appeared in a human form and spoke in words loud enough for Mary to hear and understand.

Mary had to make a decision. The word fiat was the answer. This word means, "Let it be done to me as you say." A fiat is a commands. With Mary's fiat, the agreement is made to accept the Will of God, and with that, Mary became the Mother of Jesus.

The second floor of the Basilica in Nazareth also is a church that has part of the floor removed so that one can see the altar and cave on the first floor.

The third floor is a parish church. This segment of the large Basilica has paintings, mosaics, and tile pictures of some of the appearances of Mary throughout the world. This church was the largest Catholic Church for the Christian Arabs.

Because of Mary's fiat, Christ came into the world. Because of our own fiat, we too can beget Christ in our hearts.

Fiat is a Latin word meaning "Thy will be done," We Christians say those words every time we say the Lord's Prayer. Fiat - may it so happen!

Whenever we say those words in the Lord's Prayer, we may think of Mary as She submitted Her Will to the Will of God, the Father.

More important would be if we, like She, did completely accept the Will of God in all things and executed His Will. Really, there is no other way to live, for us to act, except to agree with God's Will to live according to His Will.

The Lord's Prayer should not be empty, thoughtless words. As Mary accepted the Will of God and all the responsibilities, may we too have the courage and wisdom to do more than just say "Thy Will be done," but also, to do it.

May Mary help us in this matter and may the grace of God be with us always to do His Will, for in doing His Will is our happiness and salvation.

A MOTHER'S LOVE

There is a legend told by the Brazilian women to their children of the love of a mother for her son and this love is like the love of the Blessed Mother.

There was a boy who fell in a passionate love with a bad woman. Because he loved her body, he became her slave. He did everything to please her and all she ordered him to do, even the most difficult.

One day she told him, "I want you to do something special for me. Go to your mother, tear out her heart, and bring it to me". The boy was shocked and said, "No, I will never do that", "Then go from here " she said, "for you cannot be my lover any longer."

The boy was madly blind with passion. Even though he hated the thought of killing his own mother, yet the power of sin and the devil over him influenced his mind so much that he went home and killed his mother. He took her heart and wrapped it in a towel. Now crazed and bewildered, he sped to his illicit love. On his way cutting through a mountain pass, he stumbled and fell hard striking a rock with his face. As he laid there he heard a voice, a voice from the bleeding warn heart he carried in his hand. In a soft tender loving tone he heard, "Did you hurt yourself, my son?"

The love of the Blessed Mother for Her children is Just like that. Her heart is pierced every time Her Son is offended grievously. Every mortal sin causes Her grief. Every mortal sin is a serious insult against Her. She bewails and laments that Her children are so ungrateful, so rude, so cruel. But yet the bleeding heart of Mary loves Her children, She prays for them, She begs special graces for them, She bring about cures and favors for them, She holds back the fire of hell from them, She opens Her heart and the gate of Heaven for them.

O Mary, open Your heart and the gate of Heaven for me, too. I need Your loving heart for in my weakness and lack of presence of mind, I forget You and I insult You and Jesus by committing sin. Mother, do help me. I know You love me and want my soul in Heaven. Teach me to want to want to be with You and God in Heaven.

MARY, OUR BELOVED MOTHER

Many books and articles have been written about the Mother of Jesus, Her concerns for all peoples, and of Her appearances to a vast variety of people and in many favored areas of the world.

Whether the authors wrote doctrine, history or devotional material, Mary is pointed out as Someone who loves us, cares for us and wants us to follow Her Son.

Knowledge of all that Mary is and did may be profitable, but far above knowledge is our love of Her. That She loves us is a foregone conclusion. Mary does love us and prays for our salvation. How could She do otherwise since She is Our Mother, who wants us to share eternal life in Heaven.

There are many stories and legends concerning the Mother of Jesus. Every age and every people have their own accounts of Mary and how She supports Her people. We can read these writings and be edified and be motivated to venerate and love Our Blessed Virgin Mary. Among the many devotions is the dedication of Saturdays to Mary, Our Mother. In the Sacramentary, the book used at Mass containing the Mass prayers for the day, season, sacraments and feasts, there is a section for Our Lady,

We are requested to make the First Fridays in honor of the Sacred Heart of Jesus and we are urged to participate in the Masses on Saturdays, especially the First Saturday of the month, which are in honor of the Blessed Mother and Her Immaculate Heart.

There is a pious legend as to the sacredness of Saturdays and their relation to the Blessed Virgin Mary. This legend states that every Saturday has to have at least one moment of sunshine because Saturdays were the days Our Lady did the laundry especially the washing of diapers used for the Infant Jesus. Now She comes to help all mothers in the laundry chores in having the wash dry quickly by a moment of sunshine on Saturdays.

Is it strange for Mary to love us? Mary is the most perfect of all human beings. She is the model of love and She imitates the love of God Who loves us so much that He gave His only begotten Son. She too gave us Her Son, Our Lord.

As God in His love for us and as Jesus in His love for us want our love in return so does Mary. Her love by its nature wants our love.

132

Love is to return to the one who loves us. It must come from someone first and then is returned. This is also true in human love. One party starts the heart to beat and the other party corresponds.

God loved us first. He wants our love. Jesus loved and loves us for He told us so. Jesus thirsts for our whole love.

Mary loved us long before we were born. Her love wants our love in return. May our hearts be open to Mary today and everyday of our lives. May the various devotions we have express our love of the Virgin Mary.

O Mary, help me to love You and through this love come to love Your Son and the whole God-head with my whole heart, whole soul, whole mind, and whole strength.

MARY, OUR MOTHER

"Woman, behold Thy son." "Son behold thy Mother."
(Jn. 19, 26-27)

During the crucifixion of Her Divine Son, Mary received an unusual privilege from Jesus. This distinct honor is called the Universal Motherhood of Mankind.

Our Lord knew His end was coming. As Our Lord looked down upon the small group of the faithful who were near the cross, He saw the pain His Blessed Mother was enduring. Truly this is the time when the sword pierced Her heart as was prophesied by Simeon.

Since death was near, Christ had to complete His last will and testament. Already He committed His blood to the Church, His garments to the enemy, a thief to Heaven, and soon He would commend His body to the grave and His soul to His Father. There were only two beloved treasures remaining - His mother and His beloved disciple John. "Woman, behold Thy son." "Son, behold thy Mother." "And from that hour," writes St. John about himself, "The disciple took Her to his own."

These words of Christ have a much greater meaning than what they seem at the moment. The Church, yuided by the same Holy Spirit Who inspired St. John to write these words, holds that St. John represented all the redeemed of Christ. By giving Mary to John, Christ gave Her to all of us.

The Blessed Virgin Mary is truly our spiritual Mother, for She is the Mother of Jesus Who by His passion and death makes it possible for You and me to be the adopted children of God. It is Mary Who cooperates with God in giving us Jesus Who also is our supernatural life and food.

As a true Mother, She takes care of us. She shows Her love for us by obtaining graces for us. She constantly intercedes for us. She appears at times upon this earth bringing consolation, direction, graces and cures to Her children.

Mother of God and Our Mother help us to love You and Your Son above all. This we do when we avoid sin, receive the

Sacraments, recite the Rosary, Litany, and the "Hail Mary". As
Your true lover may we never worry about our salvation, for
you are praying for us sinners now and at the hour of our
death.

"O Mary, my Mother, be gracious to me."

MOTHER OF MOTHERS

Cardinal Mindszenty, of whom we read and heard so much since the communistic power of Hungry arrested him, wrote a book entitled "Our Mother in Heaven". In this book, he extols the virtues of Our Lady and extols the virtues of all women, and in particular, an earthly mother.

According to the Hungarian Primate, all newly wedded couples of the sixteenth century were placed under the protection of the Blessed Mother and were given jewelry reminding them of this protection. The young bride was in particular placed under special protection of the Blessed Virgin.

Good mothers, he says, are sisters of the Blessed Virgin Mary. They share similar sorrows and joys. They cooperated with God in creation, in bringing a new life into the world, in caring for and nursing a child of God, and in training the offspring to fulfill the Will of God.

Every good and virtuous mother shares in the beauty of the Blessed Mother. In fact the face of a mother is radiant with beauty which alone is distinctive. Motherhood adds a particular beauty to a woman. This beauty comes from sharing in the comeliness of Our Lady.

Somehow when we think of the beauty of our own mother, who is in our mind the ideal of an earthly woman, we attribute to her qualities of the Blessed Mother. In fact, often our minds blend the virtues and perfections of our own mother with that of the Mother of Mothers. If by chance our mothers have imperfections, our minds purify them and even raise their attributes up to a very high degree of perfection. Even though our love in a way elevates our mother, nevertheless we know her limitations and place her under the protection of the Blessed Virgin. In particular, the expectant mother needs Her protection. Mary knows of the anguish and longing of a woman for a child to be born. Mary knows of the mother's love for a child and her longing to take him to her bosom.

O Mother of Mothers, intercede for all of us, but in particular
take care of Thy sisters, our mothers. Help each mother at the
moment of delivery. Keep them and their offsprings safe and
guide them to Thy Son. Help those who want children to be
fertile. Change the minds of all who refuse to have or want to
abort children. My all women realize the glory of motherhood.
May all mothers share in Your Joy and glory while they are on
earth and grant them eternal happiness with You and Your Son
O, Mary, pray for all mothers and their children.

DEVOTION TO THE HEART OF MARY

The month of August is dedicated to the Immaculate Heart of Mary. In 1942 the Holy Father consecrated the whole world and especially Russia to Mary's Immaculate Heart.

Devotion to the Heart of Mary was founded in the beginning of Christendom and is intimately connected with the Sacred Heart of Jesus. But the devotions as we know them today are rather recent for in the thirteenth century they were started by St. Gertrude and her sister St. Mechtilde. St. John Eudes in the seventeenth century writes about this form of veneration. Then at Lourdes and Fatima the devotion to the Immaculate Heart gets its real impetus and this in the 19th and 20th centuries.

The heart is the seat of passion and of love. Every emotion affects the heart; our life depends on it. Mary's heart loved God above all, Her heart was pierced by the Seven Sorrows in Her love of Christ, and Her heart is moved by love towards us all.

At Fatima, Mary showed Her heart to the three children. Artists paint Her heart surrounded by a garland of roses, flames of fire, and lilies rising from the top, and a sword thrust through Her heart.

The rose is Mary's special flower. She showers rose petals, She made roses bloom out of season at Guadalupe, She appeared at Lourdes at the rose bush. She is the Mystical Rose.

The fire on Her heart is the love She has for us.

The Immaculate Heart is a heart most pure symbolized by the lily and is full of love. This heart is the model for our hearts.

Our hearts are to be immaculate, i.e., without sin and any adherence to sin; but rather a hatred of sin and a fleeing away from sin.

Our hearts, too, should burn with love of God and fellowman. Mary's Heart which loved God and loves each and everyone of us is a model for every Christian and especially for us Catholics.

Take a good look at the painting of the Immaculate Heart of Mary. Just glance at the somber face but concentrate on the Heart. You can read from that Heart as well as I can. You can see Her love for us. You can see Her concern for us. You can see the pain She bears for us because of our lack of love of God, of Jesus, of Her, and of our neighbor.

O Mary, teach us how to love God and our fellowman. Keep us pure and undefiled. O, that we may have Mary's heart with which to love Our Lord and our neighbor.

THE PROMISE OF THE FIVE FIRST SATURDAYS: "I promise at the hour of death to help with the graces needed for their salvation, whoever on the first Saturdays of five consecutive months, shall confess and receive Holy Communion, recite five decades of the Rosary and keep me company for fifteen minutes while meditating on the fifteen mysteries of the Rosary with the intention of making reparation to me." (Words of Our Lady to Lucia, Dec,10, 1925).

PRAYER: *O God of infinite goodness and mercy, fill our hearts with a great confidence in our Most Holy Mother, whom we invoke under the title of the Immaculate Heart of Mary, and grant us by Her most powerful intercession all the graces, spiritual and temporal, which we need. Through Christ Our Lord. Amen.*

HOPE OF VICTORY WITH MARY

From time to time the world seems to turn against God. A vast number of people begin to hate God, His Church, and its members. This happened in the first century of Christianity, in the fourth and fifth century with its heresies concerning Christ, in the sixteenth century with the Protestant Revolt and now today in the form of communism and Neo-paganism.

Not only does it look bad for Christianity, but it is bad for everyone. More and more people have fallen under the yoke of communism. Nearly half of the world was engulfed by it. Untold sufferings are being endured. Many martyrs are being made. Also, there is a world campaign against private schools. Here the Catholic church is attacked because she has a great number of such schools. Even in some of the so called Catholic countries, the government is giving the Church a hard time because of its schools.

There is a campaign on right now against God, against the Catholic Church which is His great defender and against moral law. The devil, his followers, and atheists are making an all out drive for success.

This confusion in the world cannot last too much longer. God and His Church will triumph. This has happened before and it will happen again.

Pagan Rome hated Christ but through the intercession of Mary, Rome was converted. All the heresies were defeated through Mary. The whole living Church turned to Her for help. Prayers and mortifications were offered to God through Mary's hands. Today Our Blessed Mother asks us to pray, to pray continuously for victory. And victory shall be ours. For She gives us hope, as Christ gave us hope of final victory when He said, "There shall be one Shepherd and one flock". "My heart shall triumph, Mary said at Fatima.

Neither God nor Our Mother will stand for such persecution of the Church, the denial of truth, the mockery of Moral Law. The blood of the faithful has moved the Heart of God. Mary's Heart has been broken by these events. Pity has stirred Her. Surely our prayers must be as intense today as they were in the first centuries of the Church.

The Holy Father begs us to turn to Mary in this present crisis. We are to ask for help. We are to pray for help. We are to stop sinning. We are to spread the faith. We are to sanctify ourselves and the souls of others. We are to become real lovers of God and zealous for the honor and glory of God. Others are to see the sincerity of our love and faith and thus be converted to God by our example.

This present day success of atheism and the devil is only a short lived one. Soon the Queen of Victory shall conquer.

*O Mary, our Mother, tarry no longer. Please end this confusion.
Bring the world to its knees before Christ. Stop this persecution.
Grant us peace, O Lady of Peace. We Join You in prayer before
the throne of God that Your Immaculate Heart will have a
speedy triumph.*

LIVING IN THE PRESENCE OF MARY

Some of the saints enjoyed a special grace of living in the company and
presence of Our Lady. Saint Philip Neri was one of these. His mind was aware
that he was near Our Lady at all times. He knew that She saw him, loved him
and looked after him. He enjoyed living in what spiritual writers call, "dwelling
in Mary's fair Soul".

In our daily lives, in the natural order upon this earth, we in a way live in
the soul of our earthly mother. Her influence upon us is terrific. We are
thoughtful as to what mother taught us,"Oh, I cannot do that," we say, "mother
taught me better than that." Her influence endures all the days of our life. She
knows our ways, our thoughts, and our acts. She sees us and guides us. Her love
for us keeps her interested in us. And we are continuously aware of all this
influence of mother upon us. We are conscious of our mother's presence and
her person is upon our minds most often. In fact we live, as it were, "in the soul
of our mother".

In like manner, the great spiritual people live in the "Soul of our Blessed
Lady." They have acquired the habit of living with Our Lady. They have added to
the morning prayer where they offer themselves and all acts—through the
Immaculate Heart of Mary. Her intentions and desires become theirs. They have
united their love with Hers. They have willed as She willed. They have let
themselves be influenced by Her so that they may love Christ even as She loved
Him.

This indwelling, so to speak, in Mary's Soul and She in our hearts primarily
springs from the intimacy of intellect and the heart. Our knowledge of Her urges
us to pray to Her, to ask for help; our love fosters devotion and sacrifice. Mary
knows our needs and She hears our prayers and obtains graces for us. Her love
for us, Her children, is manifested in the care She shows for us and the help She
renders us.

*O Mary, teach me to be alive in Thy presence. Take me into Thy
bosom. Make me cognizant of Your watchful and protective eye.
May I invoke Thee most often. Make Thy influence guide my
every thought and word and deed for God's glory. Bear hard
upon my mind to think, "What will my Heavenly Mother say to
this I'm to do or am doing. Keep me in Thy sweet soul." As you
and I live in the presence of God, so too we live in the presence
of Our Blessed Mother for She knows everything that pertains to
Her. My gracious Queen may I feel Your presence today and
every day of my life.*

IN SPREADING THE WORK OF MARY

From the earliest days when we began practicing our faith, we learned to pray to the Mother of Jesus. We were told who She was, what She did for our salvation and we began to love Her and admire Her.

The greatest admiration shown to anyone is imitating that person. The greatest veneration we can give to the Blessed Virgin Mary is to imitate Her and follow in Her footsteps.

The Blessed Virgin Mary was most solicitous in Her devotion to Her Divine Son and in the service of Him. Her whole life was lived solely for that purpose. Her prime concern was to serve God and She willingly used Her time, efforts, and talents doing just that.

In imitating the Mother of God, we too, should serve God in everything and at all times. What good will it do us if we win the whole world and suffer the loss of our souls?

Definitely then in our love of God and imitation of His Mother, Christ and His work should be of utmost interest to us by:

1. The spreading of our faith and knowledge of Christ-we are home missionaries.
2. Contribute to foreign missions or go to the missions.
3. Spreading knowledge of God by writing, Crucifixes, paintings, Rosaries, and other Sacramentals. A friend of mine gives each of her children a Crucifix and two large holy pictures as wedding gifts-she had nine children.

Imitation of Mary in charitable works include the spiritual works of mercy too. Who is going to comfort the afflicted, instruct the ignorant, counsel the doubtful? Who is to soothe the pains of a neighbor's heart? To give them love and hope, to smile instead of frown, to speak well of others rather than spread scandal, to swallow pride and love in peace and harmony rather than to be irritated, infuriated, angered?

Are we not to be tolerant of others' weaknesses and shortcomings? Or are we to be so sensitive and inflated with self-importance that at the least sign of an inadvertent act, or remark we sever our relations with our fellow child of God? We are hurt by the cutting retorts of our fellowmen. We are wounded by their actions. So what? So was Our Lord. So was Our Blessed Lady. What did Our Lord do? "Forgive them Father for they know not what they do." Our Lady whom we entitle, Our Lady of Mercy, for She is most merciful, imitated Our Lord in this regard and prayed for the offenders. Our imitation of Our Lord and Our Lady is to be fruitful bringing harmony and peace back into our relations with our fellowman. This is most difficult at times, but it can be done.

O, Mary, in my imitation of Thy Son and Thee, teach me to be most charitable to my less fortunate brother or sister. Give me the courage to give him a helping hand. Fill my mind with kindness and love. Make me realize that by imitating You and serving my fellowman, I am serving Thy Son, my Lord and God. See to it, O Mary, that I may hear those glorious words from the lips of Thy Son, "Come, Blessed of my Father, possess the kingdom of Heaven forever."

OUR LADY OF PERPETUAL HELP

One story of the devotion to Our Lady of Perpetual Help is very interesting. It began about the middle of the fifteenth century on the Island of Crete. One day a merchant took a beautiful picture of the Blessed Virgin holding the Infant Jesus from the island church where the faithful venerated the picture for years. Whatever prompted the man to take the picture is not known, but he took it and hiding it among other merchandise, he sailed for Italy.

While on high seas, a violent storm broke loose. Usually such a tempest meant destruction for the ship unless it reached some harbor. The vessel could not reach any port. All the people on board began to recommend themselves to God and to His Blessed Mother. At once, most unexpectedly, the sea became calm and the voyagers safely landed in Italy.

It was in the year 1496 or 1497 that this merchant came to Rome to sell his wares. But before he could get out of the city, he fell seriously sick. He begged a friend to nurse him. But even the most efficient ministrations of his friends could not help the merchant. Seeing that death was at hand, he called his friend and asked him to fulfill the promise of a dying man. His proposed promise was: "Since my death will prevent me from bringing the picture to the place for which it was destined and there restoring it to public veneration, I beg you to have it placed in whatever church you may think most suitable, in order that it may again receive the homage of the faithful."

Since there are many churches in Rome, the question as to where to place the picture befuddled the man. The Blessed Mother appeared to a little child and expressed the desire to have the picture placed between the two large churches of St. Mary Major and St. John Lateran. Thus the Church of St. Matthew received the painting. The Augustinian Fathers, who were in charge of the church, made a triumphant procession through the streets of the Eternal City and placed the picture in their church where the Blessed Mother was to be venerated for many years. Here the Blessed Virgin performed many miracles and attracted people from all over the world.

But in the year 1789 revolutions swept over Europe and many churches were destroyed by hordes of merciless fanatics. Among those churches destroyed was St. Matthews. The good Augustinian Fathers were able to save the beautiful miraculous picture of the Perpetual Help. This picture was not seen in Rome again until 1866 when it was again exposed for public veneration. This time the painting was placed in a newly built church over the ruins of the old St. Matthew's church. This church is under the care of the Redemptorist Fathers today.

When the Redemptorists learned of their treasure, they formed a most solemn procession through the streets of Rome. It was on the twenty-sixth of April 1866, that this Blessed Mother of Perpetual Help was borne through the streets to the delight of all the inhabitants. The whole city was decorated for this event.

Ever since that day, the holy enthusiasm which inflamed the hearts of the Roman people has enkindled a fire of love and devotion in the hearts of all the faithful throughout the world for Our Dear Mother of Perpetual Help.

In many American churches the fire of love for the Blessed Lady of Perpetual Help was started long ago. Every week on different days in the evening at 7:30 prayers are said in Her honor, petitions are asked, and graces and favors are received. Oh, if only all the hearts knew what favors and graces that can be theirs, they would overcrowd every church honoring Our Lady of Perpetual Help.

The Blessed Mother is ready to help Her faithful at all times. She is the Perpetual Help of Christians. She is the Comfort of the Afflicted. She is the Mother of Divine Grace. Through Her come all the graces which we have received or will receive. Mary is the Almoner of God.

We all need graces and we all need Divine favors. The place to petition for them is at the feet of Our Lady. O Lady of Perpetual Help, pray for us now and at the hour of our death. With the help of the graces which flow through Your hands, we shall be especially nourished in our spiritual life.

O Mother of Perpetual Help, bring all the wayfaring children back to the church. Grant them the grace to embrace Your Son, love Your Son, live according to the will of Your Son and pray that they and all of us may see Thee and Thy Son forever.

In prayer, O Blessed Mother we ask for peace of mind for ourselves for our families, for our nation and for all the nationas in the world. Please stop all wars, strife and anger. How can we have JOY if we have the spirit of strife? We need peace. Grant us peace that we may have joy and live in happiness now and forever.

BLESSED MOTHER'S AID TO PEACE AND JOY...THE HOLY ROSARY

St. Peter advised us with these words, "Should anyone ask you the reason of your hope be ever ready to reply". Our hope for a peaceful and joyful life comes from God Himself. It is a gift won for us by Jesus. This gift is bestowed upon us through the power of the Holy Spirit.

When the Holy Spirit descended upon the Apostles, they were convicted in their belief in Jesus who promised them victory and eternal joy in Heaven. This joy and promise of Our Lord, of eternal life was given to us through the teaching of the Apostles, our parents and the Church.

Hope is that trust of obtaining what was promised. We do want peace, joy and eternal life. But hope is based upon faith. We are to believe in God, in Jesus and in every thing Jesus said. Jesus said He would give us the Holy Spirit, He said He would prepare a place in Heaven for us. He said we are to keep the Commandments and we are to love another as He loves us. Therefore we are to know Jesus, the articles of our faith, and be ready to defend our faith even to the point of suffering. All who truly love God and abide by the words of Jesus, will accept any cross, be loyal to Jesus and eagerly await His coming to take us to Heaven.

Faith, hope and love are to be exercised by good works. We are to love our fellow man. We are to hope for all graces now and for the reward of Heaven. We are to believe in Jesus and everything He said.

An excellent way of reviewing our faith is the daily recitation of the Holy Rosary. Our Blessed Mother wants us to say the Rosary. She has requested the Rosary to be said every day. She said the Rosary at Lourdes and at Fatima. In Medjugorje the Rosary is said most often. We place a Rosary in the hands of the body which lays in the casket. Why has this custom arose? We think this Rosary will help that soul get to Heaven.

Reciting the Rosary is a good review of our Faith, By saying the Rosary we recall the sacred mysteries of the life of Jesus and Our Blessed Mother. As we recite the Rosary we come into the very lives of Jesus and Mary as if we were in Their company. As we recite the Rosary, we begin to feel very close to Jesus and Mary, we begin to know them better, we see Their concern for us and Their love for us. It is a wonderful feeling to be in the company of Jesus and Mary.

We all should know the 15 mysteries. We all should teach others these mysteries. We should be learned enough to defend our belief and be ready to express the reason for our actions and the hope which comes to us from our faith and love. May We all recite the Rosary daily and may our faith become stronger, our hope more expressive and our love more in conformity with that love which Jesus wants us to have.

ROSARY - THE FIFTEEN PROMISES OF MARY TO THOSE WHO RECITE THE ROSARY:

1. Whosoever recites the Rosary faithfully shall receive signal graces.
2. I promise My special protection and the greatest graces to all those who shall recite the Rosary.
3. The Rosary shall be a powerful armor against hell, it will destroy vice, decrease sin, and defeat heresies.
4. It will cause good works to flourish; it will obtain for souls the abundant mercy of God; it will withdraw the hearts of men from the love of the world and its vanities, and will lift them to the desire for Eternal Things. Oh, that souls would sanctify themselves by this means.
5. The soul which recommends itself to Me by the recitation of the Rosary shall not perish.
6. Whoever recites the Rosary devoutly, considering its Sacred Mysteries shall never be conquered by misfortune. He will not perish by an unprovided death; if he is just he shall remain in the grace of God and be worthy of Eternal Life.
7. Who shall be true to the Rosary shall not die without the Sacraments.

8. Those who are faithful to recite the Rosary shall have during their life and at their death the Light of God and the plentitude of His Graces; at the moment of death they shall participate in the Merits of the Saints in Paradise.

9. I shall deliver from purgatory those who have been devoted to the Rosary.

10. The faithful children of the Rosary shall merit a high degree of Glory in Heaven.

11. You shall obtain all you ask of Me by recitation of the Rosary.

12. All those who propagate the Holy Rosary shall be aided by Me in their necessities.

13. I have obtained from My Divine Son that all the advocates of the Rosary shall have for intercessors the entire Celestial Court during their life and at the hour of death.

14. All who recite the Rosary are My sons and daughters, and brothers and sisters of My only Son Jesus Christ.

15. Devotion to My Rosary is a great sign of predestination.

ITS PROMISED FULFILLMENT:

"In the end My Immaculate Heart will triumph, Russia will be converted, and there will be PEACE!"

- Our Lady of Fatima

THE ANGELUS

Recently in a Catholic paper there was an account of a South Seas native ringing a bell every morning, noon and evening. Since he was the only Catholic on the island, others asked him what was the meaning of his bell ringing. He said: "I am ringing the Angelus."

What is the Angelus? To some it means the beautiful painting of French peasants, a man and his wife, pausing during their work in the fields and bowing their heads in prayer. True, this is a beautiful painting worthy of all peoples admiration. But it is not the Angelus.

The Angelus is the Special Prayer which is to be said every morning, noon, and evening in memory of the adorable mystery of the Incarnation and to salute the Virgin Mary. It is a call to adore the Incarnate Word and to venerate the Blessed Virgin.

This prayer was introduced into the Catholic Church by the fervent and zealous client of the Blessed Mother, St. Bonaventure. It was this St. Bonaventure who during the General Chapter (a special meeting of monks) of the Franciscan Order held at Pisa in 1282 ordered his brethren Franciscans to ring the bell every morning to remind the faithful to honor the Incarnation of the Son of God and to salute the Virgin Mary. Later, various Popes approved and highly recommended this pious practice and enriched it with indulgences.

Today, all Christendom sings the praises of God in gratitude for the profound Mystery of the Incarnation of the Eternal God, and in honor of the virginal Maternity of the Blessed Virgin three times a day. Saying or singing the Angelus is an unceasing act of thanksgiving to God for the great gift of the Incarnation of His own Son. The Angelus Bell is rung in most churches at 6 A.M., 12 noon, and at 6 P.M. It reminds to say the Angelus. The bells don't pray for us.

How is the Angelus said? The following is the correct form for the Angelus. It would be highly profitable for all Catholics to learn this prayer and say it every day at the proper time.

> *The Angel of the Lord declared unto Mary. And She conceived by the Holy Spirit.*
>
> *"Hail Mary"......*
>
> *Behold the Handmaid of the Lord. Be it done unto me according to Thy word.*
>
> *"Hail Mary"......*
>
> *And the Word was made Flesh. (At these words genuflect if you are standing). And dwelt among us.*
>
> *"Hail Mary"......*
>
> *Pray for us, O holy Mother of God.*
> *That we may be made worthy of the promises of Christ.*
>
> *Let us pray; Pour forth, we beseech Thee, O Lord, Thy grace into our hearts; that, as we have known the Incarnation of Christ Thy Son by the message of an angel, so by His Passion and Cross we may be brought to the glory of His Resurrection. Through the same Christ Our Lord, Amen.*

At Easter Time the following is to be said:

> *Queen of Heaven, rejoice, Alleluia. For He Whom You didst merit to bear, Alleluia. Has risen as He said, Alleluia. Pray for us to God, Alleluia.*
>
> *Rejoice and be glad, O Virgin Mary, Alleluia. Because the Lord is truly risen, Alleluia.*
>
> *Let us Pray; O God, Who by the Resurrection of Thy Son, Our Lord Jesus Christ, hast vouchsafed to make glad the whole world; grant, we beseech Thee, that, through the intercession of*

the Virgin Mary, His Mother, we may lay hold of the joys of eternal life. Through the same Christ Our Lord. Amen.

Five "Hail Mary's" may be said instead of the above two prayers and the same indulgence of 10 years is gained for each time the Angelus is said. A plenary indulgence is gained under the usual conditions of confession and Holy Communion if this devout practice is continued for one month.

OUR LADY OF EVERYDAY

Safeguard our purity, safeguard our youth, safeguard our souls, safeguard our marriages... The following prayer is offered to all. Please recite it daily... better, commit it to memory and pray it daily. All will find consolation, strength and self-mastery through the help of Mary, the Virgin Mother of God, who desires our holiness and love.

I venerate Thee with all my heart, O Virgin most holy, above all angels and saints in Paradise, as the Daughter of the Eternal Father, and to Thee I consecrate my soul with all its powers.

"Hail Mary"......

I venerate Thee with all my heart, O Virgin most holy, above all angels and saints in Paradise, as the Mother of the only begotten Son, and to Thee I consecrate my body with all its senses.

"Hail Mary".......

I venerate Thee with all my heart, O Virgin most holy, above all angels and saints in Paradise, as the beloved Spouse of the Spirit of God, and to Thee I consecrate my heart and all its affections, imploring Thee to obtain for me from the Most Holy Trinity all the means of Salvation.

"Hail Mary".......

MEDITATION AID

Mary's Poverty

"Blessed are the poor in spirit, for theirs is the kingdom of Heaven."

Mk.5, 3.

Detachment from earthly possessions:

A. Our Lord was detached—poor
  1. poor birth
  2. Carpenter working with St. Joseph
  3. small home
  4. during public life—poor
B. Mary—perfect example of Christ
  1. She imitated Christ
  2. loved poverty and showed it
     a. Her gift to God at presentation
     b. given to poorest of Apostles
  3. Mary our example
     a. perfect example for us to follow.
     b. She knew riches belong to God
     c. She learned of poverty
     d. God giveth and He taketh

Mary Our Salvation

After the seven years of plenty in Egypt, came the seven years of famine. The people came to the Pharaoh for food. He sent them to Joseph. As the Egyptians came to him, they would say,"Our salvation is in thy hand." Gen. 47, 25.

To the Catholics all throughout the ages, the Blessed Virgin Mary was and is our salvation, for through Her came salvation Our Lord and Savior.

We call a person savior who saves us or liberates us from some evil. Our Lord Christ is the one necessary Savior of our soul. But also the Blessed Virgin Mary who imitated Christ in all things is our salvation, but a secondary one. She as Christ is interested in the welfare of our body and soul. She cooperated with Christ.

  1. Christ cured all kinds of sicknesses and afflictions. So has Mary. Look at the great shrines of Mary throughout the world. Thousands were cured there.
  2. Soul's troubles and illness. St. Francis De Sales and his temptations of the devil and his depression. Saints relied heavily upon Mary.

Mary's Charity

A. Love follows the knowledge of goodness: things good, liked and wanted; persons good, loved and wanted.
B. Mary's love for God was very great because Her knowledge of God was great.
  1. Studied about Him while in Temple.
  2. Angel of God told Her many truths.

3. Life with Christ taught Her much.
4. Had divine inspirations.

Thus knowing God more than others, Her love was far greater.

C. Being full of Grace from the first instant of Her life, She had a great abundance of the gifts of Faith, Hope and Charity. This love increased as She grew older for She saw and understood more about God.

D. This love of God was shown in Her love of neighbor:
   1. Visit with Elizabeth
   2. Concern at wedding of Cana
   3. To the Apostles, the first Christian was a great consolation and help and courage. She believed in Her Son.
   4. Offered Son as man's salvation

E. Incentive for us to love God and neighbor.

Mary's Humility

"Learn of Me, for I am meek and humble of heart."

A. Mary is a perfect copy of Jesus. As God, He humbled Himself and became man. Mother of God—remained in seclusion, silence, and humbleness as the servant of God.

B. Privileges of Mary—gifts—graces and honor.

C. No credit to Herself—the "Magnificat".

D. Her humility:
   1. Obscurity in life
   2. In background in Christ's life
   3. Silence and prayer
   4. Submission to the Jewish laws of purification and going to the Temple
   5. Seeing Christ suffer and die.

E. "Humility greater than Purity." St. Bernard. (Greatest works accomplished who is most humble and rests all hope and trust in God.) — St. Thomas Aquinas

F. Love of children as seen from Her earthly appearances.

MARY IN POETRY, ART AND MUSIC

Many poems have been composed concerning Our Blessed Mother and our love of Her. Among them is one which was a favorite of Bishop Fulton J. Sheen. He would enthrall his audiences with his most unique recitation of "Lovely Lady Dressed In Blue". Probably you have heard him on stage, on radio and or on television as he rendered his love of Mary and stimulated people to love Her. All who have heard the bishop recite this poem were moved by the words, by his expressions and by his love.

146

Lest you have not heard this poem or have not read it, it is presented here for your edification and awe. May Our Lady fascinate you to love Her Son and to love Her. She is not only the Mother of Jesus but She is our Mother too.

Lovely Lady dressed in Blue,
Teach me how to pray!
God was just Your little Boy,
Tell me what to say!
Did You lift Him up, sometimes,
Gently, on Your knee?
Did You sing to Him the way
Mother does to me?
Did You hold His hand at night?
Did You ever try
Telling stories of the world?
O! And did He cry?
Do You really think He cares
If I tell Him things —
Little things that happen? And
Do the angels' wings Make a noise? And
Can He hear me if I speak low?
Does He understand me now?
Tell me...for You know?
Lovely Lady dressed in blue,
Teach me how to pray!
God was just Your little Boy,
And You know the way.

The love of our Blessed Lady has been expressed and will be expressed by artists for many years. From the writings of St. Luke there arises the notion that he actually painted pictures of Mary and Jesus. Paintings of the Blessed Mother have come down to us from the earliest times. The Byzantine art dominated first and then came of art of the Renaissance. These painters produced master pieces which are admired today. The art galleries are full of paintings of the Mother of God.

Among some of the favorite paintings of the Blessed Mother are: Our Lady of Guadalupe, Our Lady of Perpetual Help, Our Lady of Czestochowa, and the many of the Italian artists. A visit to the art gallery of the Vatican will convince all of the great devotion artists had of the Mother of God.

Sculptors were busy carving statues out of wood, marble, stone and metal. They are beautiful works depicting Our Lady. Michelangelo's Pietá is considered one of the greatest works of art. There are many statues of Mary in the world. Most Catholic Churches like to have a statue of Mary even if it is made of plaster of paris or of plastic. These plastic statues have found their way into many homes and they form shrines for family devotions.

Today at weddings and even funerals, one song is very much in demand that is the AVE MARIA be it of Bach-Gounod or Schubert. The Lourdes Song is also most popular. One has but to look into any church music book and there he or she will find numerous compositions dedicated to Our Lady. These hymns are sung in every language.

"We want God, O Blessed Mary"..."Vogliamo Il Dio" is sung at many gatherings of devotees of the Blessed Mother. This is a stirring emotional hymn in a good tempo. It is sung in Italy, in Puerto Rico, Poland and in the United States and who knows where else. Because of its tempo and music it should be played by a band of 46 trombones and basses.

A custom in St. Vincent Seminary, Latrobe, Pa. the "Salve Regina" was sung daily. Recently in the diocese of Pittsburgh, the singing of the "Salve Regina" developed at the final farewell at priests' funerals.

— PART IV —

CONTROVERSIES CONCERNING THE BLESSED MOTHER AND HER POSITION IN THE SALVATION OF MANKIND AND THEIR SOLUTIONS

Our doctrines on the Blessed Mother came to us from the Scripture, Tradition of the living Church, Declarations of the Ecumenical Councils, the writings of the Fathers and the and the definitions of the Pope.

Time was needed to bring to the fore the truths of our Faith and of the doctrines of Jesus Christ and the Virgin Mary.

We thank God for the faith we have today. May this faith bring us to eternal glory.

THE IMMACULATE CONCEPTION

The doctrine of the Immaculate Conception does not pertain to Our Lord, but to His Mother, Our Blessed Lady. It pertains to the beginning of Her existence as is the beginning of each person's life.

Because of the sin of Adam and Eve, every person conceived by man and woman is in Original Sin. There is only ONE EXCEPTION and that special privilege is Mary, the Mother of Jesus. We have that original sin removed by Baptism whereby we come into the family of God and are filled with sanctifying grace.

It is only proper that Mary should be with out sin from the very beginning of Her conception because She was to bear the Savior of the world, the Son of God, Our Lord. It is fitting that She should never be under the power of the devil since She with Jesus was to crush the head of the serpent (Gen., chapter 3, verse 15). That idea is portrayed in art by having a serpent under Her feet. Jesus, the Son of God, should have and did have a Mother who was absolutely free from every stain of sin.

In the Gospel of St. Luke, chapter 2, verse 26, we read that Mary was full of grace. There is no restriction on Mary as to when She became full of grace or when She lost that grace. It is the teaching of the Church that She was always full of grace from the very first instance of Her conception, She remained full of grace while on earth and She is full of grace now that She is in Heaven.

There were scholastic debates as to the exact moment when She became full of Grace. This debate was to have taken place in Paris between St. Thomas Aquinas and Blessed Don Scotus. The secretary of Blessed Don Scotus writes in his record book that when Blessed Don Scotus and he were walking down the corridor to the auditorium for the debate, they paused at a statue of the Blessed Mother. Here Don Scotus looked up at Mary and said, "O Blessed Mother You will have to help me prove to all the world that You are the Immaculate Conception". Because of Scotus' argument, he is called the Father of the Doctrine of the Immaculate Conception.

This doctrine became an article of our Faith by the declaration by Pope Pius IX on December 8, 1854.

A few years later at Lourdes, the wonders of God are revealed when Our Blessed Lady appears to St. Bernadette Soubirous. During the multiple apparitions, Our Lady told Bernadette Her name, "I am the Immaculate Conception".

Already before that date in 1830 Our Lady appears to Catherine Laboure and asks for a medal to be stamped. This medal we call the Miraculous Medal. On it is printed at Mary's request, "O Mary conceived without sin, pray for us who have recourse to Thee". These same words are printed on the Green Scapular as She spoke to Catherine Brisqueburu.

The imagery of the Gospel of today is very interesting and pleasing. We all can imagine ourselves in Nazareth in the home of Mary, which was not more than a cave, and the Angel coming to Her and announcing the wonders of God. Of course, Mary did not understand the Angel. It was only after She knew that he came from God and had a message from God that She responded yes.

This yes, or Be it unto Me according to Thy will, the Latin word is Fiat - strange, the automobile produced in Italy and in Poland, which is to respond at one's command, is called Fiat. The yes was given to God as a willing, free acceptance of His will. The first point to remember of this Gospel is Mary's submission to the will of God.But before Mary submits to the will of God the Angel announces to Her that She is full of grace. Being full of grace means that She was free from sin. Freedom of sin is freedom of bondage. The purpose of Christ is to free man from the bondage and slavery of sin. It was Moses' job to bring the Jews out of the bondage of slavery. The new Moses, Jesus, is to free us from the bondage of sin and He needs a human Mother to come into this world. In view of Mary's willingness to submit to God's will, God gave Her freedom of the bondage and slavery of sin. Consequently, She was free. Her freedom was to be used in a correct way and She does this by affirming life and saying yes to God. The whole purpose of Christian life is to affirm God's reality and life. God is real, God is life, God is love. Because Mary in Her freedom accepts to be the Mother of God, She is called the Spouse of Church. Christ unites Himself with the people of this earth through Baptism in particular, and He says, "Whatever you do unto the least of these, you do unto Me", consequently the Church is called the Spouse of Christ. Mary, therefore, is the image of the Church. She is a symbol of the Church.

A lesson for us from this Gospel and from Mary is this: Freedom from sin is a freedom to love, to affirm God in His reality, to affirm life and love; therefore, it is our duty to profess our faith in God and to love life, to want to be alive, to want to be spiritually alive, free from the bondage of sin, to promote life in every form and, above all, in imitation of Mary. We should, once we know that this is the will of God, to say as She did "Fiat - Be it done to me according to Thy Will."

IMMACULATE CONCEPTION WINDOW...
AN EXPLANATION IN ART

A special stained glass window of the Immaculate Conception is the execution of a most ingenious idea of the artist. This window as the rest of our windows are worthy of study and appreciation. (Church of St. Ignatius de Loyola, Carnegie, Pennsylvania)

The artist has combined many ideas in this portrayal of the Blessed Virgin. He combines the facial features of Our Lady of Lourdes and the clothing of Our Lady of Guadalupe. He features ideas obtained from the Books of Genesis - Chapter 3, Verse 15..."The serpent under Her feet...and of the Apocalypse, Chapter 2...The moon under Her feet and upon Her head a crown of 12 stars."

"The Lord possessed Me in the beginning", is the identifying inscription signifying Mary was in the mind of God from the beginning, because God knew mankind and his proneness to sin. As soon as Adam and Eve turned their backs on God and through pride chose a creature in place of the Creator, God came upon the scene and dealt the punishments to Adam, to Eve and to the serpent. But God gave mankind HOPE in the promise of a Redeemer Who would be born of Mary.

It is really Jesus Who completely crushes the head of the serpent, but Mary is His cooperator and worked with Her Son for the redemption of mankind. Consequently the idea came to have Mary stand on the head of the serpent and thus crush him and his wicked power. Some old texts of that passage in Genesis 3, 15, have "She shall crush the head of the serpent"...meaning the power of the devil will be conquered.

Although the interpretation of Chapter 12 of the book of the Apocalypse pertains to the CHURCH as the woman, non-the-less this passage is accommodated to the Blessed Mother.

Many symbols are used to signify ideas concerning Mary. The Halo means She is all holy. The twelve stars signify She is Queen. Roses tell us of the MYSTICAL ROSE, (Mary often appears with roses). Angels are depicted because an angel appeared to Her at the Annunciation and She was taken up to Heaven by the angels. In the painting at Guadalupe we see the head bowed and the eyes lowered, signifying Her humility of which She Herself says (Luke 1, beginning with verse 46)..."Because He has regarded the lowliness of His Handmaid".

The garments of the Blessed Mother as painted in our church window are similar to that of the painting at Guadalupe, where Mary appeared as the MOTHER OF THE AMERICAS. Because of this appearance, Mexico became Catholic and the loyal Mexican still remains loyal to Mary. This window deserves study and should command our attention most often. By study and knowledge of the Blessed Mother as to who She is, we should have a greater appreciation and love of Our Blessed Mother. This love will bring us to a deep devotion of Mary, to a frequent calling Her to our minds, to a desire to imitate Her and look to Her for direction. May She lead us, Her children, to live in glory with Jesus, Her Son, forever.

QUEEN CONCEIVED WITHOUT ORIGINAL SIN

THE CONTROVERSY: It is rather difficult to state in what year or century the Feast of the Immaculate Conception was first celebrated. By the seventh century, it was well known in the East and some writers claim it was celebrated already in Spain. But already St. Andrew of Crete who died about 720 wrote liturgical hymns for the feast while George of Nicomedia in 860 wrote that the feast was not of recent origin. Some authors claim that the feast was already celebrated in the East as early as the second century. Definitely the feast was established in the east by the seventh century.

In the West, the Feast of the Immaculate Conception is first noticed in the eleventh century as celebrated in the Anglo-Saxon monasteries. The attempts to bring the feast officially into the Church brought much discussion for many centuries. The arguments really got started when Anselm the Younger in 1240 personally introduced the feast into the choir which was called an innovation of honoring Mary. St.Bernard published a protest. He claimed that they should consult the Holy See on this matter and not act upon their own authority. From the tenor of his letter we see that St. Bernard refuted the immaculate conception of the flesh and held that the sanctification came after the conception.

Many great men were added to this controversy such as St. Peter Damian, Peter Lombard, Alexander of Hales, St. Bonaventure, and Albert the Great. Even St. Thomas was not certain. At first, he writes in favor of it then later he concludes against it. St. Thomas' great difficulty seems to have been this: how could She be redeemed without having sinned. Although St. Thomas Aquinas did not really oppose the doctrine, he did not teach it either. To him, only Jesus Christ was born without original sin but to the Blessed Virgin and all other men the original sin is due them and only by the consideration of Christ is one sanctified.

TRADITION: Every lover of God has a great love and respect for the Mother of God. This is seen in all ages beginning with the Apostles and continuing up unto the present. In their love for the Blessed Virgin, the great early lovers of God, the Fathers of the Church, often extolled Her.

In professing the sanctity of the Blessed Mother, the Father's love revolved about these points:
1. Her absolute purity and Her comparison with Eve. They called Her "the tabernacle exempt from defilement and corruption; immaculate of the immaculate, most complete sanctity, perfect justice, a virgin immune through grace from every stain of sin" (Ambrose, "sermo xxii in Ps. cxviii); a virgin innocent, holy in body and in soul, and many other such epithets.
2. In an epistle dealing with the sufferings and death of the Apostle, St. Andrew we read, "As the first man was created from the spotless earth, so was it necessary that the perfect Man (Christ) should be born of an Immaculate Virgin".

    St. Augustine, the great Doctor of the Church writes, "except for Holy Virgin Mary of Whom for the honor of the Lord, I will have no question whatsoever where sin is concerned".
3. The Syrian Fathers never tired of praising the Blessed Virgin. St. Ephraem could not find words too good for eulogizing Her. He writes: "Most holy Lady, Mother of God, alone most pure in soul and body, alone exceeding all perfections of purity...all pure, all immaculate...alone most immaculate".

4. St. Amphilochus wrote, "He who created the first Eve free from shame, created a second without spot or stain".
5. St. Bernard calls the Blessed Mother, "An enclosed garden, where the sinner's hand never entered to rob it of its flowers".
6. St. John Damascene wrote, "the serpent had no entrance to this paradise".

The arguments of the 13th and latter centuries were greatly due to the lack of clear understanding of the subject. Even the word "conception" was not well defined.

It was the Blessed Duns Scotus, the celebrated Franciscan who is known as the father of the doctrine of the Immaculate Conception, who laid the true foundations for the doctrine. He showed that the sanctification after animation should follow in order of nature and not of time and he removed the difficulty of St. Thomas of Her being excluded from redemption by the mystery of preservation from all sin through the redemption.

These arguments Duns Scotus presented to the gathering of many cardinals, bishops, priests, scholars, and lay men at Paris. This meeting was called by the Pope for a public discussion on the Immaculate Conception which doctrine attained much pro and con. There is a legend about Duns Scotus at this time which says that as he was going to the conclave, he passed a statue of the Blessed Virgin. Kneeling down before the statue, he gazed at Her and prayed, "O Mary, help me to prove to the world that You are the Immaculate Conception". The status then bowed its head in reverential approval.

Although the doctrine of Duns Scotus became the opinion of the universaries, yet it had its opposition in the Dominicans who held on to the teaching of St. Thomas Aquinas. In the year 1439 a dispute was brought before the Council of Basle. Here the University of Paris which opposed the doctrine formerly now openly professes it and asks for a dogmatic definition. After that council, the bishops declared the Immaculate Conception to be a doctrine pious, consonant with Catholic worship, Catholic faith, right reason, and Holy Scriptures and they prohibited any preaching to the contrary.

On February 29, 1476 Pope Sixtus IV by decree adopted the Feast for the universal church and granted indulgences to all who assisted at its Divine Office. In 1483, the same Pope punished with excommunication all those of either side of the controversy who charged the opposite opinion as heresy.

Since the Council of Trent did not decree on the Immaculate Conception, the controversy continued. Pope Paul V in 1617 helped to conclude the argument which was kept alive by the Dominicans by decreeing that no one should dare to teach publicly that Mary was conceived in original sin. Pope Gregory V in 1622 imposed absolute silence upon the question of the doctrine until the Holy See should define the question. To prevent any further discussion of the doctrine, Pope Alexander VII on December 8, 1661 issues his letter "Sollicitudo Omnium Ecclesiarum" in which he defined the true meaning of the word "conception" and forbade all further discussion against the common and pious sentiment of the Church. The object of the feast is the immunity from original sin in the first moment of the creation of the soul and its infusion into the body he declared.

The discussion of course was finally ended by the De Fide definition of the doctrine by Pope Pius IX on December 8, 1854.

The Holy See was besieged with petitions from all parts of the world for an official pronouncement upon this question. The universal sentiment of the Church had crystallized concerning the Immaculate Conception. The demands so grew that Pope Pius IX thought it time for the definition. He sent a circular letter on February 2, 1849 to all the bishops requesting them to send the reports of the devotion of their clergy and laity concerning the Immaculate Conception. Five hundred bishops replied in favor of the Blessed Virgin and besought the Pope to raise this devotion to a dogma.

It was on December 8, 1854 that the Holy Father, amidst all the splendor of Rome, most solemnly read the Bull "Ineffabilis Deus" proclaiming and establishing that "We define the doctrine which holds that the Blessed Virgin Mary, in the first instant of her conception, was by a singular grace and privilege of Almighty God, on account of the merits of Jesus Christ, the Savior of the human race, preserved from every stain of original sin and this is revealed by God and therefore must firmly and constantly be believed by all the faithful".

In explaining this definition the theologians state:

1. "First instant of her conception means that moment when the soul which was created by God was infused into the body of the Blessed Virgin'."
2. "Conception" here means the end of the generating act, that is the produced human fetus, and not the marital act.
3. "Singular grace and privilege of Almighty God" means that above all others God loved Mary and not by Her merit but through His free gift through a miraculous act: He made this privilege, that is, the only exemption from the universal law.
4. "Through the merits of Jesus Christ", that is, She was freed from sin due of contracting original sin by preserving Her from it; it was excluded from Her and it never was in Her.
5. "Preserved from every stain of original sin" means that with the exclusion of sin, She was in the state of original grace, justice and innocence.

THE IMMACULATE CONCEPTION: Excitement captured an entire village. Soon it spread to the countryside and engulfed the whole nation of France. Thousands upon thousands of people were crowding their way to a cove along the banks of the Gave River. The little peaceful town of Lourdes in southern France was no longer quiet. It was full of people and activity. The cause of this activity and excitement were the apparitions of the Blessed Mother to a little girl by the name of Bernardette Soubirous.

Bernardette was fourteen years old when she received the special favor from God to see the Blessed Mother. This young girl of poor French parents went out with a couple of girls on the February 17, 1858. The girls waded across the water leaving little Bernardette at the bank. Just then as she was alone, she was startled by seeing a most lovely Lady in a grotto of the nearby rocks. This beautiful Lady was surrounded by a halo of bright light. This Lady was clothed in a pure white robe, with a blue girdle around Her waist, and a long white veil on Her head. A Rosary of white beads hung from Her right hand. The cross of the Rosary was of gold. This Lady smiled to Bernardette. This was the first appearance.

There were at least eighteen appearances of the Blessed Mother on that same spot during the year of 1858. Crowds of people gathered there at the cove to witness the appearances, but only Bernardette was able to see the Blessed Mother. On one of the visits of the Virgin, on March 25, the Feast of the Annunciation, upon repeated petitions by the little girl, the Lady answered, "I am the Immaculate Conception".

There was no doubt after these words were heard as to the identity of the Lady who as appearing at Lourdes. The Blessed Mother came with her message to Bernardette who was to spread the devotion of Mary. To prove beyond doubt that She really appeared there, countless miracles were performed at Lourdes. Even to this very day miracles occur there. Mary, the Immaculate Conception, is honored greatly at Lourdes.

DOGMATIC PROOF: The Sacred Scriptures do not contain any explicit statements concerning the Immaculate Conception, but it does contain implicit statements. These statements in the light of tradition most certainly persuade the acceptance of the dogma of the Immaculate Conception. The first Scriptural passage for this dogma is from the Book of Genesis, Chapter 3, verse 14: "I will put enmity between thee and the Woman, and thy seed and Her seed: he shall crush thy head, and thou shalt lie in wait for his heel". These are the words of God Who is on the scene judging Adam, Eve, and the serpent immediately after the fall.

The Church from all times interpreted this passage to mean that Mary, the Woman and Her seed, who is Christ, have a constant enmity between the serpent who is the devil and his seed which is sin and sinners and will triumph over the devil and sin.

Using this passage to support them, the theologians proceed to argue thus: the same enmity exists between the Blessed Virgin Mary and the devil as exists between Christ and the devil. But the enmity between Christ and the devil is absolute, perpetual, and essential. Therefore the enmity between the Blessed Virgin and the devil is absolute, perpetual, and essential. But this could not be true if the Blessed Virgin was for a moment through the original sin subjected to the devil. Therefore it is true that from the very beginning of Her conception She was free from original sin.

The victory of the Blessed Mother over the devil is the same as the victory of Christ. But Christ's victory over the devil was perfect. Therefore also the victory of the Blessed Virgin Mary over the devil was perfect which requires that the Blessed Mother be immune from original sin. Again this would have been impossible if She were for the smallest moment under the taint of original sin.

This same argument is presented by Pope Pius IX in his famous Bull the "Ineffabilis Deus": "The most holy Virgin, being joined with Christ by a most close and indissoluble bond, with Him and through Him held an everlasting enmity against the venomous serpent and from His plentitude She triumphantly crushed his head with Her immaculate heel."

The Archangel Gabriel comes to help us out in this question, too, for we read in the Gospel according to St. Luke, Chapter 1, verse 28: "Hail full of grace, the Lord is with You, blessed art You among Woman. " The "full of grace" admits no restrictions of grace. This means a plenitude of grace intensively and extensively. Therefore there was never a moment when the Blessed Virgin was devoid of grace. This could not be true if for a slightest moment She was under the stain of original sin.

Even the enemies of the Catholic Church have to recognize the immaculate purity of the Blessed Mother. Luther wrote, "One could not say to Her, 'Blessed Art You', if She had at anytime been subject to malediction". Zwingli, too, called Mary the: "Eternal Pure Maid".

Reason helps to convince us of the Immaculate Conception of the Blessed Virgin Mary. It is most fitting that Christ should be born from a Mother most pure and immaculate, that She would be worthy of His Sanctity and that She should be preserved from the original sin since She was to be the Cooperatrix in the work of Redemption. Too, the Most Holy Trinity should not permit a Person who was so intimately connected with the Holy Trinity to have anything displeasing in Her.

St. Thomas Aquinas gives a very logical explanation for the Immaculate Conception. He says (111 q.27, a 4.) "Those whom God chooses for anything, so prepares and dispositions them, that to what they were chosen, they are found suitable". But the Blessed Virgin was divinely selected to be the Mother of God. Therefore we cannot doubt that God did make Her suitable for the task. The Mother of God would not have been suitable if She would have sinned at anytime.

THEOLOGICAL CONCLUSIONS: The Blessed Mother never committed an actual sin, neither mortal nor venial. The Council of Trent openly made this proposition. This impeccability was caused from the special privilege of God by granting Her the plentitude of grace.

The grace given to the Blessed Virgin was greater than that given to any other creature because the dignity of the divine maternity is greater than any received by angels or men.

Grace was increased in Mary through the reception of the sacraments. Probably She received baptism although She needed not to be baptized, She surely received the Holy Eucharist and was Confirmed. Also grace was gained because of the Incarnation and through good works She performed.

The Blessed Virgin experienced no motion of concupiscence since concupiscence is a result of original sin.

O, Mary, most pure and holy, help us to live in the love of God, help us to avoid sin and help us to gain more grace by the frequent reception of sacraments.

Hail, holy Queen, mother of mercy,
our life, our sweetness, and our hope.
To you do we cry,
poor banished children of Eve.
To you do we send up our sighs,
mourning and weeping in this vale of tears.
Turn then, most gracious advocate,
your eyes of mercy toward us,
and after this exile
show to us the blessed fruit of your womb, Jesus.
O clement, O loving,
O sweet Virgin Mary.

Loving mother of the Redeemer,
gate of heaven, star of the sea,
assist your people who have fallen
    yet strive to rise again.
To the wonderment of nature you bore your Creator,
yet remained a virgin after as before.
You who received Gabriel's joyful greeting,
have pity on us poor sinners.

The Memorare

Remember, O most gracious Virgin Mary, that never was it known that any one who fled to thy protection, implored thy help, or sought thy intercession, was left unaided. Inspired with this confidence, I fly unto thee, O Virgin of virgins, my Mother. To thee I come; before thee I stand, sinful and sorrowful. O Mother of the Word Incarnate, despise not my petitions; but in thy clemency hear and answer me.

Amen.

    Because Mary gave birth to Jesus, She has to be the most important of all Mothers because of Whom She gave birth. No son, born of a woman, could be of greater dignity and importance than Jesus. It is because of Jesus that Mary receives all her honor and distinction. Being the "Mother of Mothers" is one of Her signs of glory.

    All mothers do well to imitate Our Blessed Lady, a very noble act of love. Mary lived a total submission to the Will of God. "Behold Thy Handmaid, be it done to me according to Thy Will." Every mother should glory in bringing a child into the world for she cooperates with God in an act of creation and gives her offspring an opportunity to know God, love Him, and to be with Him for all eternity. She gives him a chance to see and enjoy God's creation in all its beauty and goodness. It is good to be alive. But it is better to gain Heaven. Mothers should rejoice in seeing their children grow to the knowledge and love of God, live a good moral and religious life, and have the assurance they will live in Heaven.

O Mary, help all mothers to rejoice in their children. Bring both mother and child to the glories God prepared for all who love Him.

MARY THE MOTHER OF GOD CONTROVERSY

All of us Catholics most readily believe that the Blessed Virgin Mary is truly the Mother of God. The slightest suspicion against this truth does not even enter into our minds. The Gospels openly teach that the Blessed Mother gave birth to Jesus Who is true God and man. This is the precise teaching of the Church. That the Blessed Mother is the true Mother of God is a truth which Catholics cannot deny without falling into heresy. Knowing all this, we wonder how anyone could doubt the Divine Maternity of the Blessed Virgin Mary.

Yet, the Divine Maternity of the Blessed Mother was not only doubted but even denied in the early centuries of Christianity and it is also denied today. All who deny the divinity of Jesus Christ will also deny the Divine Maternity of the Blessed Virgin. Among the moderns are many of the so called Christians who refuse to admit that Jesus is God. In the older days. in the fourth and fifth centuries, there were some who denied this prerogative of the Blessed Virgin. This group of heretics were called Nestorians after their leader.

Nestorius was the Metropolitan bishop of Constantinople. He came from the school of Antioch which stressed the humanity of Jesus Christ. Since all the theological terms which we have today were not yet coined, this school made up its own. The difficulty here was the explanation of the Incarnation. Just what was the relation between the humanity of Christ to His divinity?

Diodor, one of the teachers in this school, tried to explain it as the indwelling of one nature in the other as the indwelling of a statue that is placed in a temple. His student, Theodore, called this union a moral union as exists between the husband and his wife who are "two in one flesh". Others of that school called it a permanent union but refused to admit a complete unity of both the divine nature and human nature in one person.

Therefore, they could not see their way through to call Mary the Mother of God, but only the Mother of Christ although the term Mother of God was already applied to the Virgin Mary by Origin, a second century father of the Church. Nestorius, being the student of Theodore, followed his teacher in denying the Divine Maternity of the Blessed Mother and proclaiming that She was only the Mother of Christ's humanity.

One year after he became the Patriarch of Constantinople in 429, Nestorius began to preach publicly against the word "Mother of God" (Theotokos). During his first year as the court bishop to Emperor Theodosius II, Nestorius made a reputation for himself as a great preacher and defender of the Catholic

Church. He even persecuted heretics. Now with his reputation made, he attacks the usage of the words "Mother of God" and orders his priests to preach against it. A certain layman by the name of Eusebius opposed the bishop in his teaching and later a group of people organized against the bishop, took the name of "Mother of God" as a test for all true Catholic orthodoxy and appealed to St. Cyril of Alexandria to defend them against Nestorius. His statement that, "if Mary is called the Mother of God, it means that She is a goddess and such an opinion must be condemned by the Catholic Church, aroused the people against him.

St. Cyril submitted the controversy to the Pope. Pope Celestine called a synod in Rome and thereafter examining the whole affair condemned Nestorius and threatened him with excommunication. St. Cyril was to see to it that the Constantinople Bishop would recant. Nestorius refused and counter charged St. Cyril of the heresy of Apollinarism, which stressed the Divinity of Christ to the neglect of His humanity.

To settle this controversy Emperor Theodosius II invited bishops to meet in council at Ephesus for the feast of Pentecost 431. Pope Celestine sent his delegates with a letter stating that the Council was only to confirm what had already been decided upon in Rome in 430.

The Council of Ephesus was not a quiet one. Nestorius and his partisan bishops refused to meet with St. Cyril and his group of bishops. St. Cyril and his group meet in a Cathedral dedicated to the Blessed Mother and there they condemned Nestorius and his teaching and excommunicated him unanimously. The whole city celebrated the event in the evening "with parades and fireworks". However the Council was not over, for Candidian, the Emperor's representative, declared the session invalid. Two more sessions were held and the outcome was sent to the Emperor and the people of Constantinople. But Nestorius also sent messages which appeared that he was right and St. Cyril wrong. Since the roads were blocked by Candidian and Nestorius's men, the others of the Council had to dispatch an old man who would not be suspected and had him carry the message in a hollow cane to the Emperor who accepted their decisions and the doctrines of Christ being one person in two natures and the word "Theotokos" which means Mother of God.

The important canon passed by this Council in 431 and then approved again in 451 at the Council of Chalcedon and in 553 at the Second Council of Constantinople pertaining to the Mother of God is this one: "If anyone does not profess that the Emmanuel is truly God, and therefore the Blessed Virgin is the Mother of God, let him be an anathema".(Can.l). The Council of Constantinople states in Canon 6:" If anyone says that the Blessed Glorious ever Virgin Mary is abusively or not truly the Mother of God, let him be an anathema".

The Council of Ephesus and the Council of Chalcedon settled the Catholic question once and for all about the doctrine of the Mother of God and the Person of Christ. From then on we know exactly and we believe that the two natures of Christ, the divine and the human, are intimately united into one Person who is the Divine Son of God, the Second Person of the Blessed Trinity. This same Son of God was born in time of the Blessed Virgin Mary, the glorious Mother of God.

The Catholic Church gives proof for the truth that the Blessed Virgin is the Mother of God by giving arguments from Holy Scripture, from the living faith of the Church which we call Tradition, and from natural reason.

THE ARGUMENT FROM HOLY SCRIPTURE: It is a universal accepted fact that the woman is said to be the mother of the child which she had conceived and to whom she gave birth. But the Gospels clearly state that the Blessed Mother did conceive and gave birth to Christ Who is truly the Son of God. Therefore She is the Mother of God.

The following is the account of the conception of Our Lord in the Virginal Womb of the Blessed Virgin. "And in the sixth month, the Angel Gabriel was sent from God into a city of Galilee, called Nazareth to a Virgin engaged to a man whose name was Joseph, of the house of David; and the Virgin's name was Mary." (Read for yourself St. Luke 1, 26-39.)

Even St. Joseph did not know at first that the Holy Spirit, the active principle in the Incarnation to show God's love for man, activated and fertilized the Virgin Mary by His supernatural overshadowing. St. Matthew describes this very well. Now the generation of Christ was in this wise." (Read for yourself. Matt. 1, 18-25.)

Even before Jesus was born, the Blessed Virgin is called the Mother of the Lord by St. Elizabeth who was inspired by the Holy Spirit. "And Elizabeth was filled with the Holy Spirit and she cried out with a loud voice, and said: 'Blessed art thou among Woman, and blessed is the fruit of Thy womb. And whence is this to me, that the Mother of my Lord should come to me'?" (St. Luke 1, 41-43)

There should be no question as to the identity of the Mother of Jesus. St.Luke very explicitly states that Mary is the Mother of Jesus. The narration of the Nativity proves this. (Read Chapter 2 from verse 4 to verse 18).

Then again in verse 51 chapter 8, St. Luke calls Mary the Mother of Jesus: "And He went down with them, and came to Nazareth, and was subject to them. And His Mother kept all these words in Her heart."

The Person whom Mary brought into this world is truly the Son of God. If any one denies that Jesus Christ is God, that person does not know the Gospels nor has he ever heard the convincing evidence presented therein for the divinity of Christ. The whole Gospel was written for that purpose as St. John says most emphatically, "But these are written, that you may believe that Jesus is the Christ, the Son of God; and that believing, you may have life in His name". (St.John 20, 31).

SECOND ARGUMENT FROM SACRED SCRIPTURES: The same person was born in time of the Blessed Virgin Mary as was generated from eternity by God the Father. But the Son of God, the Word of God is generated by God the Father from all eternity. Therefore He who is born in time of the Blessed Virgin is the Son of God and consequent the Blessed Virgin Mary is the Mother of God

St. Paul in the Epistle to the Galatians states, (v.4): "But when the fullness of time was come, God sent His Son, made of a Woman, made under the law".

This "made of a Woman", explained St. Bede, is rightly used because Christ takes His body from the body of His Mother and not from nothing.

TRADITION PROVE THE DIVINE MAJESTY OF THE BLESSED VIRGIN: From Apostolic times the faithful always believed that the Blessed Virgin was the Mother of God, the Mother of Jesus Christ. That fact is stated in all the Professions of Faith and Creeds. The Apostles Creed contains this truth and so does the Nicene Creed. The early fathers of the Church wrote of this fact. St. Alexander of Alexandria used the word "Theotokos", Mother of God, already in about 316. Finally St. Cyril of Alexandria settles the question of the Divine eternity in the Council of Ephesus and which settlement was confirmed in the Council of Chalcedon in 553. From that day on all Catholics must believe this truth of the Divine Maternity of the Blessed Virgin Mary; otherwise they are heretics.

REASON AIDS OUR PROOF: Our reason argues in favor of the Divine Maternity of the Blessed Virgin in this way: A person is born and not some kind of nature; but the person to whom the Blessed Virgin Mary gave birth is God, for Jesus is the Son of God subsisting in the human nature; therefore, we truly and properly say that the Blessed Virgin Mary is the Mother of God.

St. Thomas Aquinas comes to our reason's help by saying, "If anyone wishes to say that the Blessed Virgin should not be called the Mother of God because from Her was not taken the Divinity of Christ but only His body, then by this he shows his ignorance. For by this is a Woman called the Mother of Someone, that His whole being is taken from Her. For a man consists in the union of body and soul and more so is a man a man, because of the soul than because of the body. The soul however is in no way taken from the mother for it is created immediately by God. Thus therefore, the mother of anyone is the mother from whom his body is taken. Thus, the Blessed Mother is the Mother of God, for from Her is taken the body of God".(Com.Theol.c.222)

CONCLUSIONS DRAWN FROM THE THESIS:

1. Although all three Divine Persons do all thing together, yet we attribute certain tasks to an Individual Person because of His prerogatives. Because the Holy Spirit is the sign of God's love to man, to Him it is attributed as the Active Principle Who fertilized the Virgin Mary by overshadowing Her and by which action She conceived.
2. The Divine Maternity is an infinite dignity because Christ, the God-man, the fruit of Her maternity, is infinite. St. Thomas states, "The Blessed Virgin because She is the Mother of God, has a certain infinite dignity from the infinite Good, Who is God; and on account of this She cannot do anything better just as there cannot be anything better than God".
3. The Divine Maternity is the root and final cause of all the grace and privileges which were given Her. God selected Her to this special office and it was necessary that He gave Her all the graces and privileges in order that She could fulfill Her office.

QUESTIONS CONCERNING OUR BLESSED LADY, MARY, THE MOTHER OF GOD

WHAT IS UNDERSTOOD BY THE VIRGIN BIRTH?

This is the doctrine which states that Jesus was born of Virgin Mary without prejudice to Her virginity. We consider Mary's Virginity under three aspects:

1. Mary a virgin before the birth of Jesus:

Both St. Luke and Matthew testify to this: Luke Chapter 1, v. 34 "Know not man". The Angel informs Mary, "the Holy Spirit shall come upon Thee and the power of the most High shall overshadow Thee, and therefore, the Holy One shall be born of Thee shall be called the Son of God". St. Matthew writes in Chapter 1, 18-25 that Mary was with Child from the Holy Spirit before She and Joseph came to live together. The Angel informs Joseph what had happened. St. Matthew then quotes the Isaian prophecy "Behold, a Virgin shall be with Child and give birth to a Son and they shall call His name Emmanuel". Matt. 1, 23. The early Fathers of the Church confirm this truth and this truth is part of the Apostles Creed.

2. Mary remains a virgin during the birth of Jesus.

Matt. 1, 23 "Behold a Virgin shall be with Child and give birth to a Son.." means that She will remain a virgin though bearing a Son. The Apostles' Greed also has this meaning. The interpretation of Ezechiel 44, 2 refers to Mary and Her virginity. Tradition claims there was no childbirth pain. St. John Dmascus testifies the faith of the Greeks as "no pleasure preceded this delivery, no birth throes accompanied it".

3. Mary remained a virgin after the birth of Christ.

Council of Constantinople 553 incorporated "ever virgin" into the Creed. Lateran Council of 649 declared Her perpetual virginity: "If anyone refused to confess, in accordance with the Holy Fathers, that Mary was properly speaking and of a truth the Holy Mother of God and always an Immaculate Virgin.. ..that She conceived of the Holy Spirit without seed and gave birth without corruption, Her virginity remaining inviolate also after parturition, let him be anathema" The sixth Ecumenical Council of Constantinople 680 decreed: "The virginity of Mary...remained before, daring and after parturition."

BROTHERS OF JESUS.... Matt. 13, 55... "Is not His mother called Mary, and His brethren (brothers) James and Joseph and Simon and Jude? And His sisters, are they not all with us?"

Read these Passages: Matt. 12, 46; 13, 55; Mk. 3, 31; 6,3; Lk. 8, 20; John 2, 12; 7, 3; Acts 1, 14; Gal. 1, 19. Why did Jesus bequeath His mother to John - "Son, behold thy Mother" to take care of Her if She had other children? This would be an affront to their obligation and duty. Strange, the brothers of Jesus are never called the sons of Mary. Jesus alone is called the Son of Mary. Could they be the children of St. Joseph through a previous marriage? This idea has been refuted ever since the time of St. Jerome, because the universal Christian belief is and has been that St. Joseph, like his holy Spouse, abstained from carnal intercourse throughout his life. The simple explanation of "brothers" as used in both Testaments is a synonym for kinsman. These brothers could be the relatives of Mary. St. James the Less, who is Called "the brother of the Lord" was a son of Cleopas and Mary and not of Joseph and Mary. St. Jude was probably a cousin of Our Lord.

Problems: "Before They came together....." means dwelled together under the same roof. Even if the term were used in the sense of marital intercourse, St. Jerome states that "before They came together" does not follow that They came together afterwards. Scripture merely intimates what did not happen.

Joseph know Her not "till".....the word till does refer to what has happened and not what will happen.

"First born" denotes a mother's first born child no matter whether it is followed by others or remains the only one. St. Jerome points this out in his writing.

The Fathers regarded the denial of the perpetual virginity which is so rooted in tradition as an insult to Our Lord Himself.

St. Thomas Aquinas lists these reasons for the perpetual virginity:
1. The unique character of Christ as the only begotten Son of God.
2. The honor and dignity of the Holy Spirit, Who overshadowed Her virginal womb.
3. The excellency of the title of Mother of God.
4. The honor and chivalry of St. Joseph, who was commissioned to be the protector and guardian of his chaste Spouse.

Surely, St. Joseph knew who his Wife was and who lived in Her womb for nine months and therefore his honor and dignity would not permit him to enter where the Son of God lived. Out of respect for God and Mary he honored Her, guarded Her and respected Her.

WHY WAS JESUS BORN OF A MARRIED WOMAN INSTEAD OF A SINGLE MAIDEN?

1. She needed a guardian, protector and breadwinner.
2. to prevent Her being accused of adultery or even killed as an adulteress.
3. to give Jesus a natural family rearing and the whole family to be an example of family life for us.
4. to even deceive the devil in thinking that Jesus was only human.

The Blessed Virgin Mary is our Mother.....this under a five-fold title:

1. By our relationship with Christ, because She is the Mother of the Son of God, Who became our brother according to the human nature and Who according to Grace adopted us to be the sons of God and to be His brothers.
2. By the title of Cooperation in our salvation, for by giving us the Son, She gave us supernatural life.
3. By the title of Consent given by Mary in place of the whole human nature to that supernatural marriage which the Son of God by His incarnation, began with human nature.
4. By the title of Love and Solicitude for our Salvation. In Her love and solicitude for us She has given us the Rosary, Scapulars, and the Miraculous Medal; She has appeared countless times to individuals and personally comforted them or corrected them; She has appeared at places such as Lourdes, Fatima, La Salette, Guadalupe, etc.
5. By the title of Heredity, because at the moment of death on the Cross, Christ gave Her to us in the person of St. John.

Woman, behold Thy Son, and Son, behold thy Mother" Jn. 19, 26-27 were the words uttered by Christ Who gave Mary to us as Our Mother. The Holy Church inspired by the Holy Spirit always held that St. John represented, at that moment, all the redeemed of Christ and that in giving His Mother to St. John, Christ gave Her to all men.

SPECIAL DIGNITY OF THE BLESSED MOTHER:

1. She claims the one and same Son as the Father. She, who is the Adopted Daughter of God, becomes the Mother of His Son and obtains for Herself the title of Lady, that is, "in becoming the Mother of the Creator, She became the Mistress of all His creatures". (St.John Damascus, De Fide Orthod, 4, 14.)
2. In relation to the Son, the Son is the true Son of His Heavenly Father and of His earthly Mother.
3. In relation to the Holy Spirit, She is the Spouse of God. There are reasons why we honor the Blessed Virgin. This special honor and love is called Hyperdulia, which means the greatest veneration given to a human. Dulia or veneration is that respect and love we give to all the other saints.

Our Hyperdulia is expressed in many forms of expression of our love, respect, and honor...our prayers, our devotions, our veneration of the icons and statues of Mary, the Marian shrines and processions, the use of the devotional such as Rosaries, medals, Scapulars, pendants, etc., the Angelus, hymns, Office or Breviary of the Blessed Virgin Mary.

The "Hail Mary" recited or sung is a favorite form of our love of Mary. Our love of the Mother of God is expressed in many ways because it is easy and fitting for us to love Mary and to tell Her we love Her. Our love is reciprocal for the love She has for us, Her children under Whose protection Christ placed us.

O Mary, Our Mother, take care of us, Your children. We need Your maternal care, Your tender touch, Your watchful eye. Protect us daily and lead us along the path of life. See to it, Mother, that we join You and remain with You for all eternity. Mary, pray for us now and at the hour of our death.

BLESSED VIRGIN MARY'S INCREASE OF GRACE

We speak of the Blessed Virgin Mary as being full of grace. The archangel Gabriel tells us "Hail, full of Grace". It is a certain theological truth that the amount of grace She received because of Her position as Mother of God was more than that of all the angels and saints. Even though She was full of grace, nevertheless it was increased.

Sacred Scripture records a definite incident in Her life where She received an increase of grace. This was Her confirmation on Pentecost Sunday.

After Our Lord ascended into Heaven, Blessed Mary went with the Apostles and faithful into the city of Jerusalem and remained for ten days in the Last Supper room praying and awaiting the Holy Spirit. On Pentecost, "suddenly there came a sound from Heaven, as of a mighty wind coming, and it filled the whole house, where they were sitting. And there appeared to them parted tongues as it were of fire, and it sat upon every one of them". (Acts 2, 2-3)

As to the other sacraments, it is certain She received the Sacrament of Holy Eucharist, and probably Baptism although She did not need to be washed from any sin since She was free from all sin. As to Her marriage, we know that it was definitely a true and real marriage according to the Old Law. It was a true natural contract. Whether Christ raised it to the dignity of a sacrament is not known.

Although Blessed Virgin Mary was full of grace nevertheless She increased the grace in Her by doing meritorious good works which She offered up to God, by the Incarnation itself which gave Her the proportionate grace of the Mother of God, and by the reception of the sacraments.

From Mary we are to learn to increase the grace we have in us by doing good works. Each morning we should offer to God everything we think, say, do, enjoy, and suffer for His honor and glory and our own salvation. Being charitable and doing good to others and by the frequent reception of the Sacraments we gain more abundant grace. We all can go to Confession at least once a month, but it would be better to go every week. We all can go to Holy Communion every Sunday but it would be better to receive Our Lord's Body and Blood daily.

O, Mary, inspire us to receive Your Son most frequently in Holy Communion. Help us to increase in all graces by receiving the sacraments and doing supernatural acts. Help us to present our good works to Jesus so that we can become more holy and pleasing to You and to Jesus, Your Son and Our Lord and God.

O, Mary, be our consolation and love now. Be sure we have the grace of receiving the sacrament connected with the anointing of the sick. When we are about to enter the Kingdom of God to meet Him face to face, be at our side, O Mary Our Mother.

THE ASSUMPTION OF THE BLESSED VIRGIN MARY

November 1, 1950 will be long remembered as the day of the definition of the of the ASSUMPTION OF THE BLESSED MOTHER. On that day, the Holy Father as the infallible teacher of the Church in matters of faith and morals, proclaimed that the Blessed Virgin upon Her death did not decay in body as is the common lot of mankind, but shortly after Her death, was BODY AND SOUL taken up to Heaven. Thereby She experienced the resurrection of the body long before the general resurrection and judgment. From this day on every Catholic must believe this truth or be considered a heretic.The following are the actual words of the Papal Bull, "Munificentissimus Deus" which defined the Dogma of the Assumption.

"After we have time and again offered supplication to God and have invoked the light of the Spirit of truth, for the glory of Almighty God, who has lavished His special benevolence upon the Virgin Mary and for the honor of His Son, the Immortal King of the ages and the Victor over sin and death, in order to increase the glory of His AUGUST MOTHER and for the joy and exultation of the entire church, by the authority of Our Lord Jesus Christ, we pronounce, declare, and define that it is a divinely revealed dogma that the Immaculate Mother of God, ever Virgin Mary, when the course of Her earthly life was finished, was taken up body and soul into Heavenly glory". Pope Pius XII.

Upon what facts could the Pope declare this truth? It is true there is no explicit statement in the Holy Bible concerning the Blessed Mother's Assumption in just these particular words, but there are certain passages which explicitly refer to Her universal triumph with Christ and implicitly to Her triumph over sin, concupiscence and death. Her complete triumph over sin was in Her Immaculate Conception, which is a dogma of the church. Her triumph over concupiscence was in Her Virginal Maternity. It is a dogma that the Blessed Virgin was a virgin before the birth of Christ, during the birth and after the birth. She is the ever-virgin Mary. Now it remained for the Church to declare Her complete triumph over death by the defining formally Her Assumption, which is the inevitable result of Her association with Jesus.

1. The faithful believed in the Assumption of Mary from the Apostolic times, but only in the 6th century did the Church openly and explicitly hold that the Blessed Lady was assumed into Heaven and there Her body and soul reunited and there she lives with Her Divine Son in all His Divine glory.

2. This doctrine is based solidly upon the theological principles of Holy Scripture and Tradition of the Church. Truly, the church could not be wrong believing in this truth or else the Holy Spirit would not be keeping up to the promise of remaining with the church forever and

Christ's words would have fallen through for He did say "And the gates of hell will not prevail against it".

3. The tradition of the Church on this doctrine is based primarily on St. John Damascene, a doctor of the Church who was born in Damascus about 675. But even before his time, already others wrote concerning this truth, for example, St. Modestus, the patriarch of Jerusalem 631-34: St. Gregory of Tours 538.

St. John Damascene wrote the following: St. Juvenal, Bishop of Jerusalem, at the Council of Chalcedon (451) made known to the Emperors Marcian and Pulcheria, who wished to possess the body of the Mother of God, that Mary died in the presence of all the Apostles, but that Her tomb, when opened upon the request of St. Thomas was found empty: where from the Apostles concluded that Her body was taken up to Heaven.

4. From the Gospels we know that St. John was given charge of the Blessed Virgin. It is a tradition that he took Her with him to Ephesus and later She returned to Jerusalem and lived in a house near the Cenacle. It was while there She died. There is a church called "The Dormition of Mary on or near the place Mary died. Also, there is a crypt at the grave of Mary, in the family tomb where Saints Ann, Joachim, and Joseph were buried. This spot is venerated by the Armenians, Moscovites Moslems as well as by the Christians as the resting place of "THE LADY MARY".

5. An apocryphal gospel entitled "Account of St. John, the Theologian, of the Falling Asleep of the Holy Mother of God" gives an account of how the Apostles were gathered miraculously from all parts of the earth for the death, burial and the Assumption of the Virgin Mother of Jesus.

6. Epipanius, one of the earliest Church writers, doubted whether the Blessed Mary ever died, but rather was taken up into Heaven. Others spoke of the Virgin's death as Her going to sleep (dormition)...and of the transition of Mary.

7. History states that the Feast of the Assumption was already celebrated in the whole church by the 5th century. (Page 484, Tanquerry-Brenior Theologia Dogmatica). The Greek Catholics, which was reunited with the Church of Rome, celebrates this feast. This means that this feast and the knowledge and belief of the Assumption was known and celebrated even before their separation from Rome in 1051.

ANTICIPATION OF THE GENERAL JUDGMENT: In the Bible we read of several persons who were resuscitated, for example Lazarus, and the great number who arose at the time of the Crucifixion (St. Matt. 27,52). Then there were Enoch and Elijah who did not suffer death at all but were taken up into Heaven. Here are examples of the anticipation of the general resurrection of the body which is to occur at the end of the world, which truth we believe. Therefore it is most fitting that God Who privileged Mary to be the Mother of Christ and granted Her many graces and privileges that He, too, granted this privilege of the anticipated resurrection to Mary.

THEOLOGICAL PROOFS FOR THE ASSUMPTION
OF THE BLESSED VIRGIN MARY, MOTHER OF JESUS

1. Psalm 15,10 "Thou wilt not leave my soul in hell nor wilt Thou give Thy Holy One to see corruption". St. Peter in Acts 2,27 and St. Paul in Acts 13,35 in quoting this psalm verse attribute it to Christ. Yet the flesh of Christ was taken from that of Mary since She is the Mother of Christ whose body knew no corruption after the crucifixion. Therefore, it is fitting that Her body should not suffer any corruption either since Her glory is that of sharing in the glory of Her Son.

2. Death and corruption is the result of sin. But there was no sin in Mary for She was immaculately conceived and was a perpetual virgin. Therefore, She could not be punished for a guilt of which She was freed. St, Andrew of Crete (d.720) wrote, "As Mary's womb was in no wise corrupted by parturition, so Her flesh did not perish after death". But Mary did die. She died as Her Son did, voluntarily for our benefit to show us how we too are to die. She did not suffer any pain nor disease or concupiscence which are the results of original sin of which sin She was free.

3. The linking of Mary to the Ark of the Covenant and the Church give other proofs. Psalm. 131,8 "Arise, 0 Lord, into Thy resting place; Thou and the Ark which Thou has sanctified". The famous text of the Apos. 12 "The temple of God was opened in Heaven and the Ark of His testament was seen in His temple...and a great sign appeared in Heaven; A woman clothed with the sun, and the moon was under her feet and upon her head a crown of 12 stars". This passage probably and primarily refers to the Church, but from the earliest times this text was thought to refer to Mary and also She was always considered as a type of the Church. Eusibius quotes a letter in which the figure is taken from the Virgin Mother of Christ in reference to the Church, "created in the Virgin Mother the Church by martyrdom for those whom she brought forth as dead she recovered again as living". This was sent by the Christians of Vienna and Lyons in 177 (Msgr. Smith..Register Aug. 1950). St. Augustine (born 354)says "The woman in Apos. 12 signifies the Virgin Mary who being inviolate brought forth our Inviolate Head. She also exhibits the figure of Holy Church in Herself, as while bearing a Son, She remained a virgin, so also it in every age bears His members and does not lose virginity".

   The arguments of the ARK and the CHURCH for Mary become more conclusive from the Apoc. 11,19 which is an introduction to the rest of the chapter 12 on the woman. It states "and the temple of God in Heaven was opened and there was seen the Ark of His covenant in His temple. Every student of the Bible will admit that the Ark has reference to Mary. Mary was called the Ark by St. Ambrose, St. Ephraen the Syrian, and others already by the 4th century. Since the 12th century Mary has been called the Ark of the Covenant and this term has been placed in Her Litany of Loreto.

4. Rev. Garrigor-Lagrange in his book "Christ the Savious" gives the following reason for the Assumption: Tradition is the voice of the living church and not only of the past. But in recent years there have been vast petitions begging the Holy See to declare this as a dogma. (In reports from Rome 98.2% of the world's residential bishops expressed approval to the questionnaire sent to them by the Vatican. The questions were: Can the Assumption be declared a dogma? Is it advisable to do so? "Such a consensus before a formal definition has almost never been verified in the history of the Church", said Rev. W. Hentrich, S.J. who was in charge of collating the matter for the Assumption. This is not only the opinion of the bishops alone but also of the priests and laity, for the bishops were to investigate the opinions of their people. This testimony is regarded as a witness to Tradition on matters of Faith.

5. St. Anthony of Padua is sometimes called the doctor of the Assumption because of his defense of the doctrine.

6. Pope Pius IX December 8, 1854 when defining the Immaculate Conception wrote: "The fathers taught that the Mother of God is the seat of all divine graces, that She is adorned with all the charismatic gifts of the Holy Spirit, that She is in fact the infinite treasure of these very gifts and their inexhausted abyss so much so that never subject to an evil and together with Her Son, partaking of perpetual blessing, She merited to hear from Elizabeth moved by the Holy Spirit..."Blessed art You among women and blessed is the Fruit of Thy womb". But the Angel of God called her "Full of grace". Therefore She who is full of grace and the blessed among women, a special privilege from God, did not corrupt but was assumed into Heaven body and soul or otherwise the blessing would have turned into a malediction "revert to dust".

7. BECAUSE SHE IS THE MOTHER OF GOD: The Most Rev. Cuthbert Gumbinger, OFM Cap. in his article " Assumption of the Mother of God into Heaven" which appeared in "The Scapular" July-Aug. 1950 wrote, "The Divine Maternity is the foundation and the soaring tower of all Mary's graces, privileges, charismatic gifts and offices. We believe all the Church teaches or will ever teach about Mary, precisely because She is the Mother of God...therefore, She is immaculately conceived, always free from every sin and all motions of concupiscence "full of grace", in fact holier than the highest seraph She is ever a virgin; She is the Co-Redemptrix and Spiritual Mother of the human race. She died without pain; very soon after death God raised her gloriously from the dead. Her body suffered no corruptions and with Her body and soul She was assumed into Heaven where She rules as Queen of the Universe and Mediatrix of all grace...all this became She is the Mother of God. Can we conceive that after God had granted Her so many graces and privileges, He would allow Her body to turn to dust? Never.

It will be good to remember some of the arguments presented, but far better it is to LOVE OUR BLESSED MOTHER. Speak to Her. Remember THROUGH MARY TO JESUS.

EPILOGUE

There are many text books written on the Blessed Virgin Mary. The libraries, especially Catholic libraries, have a large number of books concerning the doctrines, the shrines and the devotions of the Mother of Jesus. If by chance any one may want to read more about the Blessed Mother, please visit a library.

This book is not a text book on the Blessed Mother. It was written because of the LOVE OUR PEOPLE have for Our Blessed Lady. This book may also stimulate others to express their love in positive ways of devotion. The recitation of the Rosary, the Litany and the Angelus are excellent means of demonstrating one's love of Mary.

For those who would like a summary of doctrines concerning our Mother Mary, the following pages are given. These may help one to understand Mary and Her position in our salvation.

More important than to know all of the doctrine concerning Our Blessed Mother, is love Her. She does love all mankind, She is interested in all mankind, She directs all mankind to Jesus.

As we say the "Hail Mary" may we honor the Mother of Jesus and may She be at our side when God calls us to Himself. May She present our souls to Our Lord Who will grant us a place in Heaven because we LOVE.